Editor:
Mecalux, SA
Silici, 1-5
08940 Cornellà
Barcelona (Spain)
info@mecalux.com
www.mecalux.com

© 2011 MECALUX, SA

Design and layout:
Mecalux marketing department

ISBN: 978-84-616-3528-3
Legal deposit: B-11714-2013

All rights reserved.
Its reproduction, either in full or in part, and its transmission in any format are prohibited without the publisher's prior written authorisation.

TECHNICAL WAREHOUSE MANUAL

CONTENTS

INTRODUCTION
HOW ARE WAREHOUSES CURRENTLY DESIGNED AND WHY? 15
Rapid response to the market
Facilitating understanding

FOREWORD TO THE TECHNICAL WAREHOUSE MANUAL 19
What information can be found in this book and what concepts are explained?

CHAPTER 1
CONCEPTS COMMON TO ALL WAREHOUSES 23
1.1 What is a warehouse? 23
1.2 Classification of warehouses 23
1.3 What happens in a warehouse? 24
1.4 What elements are involved in a warehouse? 24
1.5 What information is required to plan a warehouse, and how is it important? 24
1.6 What are the different parts of a warehouse? 30
1.7 Flows of materials within a warehouse 35
    1.7.1 What is a unit load? 36
    1.7.2 Types of flow 38
        Simple flow 38
        Medium flow 39
        Complex flow 39
    1.7.3 The impact of flows on storage facilities 41
    1.7.4 Product rotation: A-B-C 43
    1.7.5 Conclusions about flows and rotation 45
1.8 Basic strategic criteria 46
1.9 Warehouse management 47
    1.9.1 What are the benefits of managing the facility well? 47
    1.9.2 Who manages the warehouse? 48
    1.9.3 How are the goods and their location managed? 49
    1.9.4 What functions does a WMS perform? 50
        Entry functions 51
        Location functions 52
        Stock control functions 53
        Exit functions 53
        Functions in complex warehouses 54
    1.9.5 The importance of radio frequency 56
    1.9.6 Automatic identification systems 56
        Barcodes 57
        RFID encoding 59

CHAPTER 2
THE LOAD UNIT, IN DEPTH 61
2.1 Grouping products into larger load units 61
2.2 Pallets and containers: General issues 63
2.3 Pallets 63
    2.3.1 Wooden pallets 63
    2.3.2 Metal pallets 69
    2.3.3 Plastic pallets 69
    2.3.4 Other plastic pallets 71
2.4 Containers 72
    2.4.1 Wooden containers 72
    2.4.2 Metal containers 73
    2.4.3 Plastic containers 75
    2.4.4 Box type containers 76
        Other types of boxes 80
2.5 Standardisation of pallets 81
2.6 Stacking goods on pallets 84
2.7 Conclusion 87

CHAPTER 3
HANDLING EQUIPMENT 89
3.1 Conventionally operated systems 92
    3.1.1 Pallet trucks 92
        Hand pallet trucks 92
        Electric pedestrian pallet trucks 93
        Electric rider pallet trucks 93
    3.1.2 Stackers 94
        Comments about stackers 95
    3.1.3 Order pickers 96
    3.1.4 Conventional forklift trucks (counterbalanced) 99
    3.1.5 Reach trucks 101
        Double-reach truck 105
    3.1.6 Side-loading reach trucks 105
    3.1.7 Turret trucks (for narrow aisles) 107
        Combi VNA trucks 109
        Guidance systems 110
3.2 Manual picking stacker cranes 111
3.3 Observations about the use of forklift trucks when planning a warehouse 112
    3.3.1 Technical specifications of the forklift 112
    3.3.2 Lifting height 114
    3.3.3 Issues related to the use of forklifts with drive-in pallet racking 116
    3.3.4 Clearances required with conventional pallet racking units for each type
    of forklift truck 118
    3.3.5 Clearances in the aisles along which the forklift trucks move 119
3.4 Automated operating systems 123

3.4.1 Stacker cranes for pallets 123
3.4.2 Stacker cranes for boxes: miniload 127
3.4.3 Automatic guided and laser guided vehicles (AGV/LGV) 131
3.4.4 Roller and chain conveyors and shuttles for pallets 133
3.4.5 Roller, belt, and band conveyors for boxes 143
3.4.6 Electrified monorail systems 149
3.4.7 Other transport systems 150
3.5 Comparison table for pallet conveyor and lifting machines 153

CHAPTER 4
STORAGE SYSTEMS 155
4.1 Palletised on racking storage 155
   4.1.1 Storage systems offering direct access to pallets 157
      When should conventional static racking be installed? 159
      When should mobile bases (Movirack systems) be used? 161
      Elevated installations 163
      The double deep option 164
      Conventional racking with automated systems 167
   4.1.2 Compact systems 170
      Drive-in racking units 172
      Push-back racking units 174
      Racking units with radio-shuttle 175
      Live storage pallet racking 176
      Compact system with automated handling and management 178
   4.1.3 Capacity differences between systems 181
      Comments on capacity
      differences between the various systems 194
4.2 Storage of individual boxes and small products 200
   4.2.1 Man-to-goods solutions 201
      Traditional racking units: M3, slotted angle and Simplos 201
      Medium-duty racking units (M7) 205
      Traditional and medium-duty racking units on mobile bases (Movibloc) 208
      Boxes and loose units on pallet racking units 210
      Live picking racking units 212
      Live picking racking units with the "pick to light" system 219
   4.2.2 Goods-to-man solutions 221
      Miniload 221
      Vertical lift module (Clasimat) 225
      Vertical carousels 228
      Horizontal carousels (Spinblock) 229
4.3 Mixed systems 234
4.4 Specific systems 244
   4.4.1 Cantilever racking units 244
   4.4.2 Racking units for reels and cylinders 248
      Reels on shafts 248

  Supported reels... 248
  Storing cylinders 249
 4.4.3 Mezzanines...249
 4.4.4 Warehouses for special and large products 253
  Sheet type goods.. 253
  A. Plastic sheets 254
  B. Wooden sheets and boards.. 254
  Tube-shaped goods 254
  A. Handling and storage of semi-rigid tubes 255
  Cylindrical type goods 255
  A. Sheet metal rolls... 255
  B. Cable reels.. 256
4.5 Where to find more information about storage solutions 257

CHAPTER 5
THE IDEAL STORAGE SOLUTION 259
5.1 What is the ideal storage solution? 259
5.2 Basic criteria for selecting the most appropriate storage system 260
 5.2.1 Capacity to be obtained 261
 5.2.2 Desired speed 262
 5.2.3 Product variety and type... 263
 5.2.4 General cost.. 263
 5.2.5 Combination of factors 266
 5.2.6 Optimisation of the factors in automated warehouses................................ 266
5.3 Order preparation (picking) 268
 5.3.1 Impact of picking on investment 268
 5.3.2 General strategies to improve picking 271
 5.3.3 Order preparation methods using the man-to-goods
 principle 271
  Order preparation at ground level...271
  A. Possible systems..272
  B. Reasons for preparing orders at ground level 273
  C. The most appropriate equipment for preparing orders at ground level 274
  Order preparation at low levels.. 274
  A. Systems for low-level picking... 274
  B. When to use low-level picking..275
  C. Equipment for low-level picking..276
  D. Position on manual picking racking units 276
  Order preparation at mid-level 278
  A. Use of mid-level order preparation 278
  B. Mechanical equipment for mid-level picking.. 279
  Order preparation at high levels 280
  A. How to perform high-level order preparation 280
  B. Equipment for high-level order preparation 281
 5.3.4 Devices to improve picking from pallets or boxes................................... 282

- 5.3.5 Picking systems in automated warehouses with products on pallets 285
  - Picking positions at the front of the automated warehouse 285
  - Picking positions on one side of the automated warehouse 286
  - Picking in annexed areas 287
  - Automated picking with robots 289

5.4 Storage of small pieces 292
- 5.4.1 Preliminary considerations in the design of a warehouse for small pieces 292
  - The importance of warehouse storage to the production chain 292
  - Obtaining sufficient capacity for current and future needs 292
  - How to increase capacity in an existing warehouse 293
  - How to obtain the highest possible rotation ratio 294
  - The effect of streamlining on the storage of small pieces 295
- 5.4.2 Key principles when creating storage for small pieces 295
  - Man-to-goods strategy 296
  - A. Racking units on a single floor 297
  - B. Racking units on several floors 299
  - C. Mobile racking units 299
  - D. Warehouses with narrow aisles 300
  - E. Live picking racking units 302
  - The goods-to-man strategy 304
  - A. Vertical lift modules (Clasimat) 305
  - B. Horizontal carousels (Spinblock) 307
  - C. Box stacker cranes (miniload) 308

5.5 Return on investment calculations 311
5.6 Conclusion 315

CHAPTER 6
THE DESIGN AND CONSTRUCTION OF THE WAREHOUSE 317
6.1 The importance of location 317
- 6.1.1 Product characteristics 319
  - Durability 319
  - Intrinsic stability 319
  - Manageability 320
- 6.1.2 Manufacturing capacity 320
  - Degree of product processing 320
  - The necessary distribution network 321
  - A. Influence of the composition 321
  - B. Influence of the distribution of the sales network 321

6.2 The design and layout of warehouses 323
- 6.2.1 Loading and unloading areas (A) 324
  - Loading and unloading areas integrated into the warehouse 325
  - Independent loading and unloading areas 328
- 6.2.2 Reception area (B) 329
- 6.2.3 Storage area (C) 331
- 6.2.4 Order picking areas (D) 332

- 6.2.5 Dispatch areas (E) 333
- 6.2.6 Service areas (F) 334

6.3 The central warehouse: functions and design 334
- 6.3.1 Factors when choosing the location of a central warehouse 335
- 6.3.2 Influence of the location of the sources of supply 335
- 6.3.3 Influence of the location of the points to be supplied 335
- 6.3.4 Functions of a central warehouse 336
  - Receipt of all products 336
  - A. Weight and size of products to be received 336
  - B. Mechanical means used for loading and unloading. 337
  - Instant quality control. 338
  - Control and inventory of the products stored 338
  - Correct storage of goods 338
  - Preparation of orders for regional warehouses 339
  - Rapid dispatch of orders 341
- 6.3.5 Design of a central warehouse 342
  - Reception area 342
  - Storage area 344
  - Dispatch area 347

6.4 Starting construction and the importance of flooring 349
- 6.4.1 Loads that flooring must withstand 350
- 6.4.2 What do we mean by "suitable flooring"? 351
- 6.4.3 The importance of the substrate 351
- 6.4.4 Composition of the flooring 352
- 6.4.5 Joints in the flooring 353
- 6.4.6 The finishing layer 354
- 6.4.7 Laying the flooring 355
- 6.4.8 The importance of flatness 357
  - Requirements for a class 400 floor (for wide and narrow aisle). 360
  - Requirements for a class 300 floor (very narrow aisle). 360
  - Requirements for class 100 and 200 floors (very narrow aisle). 360
- 6.4.9 Racking unit clearances 361
- 6.4.10 Strength, porosity, bonding, and durability of flooring 362

6.5 When should self-supporting warehouses be used? 362
- 6.5.1 Fixed-route devices 363
  - Precision positioning 365
  - Supports for fixed-route elements 366
  - A. Supports for roller conveyors 366
  - B. Supports for stacker cranes 367
  - Clearances for fixed-route devices 369
  - Clearances in working aisles 369
  - Positioning of loads on racking units 369
- 6.5.2 Use of free-moving devices 372
  - Supports for free-moving devices 373
  - Clearances for free-moving devices 373

6.5.3 The external shell for self-supporting warehouses 375
6.5.4 Combined construction systems 376
6.6 The design and construction of access points 376
    6.6.1 Greater safety.. 377
    6.6.2 Factors influencing access points 377
        The influence of just-in-time.. 377
        Large vehicles 378
    6.6.3 Design of access points for warehouses 379
    6.6.4 Construction of the road surface 380
    6.6.5 Traffic planning 380
    6.6.6 Access doors.. 381
    6.6.7 Factors that influence the layout of the docks... 381
    6.6.8 How many access points are necessary? 382
    6.6.9 Asphalt and weight 383
    6.6.10 Ramps for forklifts... 383
    6.6.11 Special features of the docks 383
        The ideal approach dock 383
        Sloping entrance area.. 384
        Closed docks 385
        Saw tooth docks 385
        Planning the approach area 385
        Heights of the docks.. 386
        Use with special lorries 387
6.7 Safety 388
    6.7.1 Fire risk 388
        Fire prevention systems at the facility 389
        Fire prevention in the racking units using sprinklers 393
    6.7.2 A safe layout within the warehouse 394

CHAPTER 7
CONCLUSIONS FROM THE TECHNICAL WAREHOUSE MANUAL 397

Logistics warehouse for the pharmaceutical industry. Source: Mecalux.

INTRODUCTION
HOW ARE WAREHOUSES CURRENTLY DESIGNED AND WHY?

Today, there are many and varied reasons why companies need to create and use warehouses. Over time, these elements have become increasingly important and strategic to the business and, by extension, to the success of many organisations.

Traditionally, warehouses have been used to ensure the greatest possible efficiency in combining the provisioning, production and demand of products and services in companies. Achieving this requires the capacity to store raw materials and products and to make these available, regardless of whether they come in packaging (such as electrical appliances, for example) or are provided loose (as is the case of spare parts, profiles, carpets, etc.).

While assembly-line production of a certain product is easy to control, as long as the right machinery is available and this is adjusted in response to new manufacturing needs, the demand for finished products is subject to irregular ups and downs, just like seasonal variations. This variability in demand can cause a common provisioning problem for both raw material suppliers and manufacturers, and for those who produce bottles and packaging.

Given this difficulty, the only solution is to anticipate any possible shortfalls in supply and, as a result, store a certain quantity of raw materials so that production is kept constantly supplied.

In addition, although just-in-time production techniques are designed to deal with precisely this variability in demand through policies to reduce fixed assets, at times it is better to stock up and order certain raw materials in bulk because of the cost reduction this offers.

To all of these factors must be added the demands of the distribution sector itself, and the changes in the different technological processes in response to these demands. All of this involves the need to plan specific buildings suitable for storage and distribution.

Rapid response to the market

Apart from meeting production-related needs, another reason for the use of warehouses is to move goods as close as possible to the points of consumption, so that the company can immediately respond to demand as soon as it materialises.

The inability to supply a market results in a series of losses, such as lower sales figures and damage to the product's image. This is why all distribution companies take great care with this issue and have appropriate warehouses in ideal locations, the aim being to obtain the greatest market penetration possible.

While ideal geographic positioning is important, no less important is the need to adapt the storage centre to the current and future needs of the company.

The design of a warehouse must be comprehensive and consider other factors in its planning as well as those already discussed. One of the most relevant is cost reduction, which is carried out after choosing the initial storage system to be used. One must bear in mind that the buildings used for these activities are designed for a depreciation period of no less than 25 years, and that they offer their maximum return approximately half way through this time period, while today technological changes take place so quickly that the facility designed can become obsolete in a mere five or six years.

Gone are the days when this type of building was constructed as economically as possible, on the assumption that it would be demolished once the warehousing system had become outdated. Today the cost of land, construction and handling systems, along with the quest for the highest possible industrial competitiveness, mean that manufacturing and distribution companies cannot cope with the financial impact of closing a facility for modification and the resulting reduction in sales this entails.

Designers of buildings intended for storage must consider a series of factors which could be decisive in carrying out modifications in response to new needs and technological changes that may arise at a later date. Some factors that could indicate sufficient capacity to adapt the building in the future are, for example, having fitted out a space for possible extensions and deciding what its initial function will be (it could be used as an operational area or overflow zone).

Unfortunately, it is true that certain factors that can influence the warehouse's later development are impossible to predict, such as land planning regulations implemented by local authorities which, of course, must always be taken into account.

Facilitating understanding

There is no doubt that proper warehouse planning is a difficult operation in which the most crucial factors are in fact out of the designer's control. At times, marketing managers at the client company are unable or simply do not know how to sufficiently anticipate real market development. In other cases, there is a communication breakdown between the people taking part in the project, primarily due to the difficulty of one party in expressing its needs or excessive use of technical jargon by others.

The aim of this book is to provide basic information on some key areas of warehouse design and construction and to help all involved by offering them an informative reference document that promotes improved coordination and, as a result, greater success in planning storage buildings. Despite efforts to clarify the concepts and premises, it should be noted that all the information in this book is subject to frequent change. Therefore, the content of this book cannot be relied on in isolation, and specialist or reference information sources now available should be consulted.

What this book does offer is an excellent starting point for understanding almost all aspects related to storage and to the buildings and facilities dedicated to this activity, while at the same time helping improve understanding of the refinements and changes that will occur in the sector in the future.

FOREWORD TO THE TECHNICAL WAREHOUSE MANUAL

Mecalux is delighted to offer you this *Technical Warehouse Manual*, which is intended to combine in a single reference document all the basic concepts about the different warehouse systems, as well as the mechanical, automated, and semi-automated resources that are necessary or useful when handling and storing goods.

To complement this, chapters have been included that set out and explain the basic essential concepts involved in designing or planning a warehouse, such as those related to the characteristics of the paving and the floors, for example. However, the book does not contain in-depth information about these technical characteristics.

Everything explained in this book is aimed to increase understanding of the storage basic concepts involved in theory and practice, thus making it possible to apply some if not all of these, depending on the level of analysis and depth desired for each aspect.

The manual is divided into different sections. In future, other more advanced or more complex solutions may be added as a result of the ongoing development of techniques.

WHAT INFORMATION CAN BE FOUND IN THIS BOOK AND WHAT CONCEPTS ARE EXPLAINED?

As you will see, a warehouse is basically structured around two different worlds: that of goods handled in boxes or loose; and that of goods handled on pallets. Although certain criteria are applied in a very similar way in both cases, there are indeed differences in terms of their handling. These differences will be addressed throughout the book.

The warehouse solution is also directly connected to how the flow of the loads takes place, i.e. the how, how much, and from where the goods are taken, such as their reception, positioning, picking and dispatch, so this manual will cover all these factors. The design will be different in each case and seldom are two systems the same, just as there are no two sets of identical needs.

As is only natural, the solution will also be influenced by the space, the physical warehouse with its dimensions and services, its location, and its use (as the main warehouse, a local warehouse, etc.). Therefore, part of this manual is devoted to explaining these conditioning factors.

Company specialising in construction machinery and tools. Source: Mecalux.

There is also an explanation on a case-by-case basis of the most convenient means of transport, as well as the procedures and machines that can be used to lift and handle goods, since without these there is little that can be done and they are crucial in determining the solution to be applied. As a result, a discussion of the possible options for these elements has been included.

An important chapter has been devoted to warehouse management. Nowadays, it is hard to conceive of a facility, regardless of its size, in which appropriate warehouse management software is not implemented.

Nor has the human factor been overlooked in this book: all warehouses, regardless of how small or automated they may be, require the labour of professionals. Their involvement and preparation will result in a better or worse performance and greater or less return from the facility.

Finally, the goods themselves are described. Their shape, weight and handling requirements undoubtedly mark the path to be followed when planning the solution.

In short, this manual is designed to include the key features of a warehouse as it develops, taking into account the new directions which will influence the logistics of warehousing from a descriptive and strategic point of view in the near future.

We at Mecalux hope that this book fulfils its purpose, helping to clarify the different warehouse systems available, and hence contribute to the study and acquisition of the elementary and fundamental information required to plan, design, and incorporate load-storage equipment and systems.

Logistics warehouse for refrigerated and frozen food products. Source: Mecalux.

CHAPTER 1
CONCEPTS COMMON TO ALL WAREHOUSES

1.1 WHAT IS A WAREHOUSE?

A warehouse is a facility that, along with storage and handling equipment and human and management resources, allows us to control the differences between the flow of goods entering (those received from suppliers, production centres, etc.) and the flow of goods leaving (those goods being sent to production, sales, etc.). Usually, these flows are not coordinated, and this is one of the reasons why it is important to have storage facilities.

1.2 CLASSIFICATION OF WAREHOUSES

At times, the economic activity of a company can require one or more types of storage facility: one for raw materials, one for semi-finished products, one for finished products, etc. All of these have to be arranged on the basis of their specific operating needs, and in accordance with the restrictions and options for each location and its surroundings.

The best way to classify the different types of warehouse that currently exist is to group them according to their common characteristics. These can be defined according to the nature of the product they are used to store, the building used, the flow of materials taking place, their location, or the extent to which their facilities are mechanised. Some examples are as follows:

According to the nature of the product. There can be warehouses specialising in coils, flammable products, profiles, small materials, spare parts, and perishables, and even warehouses that are for general use, among other possibilities.

The building itself can also be a criterion for classification. Buildings can be classified as open air warehouses, industrial buildings, basements, silos or tanks, cold chambers, self-supporting warehouses (the racking itself forms part of the building construction system), etc.

According to the flow of materials. Installations can be grouped in terms of those used for raw materials, components or semi-finished products, finished products, intermediate warehouses, bonded warehouses, for distribution, etc.

In terms of location, warehouses can be central, regional, or transit. Finally, warehouses can be classified according to the extent of their mechanisation. They can be manual, conventional, or automated.

1.3 WHAT HAPPENS IN A WAREHOUSE?

The main tasks performed in a warehouse are the receipt and verification of goods, internal transport (between different parts of the warehouse), storage and safe-keeping, the preparation of orders, the consolidation of loads, the dispatch of goods and management and information relating to stock, flows, demand, etc.

1.4 WHAT ELEMENTS ARE INVOLVED IN A WAREHOUSE?

A number of factors must be taken into account when planning a facility. The most important of these are the product to be stored, the flow of materials or goods, the space available to house them, storage equipment (such as racks and handling equipment), the human factor (personnel), and the company's management system and policies.

Based on the above, various items of information must be collected. This information, which is stipulated below, will in turn influence the various aspects of the facility and must be taken into account when developing it.

1.5 WHAT INFORMATION IS REQUIRED TO PLAN A WAREHOUSE, AND HOW IS IT IMPORTANT?

As much information as possible must be collected about the needs of the customer, the space available, and the resources at one's disposal. The information collected is limited only by the extent of planning you wish to carry out at any time.

It is not enough to simply know what the customer needs or can do: a knowledge of the options available on the market is vital. Therefore, a thorough knowledge of storage systems is required, as is an up-to-date knowledge of the equipment on the market.

We will see how the data gathered are classified. Each factor will play a role in defining the warehouse and all of them, taken together, will impact on its planning.

PRODUCT: WHAT ARE THE CHARACTERISTICS OF THE GOODS TO BE STORED?
Required information
What **unit load or units** does the company use?
What are the different **dimensions and weights** of the unit loads?
How much **of the product** needs to be stored?
How many **items or types** of products will be stored?
What is the resistance of the product to **compression and deformation**?
Is the product climate-**sensitive**?
Are the goods fire-sensitive? What safety conditions are necessary?
What are the **rotation** requirements?
Is **traceability** of the goods necessary?
Is there an article **master**?
Is **growth** forecast for the future?
This information determines…
The storage **system** to be used and the **dimensions** required for the spaces or shelves.
The **size** of the facility, the **location system, and the layout**.
The handling and resistance of the **storage equipment** used.
How **operations** will be performed.
The working **areas** to be established.
The product layout in the facility.
The organisation of **internal flows**.
Whether or not products can be stacked on top of each other.
The **stability** of the load during handling.
Whether or not there is a possibility of **collapse** (and, therefore, whether or not more space is required).
Whether or not it will be a **temperature-controlled** facility (warehouse with a negative temperature, refrigerated, or at room temperature).
The **fire alarm system** to be used.

Company involved in beverage production and logistics. Source: Mecalux.

SPACE: WHAT INFRASTRUCTURE IS AVAILABLE?
Required information
To answer these questions, it is not enough to have a plan provided by the customer. The building must be visited to confirm all information and confirm measurements.
What is the **shape** and **size** of the premises?
Are there special **characteristics or limitations** in terms of access, floors, windows, pillars, manholes, installations, lines, and energy pipes?
Are there **spaces adjoining** the premises that have an impact on it?
What is the **earth resistance**?
What **construction regulations are in force** in the area?
Are **seismic calculations required**?
This information determines…
The potential **capacity** of the facility and the **layout** of the goods inside it.
The **accessibility** available in the warehouse.
The **layout** of the space and the location of emergency exits.
The need to install **racking units with the appropriate strength**.

EQUIPMENT: WHAT RESOURCES ARE AVAILABLE?
Required information
Are there already **racks in place**? If so, how many and what are their measurements and load capacity?
Is **elevation and transport equipment** available? If so, what are its measurements, elevation height and load capacity?
Are there already **auxiliary elements**, such as boxes, pallets, etc.? What are their measurements and characteristics?
Is there a predisposition toward buying **new storage equipment**?
This information determines…
The need to integrate **new equipment**.
Limits to **capacity**.
How to best **adapt the system to the needs** of the customer.
Whether or not it would be possible to **increase capacity**.

FLOWS AND ROTATION: HOW DO THE GOODS CIRCULATE?

Required information

How will products enter the facilities, how often, and in what **quantities**?
How will the **goods be handled**?
How many **orders** will there be, and **how many lines** will each order contain?
At what point will the **order be prepared**?
How will the product be issued? Classification and quantity.
What are the requirements of the goods in terms of **rotation, quarantine**, etc.?

The products are **classified** as
  A: High rotation
  B: Medium rotation
  C: Low rotation

What are the **current needs** and those of **future growth**?

This information determines...

The required **size and layout** of the warehouse.
Whether or not additional spaces must be **set aside**, and what these will be like.
How goods are arranged **on racks**.
How orders are **prepared**.
Whether or not **auxiliary resources are required**, and what form these should take.
The **management system** to be used.
What **handling equipment** will be used, and of what type.
The **speed** of operation and preparation of the facility.

PERSONNEL: WHAT PROFESSIONALS ARE AVAILABLE?

Required information

Number of **personnel** available to work in the warehouse.
What **qualifications** will the personnel assigned to the facilities have?
Will **shifts patterns be used**? If so, how will these be **organised**?
Will there be a tendency to reduce or increase the number of people and their qualifications?

This information determines...

The **operating capacity** of the facility.
Whether or not it is necessary or possible to **improve productivity**.
Whether or not **storage systems** and **equipment other** than those already in place are required.
The measures that will be necessary in relation to **handling equipment**.

MANAGEMENT AND BUSINESS POLICY: HOW ARE THINGS DONE?
Required information
How is the warehouse **controlled**?
Is there already a **warehouse management system**? (WMS software)
What **resources** are available?
Is it necessary to **speed up orders**?
Is it helpful to **reduce stock**?
How important is **reputation** to the company, and on what is this reputation based?
Is there the potential for **investment**?
What location system is used?
This information determines…
Whether or not it will be **necessary to improve** the management system.
The most **appropriate storage and order preparation system.**
The **location system** that will need to be adopted.
The **space that will be required.**
The **quantity of stock** that can be managed.
Whether or not a reduction or increase in **personnel** will be required.
The **degree of effectiveness** of the facility.
How both the **systems** and available **resources** will be **applied**.
And, ultimately, **the success or failure** of the solution implemented.

1.6 WHAT ARE THE DIFFERENT PARTS OF A WAREHOUSE?

The factors discussed in the previous section will have a decisive influence on how the building is organised and its layout.

The simplest warehouses normally have access doors, a free area for manoeuvring and verification, a storage area where the goods are located, a control office for the management of the plant, and toilets and changing rooms for personnel.

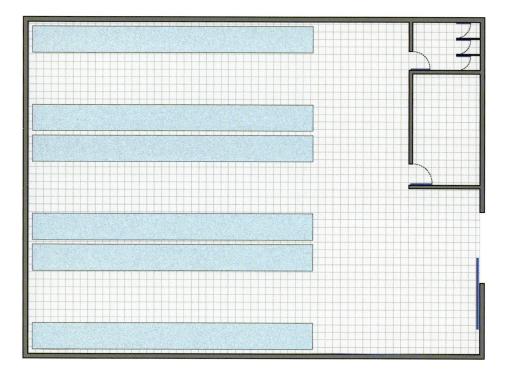

Starting with the simplest possible configuration other areas can be added, such as areas for receipt, packaging and consolidation, dispatch, recharging batteries for the forklift trucks, and loading docks, for example.

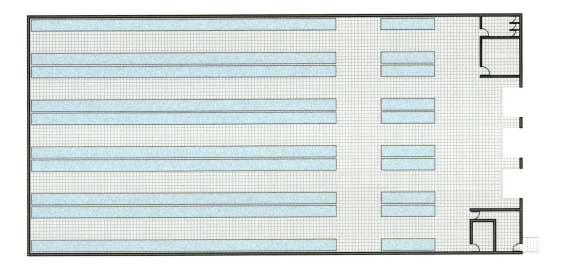

Source: Mecalux.

In turn, the warehouse can be divided into sectors according to the product being handled or working operation. The following diagram illustrates an example of this type of organisation:

1. Office and services building.
2. Loading and unloading docks.
3. Receipt and verification.
4. Dispatches.
5. High rotation or large volume product warehouse.
6. High rotation picking on pallets.
7. Warehouse for irregular products.
8. Warehouse for medium rotation components.
9. Warehouse for high rotation components.
10. Warehouse for low rotation components.
11. Warehouse for high value products.
12. Packing and consolidation area.

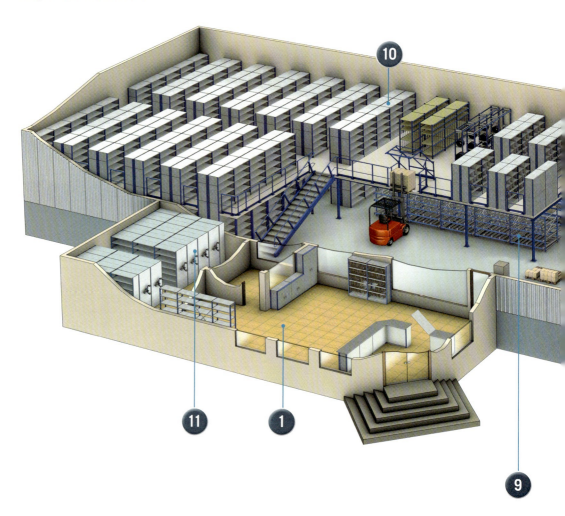

Chapter 1 - Concepts common to all warehouses

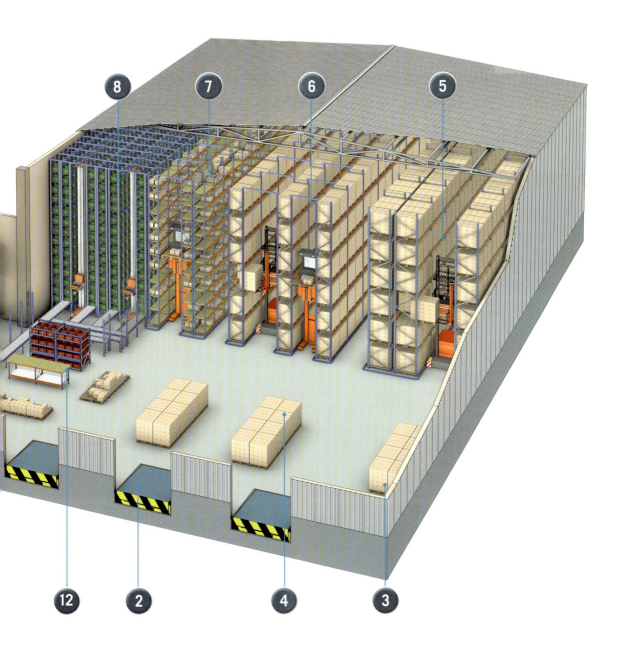

Chapter 1 - Concepts common to all warehouses

Central warehouse for the production and distribution of frozen dough for the food sector. Source: Mecalux.

The space assigned to each area must be appropriate, given the size of the land or building, the desired capacity, the operations that need to be performed, personnel and resources required, the flow of materials, and possibilities for future growth.

In any event, the customisation of the project and the design of areas within the facility will be determined from an exhaustive study of the company's needs (through the previously listed questions) and the supplier's experience in implementing logistics and storage solutions.

The entire building – its form, contents, and access – must be in keeping with the specific needs of the customer. Opportunities for growth must also be taken into account. To build a warehouse that is too close to current requirements and has no room for expansion in the future would be an error, unless it is a temporary facility or one that will not experience growth.

1.7 FLOWS OF MATERIALS WITHIN A WAREHOUSE

As explained in the previous section, the warehouse is the element of a company which, along with the storage and handling equipment and human and management resources, manages the differences between the receipt and dispatch of goods. Products and materials are stored in the warehouse on a temporary basis; everything that enters the facility sooner or later has to leave again.

Flows within a warehouse can be simple or complex, depending on the company in question, internal operations carried out with the goods, the quantity of goods, and how they are moved.

To more easily understand this section, however, an analysis the types of unit loads that can be found there is required first.

Warehouse for the manufacture of advanced digital products and applied technologies. Source: Mecalux.

1.7.1 What is a unit load?

A unit load is the basic storage and transport unit arranged on a modular support or package (box, pallet, container, etc.) to ensure efficient handling. Unit loads are handled at working points such as a general warehouse, reserve warehouse, picking warehouse, an internal element of transport, etc. As a result, in a single facility it is possible to handle just one type of unit load or various types.

The unit load can be divided into smaller elements that can also be handled. The first logical division results in **order preparation units**, which are the smallest product units for each item that can be delivered to a customer.

In turn, order preparation units can be divided into **delivery units**, which are groups that consist of sales units that allow for the optimal running of production, distribution, and sales systems. If this unit is not the same as the order preparation unit, it means that there is a wholesaler between the supplier and the retailer.

Similarly, this delivery unit can be subdivided into **sales units**, which are the smallest units of the product that the consumer can buy from a retailer.

The following diagram explains how units are divided and subdivided throughout the logistical life of the product.

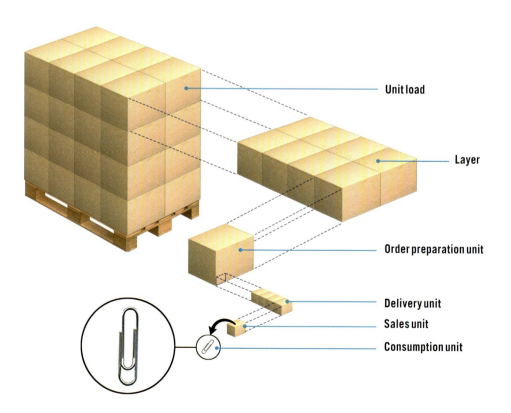

Chapter 1 - Concepts common to all warehouses

A warehouse can contain different types of unit load, such as:

The packaging box sent by the supplier.

A container into which the packaging boxes sent by the supplier are placed.

A container used to store the loose sales units.

A pallet onto which the packaging boxes sent by the supplier are placed. It can also send the goods already palletised (on a pallet).

Loose sales units can also be stored in a warehouse, without the packaging box or container. This facilitates what are called picking operations (which involve selecting units of goods to fill an order).

In these cases, the concept of a unit load is abandoned in favour of a picking bay on a shelving. In its simplest form, this picking bay can be, for example, a small pigeonhole or a compartment within a removable drawer in the rack. These two options are shown below.

Rack with small pigeonholes.

1.7.2 Types of flow

Once we are clear on the concept of the unit load and the different types of unit load, we can move on to analyse the flows, which are the movements of the units as they enter the warehouse, move around it, and finally exit.

<u>Simple flow.</u> To understand how these movements work we can examine the simplest possible flow, which takes place when units sent by the supplier are used, without dividing these up.

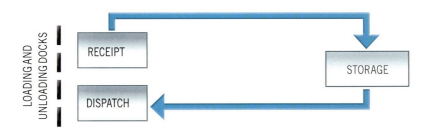

Medium flow. Movements start to become more complex with this type of flow. It is normally found in warehouses with single or combined picking operations, generally with the supply of full pallets.

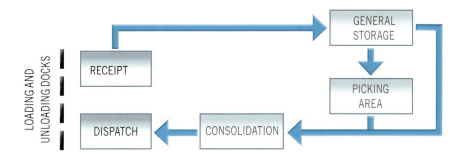

Complex flow. There are warehouses with different working areas, depending on the types of product and their consumption. They normally have intermediate handling areas and can require various operations that in turn need flows of a certain (and at times great) complexity. This diagram shows an example of this type of facility and the loading movements that occur there.

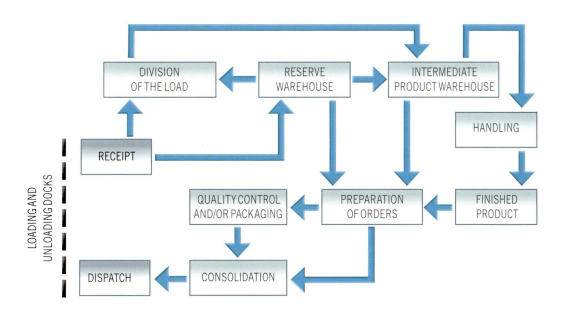

Chapter 1 - Concepts common to all warehouses

Source: Mecalux.

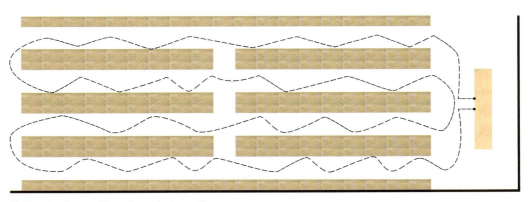

Picking warehouse with man to product operation.

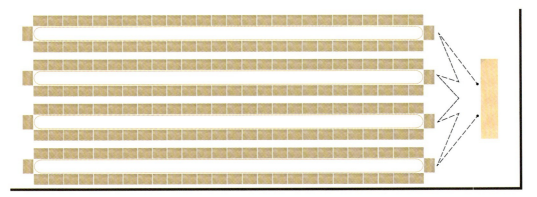

Picking warehouse with product to man operation.

1.7.3 The impact of flows on storage facilities

Each flow added to the working system represents an additional cost when it comes to calculating the overall cost of the process within the warehouse.

The greater the division of the unit loads, the greater the impact on costs. Picking operations account for the largest proportion of the total costs of the warehouse option (up to more than 60%). This is why the design of these areas is of such importance.

In addition, the larger the warehouse, the further the handling machines and personnel have to travel and the greater the final cost of the operation. In centres with a great deal of movement, it is worth analysing the possibility of introducing automation, so that the product goes to the man rather than the man going to the product.

As is to be expected, the location of items depending on their consumption and volume is basic. The closer the high demand or large goods are to the loading and unloading docks, the lower the handling costs.

A good example is a warehouse where loose units are directly prepared. As explained above when discussing unit loads, a single pallet can contain hundreds of sales units, so by moving these in a single operation it is possible to avoid the hundreds of movements that would otherwise be required to prepare each individual loose item.

All operations need a person, a machine, or both, to be performed. Therefore, it is vital to ensure that a single operator performs the greatest number of actions in a given time, or what boils down to the same thing, takes the shortest possible time for each operation. This applies to all activities in the warehouse. However, applying this principle is particularly important for picking, since this involves more movements than any other operation.

Warehouse of small pieces for hardware, industrial, DIY, and construction supplies. Source: Mecalux.

1.7.4 Product rotation: A-B-C

Another decisive factor that influences the speed and cost of operations is demand for the product or good. This is why items in most demand must be close to the loading and unloading docks. To this end, the concept of rotation is used. Products are classified as described below, according to their consumption:

A. High rotation: Units enter and exit continuously. These items are in high demand.
B. Medium rotation: Units enter and exit in smaller volumes than in A.
C. Low rotation: These are the items that spend most time in the warehouse, and are in low demand.

In most warehouses, the 80/20 rule or Pareto Chart applies. According to this rule, 80% of sales can be attributed to 20% of the products, while the remaining 20% of sales come from the remaining 80% of products.

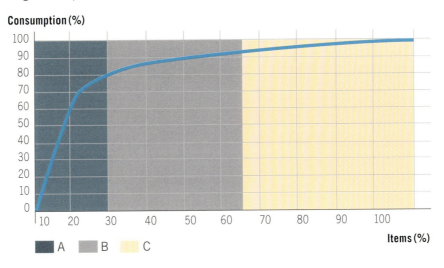

Chapter 1 - Concepts common to all warehouses

Obviously, the flow of materials has to be treated differently according to the rotation in question (A, B, or C). Here we illustrate two examples of possible applicable criteria:

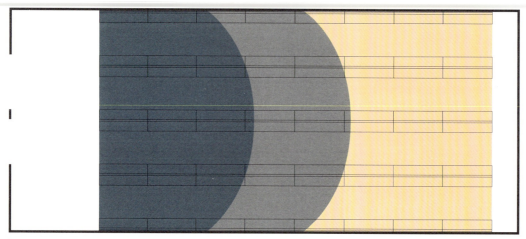

Layout of products throughout the warehouse according to rotation.

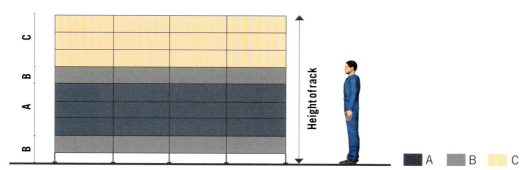

Arrangement on a rack (this normally applies to picking).

In the first example, the "A" products have been positioned closest to the loading and unloading area.

In the second example, the "A" products have been positioned in the most ergonomic part of the rack.

To arrange a warehouse in the most logical manner, each individual case must be analysed. There must also be an awareness that things may not be that simple, given that there are probably existing factors to be taken into account.

At times, to make the best possible use of the available space, it will be advisable to position products according to the storage systems used. However, in other situations, speed and the shortest possible time spent on operations will take precedence. Where feasible, a combination of both factors will be sought.

One example that demonstrates this is the standard combination of conventional and drive-in pallet racking in a warehouse, where the drive-in system is used for high rotation products.

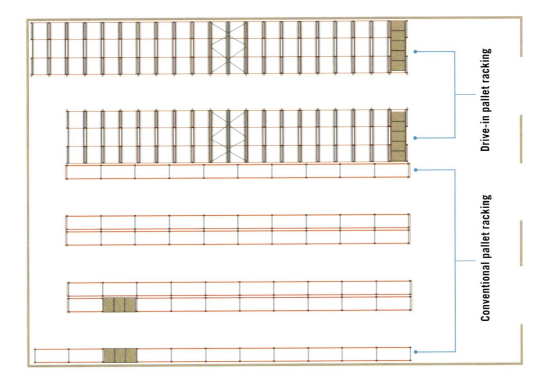

1.7.5 Conclusions about flows and rotation

Handling costs can be reduced (and therefore the warehouse made more profitable) if products are arranged in the correct manner according to their consumption, with appropriate handling, the correct order of flows, and if intermediate process points are correctly located .

To ensure that a warehouse is optimized, it is essential to choose the appropriate storage equipment, both in terms of the type of system and forklift trucks or handling equipment used.

The various storage systems (conventional, drive-in, live, etc.) explained later in this manual have different features which make them ideal in different situations.

Having a good warehouse management system (WMS) is vital for achieving the objectives set out in this section.

1.8 BASIC STRATEGIC CRITERIA

When planning and operating a warehouse, certain basic criteria must be taken into account in order to achieve the best possible and most profitable result. These criteria can be summarised thus:

- **Minimum stock levels** (except in the case of specific warehouses).
- Being able to **guarantee service** provision at all times.
- **Efficient monitoring and management**.
- Occupying the **minimum possible space**.
- Complying with **accessibility and ergonomic** criteria.
- **Minimum distance** to perform the operations.
- **Maximum performance**.
- Lowest **possible operating costs**.
- **Anticipating** requirements and offering the possibility for future **growth**.

The clearest example of how to meet these criteria can be seen in the car sector. Car manufacturers hold practically no stock of components, since it is the suppliers who supply these as and when required. This is known as the just in time procedure.

The manufacturer of the components, in turn, works with tight forecasts and short deadlines imposed by its customers. This means that in many cases the complete part is not available beforehand, rather just the elements that are assembled upon final confirmation. The final product is only stored for a few hours.

The component manufacturer must guarantee a flawless service because the entire assembly line relies on it. However, it must also work with very low prices controlled by its customer. This means that it has to reduce its fixed assets or working capital, which in turn means having the minimum possible stock controlled through good management.

In general nowadays, and not only in the car sector, the market is dominated by buyers. These specify what they want, how much, when, where, and how they want it. In this market, the only firms that succeed are those prepared to provide the best service.

The world has become smaller. Buyers can source from any continent, as long as the quality, price, and service are right. Given that Europe is not competitive with other regions on price, and given that the quality of the products in these other countries is acceptable, the only other way to compete is to offer good service.

While it is true that buyers are above all looking for the best product at the best price, the fact remains that they also place great value on good features and the supplier not failing them. For this reason, in addition to acceptable quality and a competitive price, companies that want to stay in business must offer excellent service and first-class customer care, characterised by flexibility, punctuality, variety, etc.

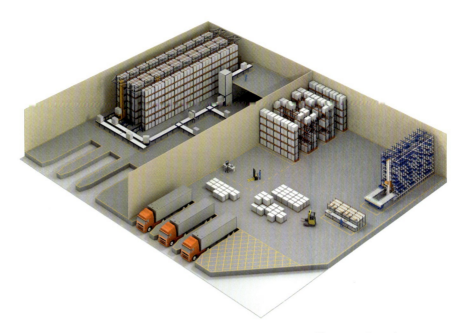

From what we have seen so far, it is clear that if a company wants to offer a good service, something must be stored somewhere along the chain (even when working with just in time systems): raw materials, components, tools, final products, etc. This means that companies require the appropriate resources and must manage these intelligently. This issue is addressed in the next section.

1.9 WAREHOUSE MANAGEMENT

1.9.1 What are the benefits of managing the facility well?

Good management of the warehouse allows a company to have the necessary stock, offer the best service, have high occupation levels for the warehouse, spend the shortest possible time on internal operations such as transport and picking, controlling stock, and optimising locations and flows, among other aspects.

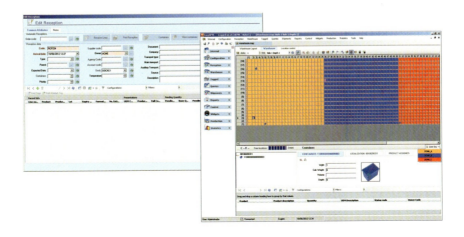

To ensure the best possible performance, the warehouse needs to be **smart**, i.e. managed logically and efficiently.

Nowadays, it is impossible to conceive of professional facilities that do not use warehouse management software (also known by its initials, WMS), which guarantees the requirements listed at the start of this chapter.

Choosing the right WMS is vital. As minimum, it must allow the company to perform the basic functions involved in managing the warehouse in a simple and intuitive manner.

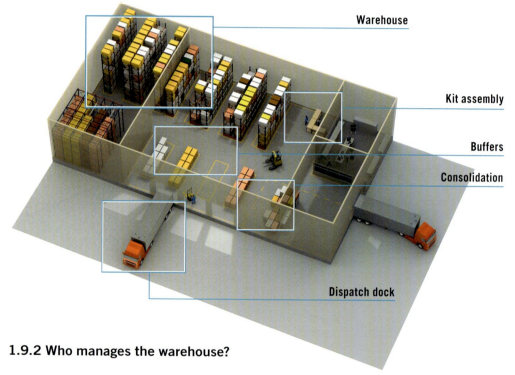

1.9.2 Who manages the warehouse?

Most warehouses are run directly by the company that owns the facilities (the manufacturer or marketer). All functions of the system can be integrated with the rest of the management of the company or run separately from, but coordinated with, the management. The WMS is only used for functions within the warehouse, and through a set of interfaces it establishes real-time communication with the company's general or central management system.

In addition, it is increasingly common for companies to outsource their logistics and storage services to **logistics operators** who, in addition to storage, can offer a comprehensive service and prepare picking, assemble components, arrange for transport, etc.

As a result, a single warehouse run by a logistics operator can hold goods from various customers or owners which have to be managed correctly. In these cases, the WMS must be able to be used on the basis of the **multi-owner principle**.

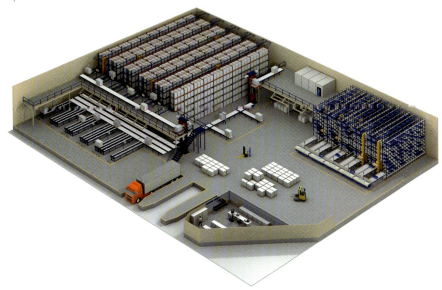

1.9.3 How are the goods and their location managed?

The management of the warehouse must be designed according to the functional analysis already performed. This functional analysis must follow the steps in the flows of materials and reflect the characteristics and type of facility and its components.

In terms of the location of the goods within the warehouse, one must take into account the classification of the products into A, B, or C, with "A" goods placed at the closest and most accessible points, as is explained in the discussion on flows and rotations in section 1.7.4.

The criterion used to determine the location of racks will determine the way of working and effective capacity. There are three ways of determining the location of each unit load.

With the **specific or fixed location** system, each item is assigned a position or a number of locations determined in advance. The great advantage of this method is the ease with which items can be located: warehouse personnel know where each item is without having to use IT tools for assistance. The great disadvantage of using this system is the loss of effective capacity, which is much lower than the physical capacity (number of locations). This issue is discussed in more detail in chapter 4.

This system must only be used in very small warehouses that do not need a management system.

With the **random location** system (also known as the chaotic, free, or varied system), goods are located in any available empty space using an approach previously established and configured (programmed) in the WMS. The classification into A, B, or C is generally taken into account. The system, into which all data have been entered (including empty spaces), tells the operator where to place goods or where they can be found.

In addition to the perfect management this provides, chaotic location allows the effective capacity of the warehouse to be much closer to the physical capacity, and can exceed 92% of the latter.

Lastly, the mixed or semi-random location system is the one most frequently-used and combines the specific and random systems, with each of these used according to the type of product or operation to be performed. Therefore, specific locations are used for high consumption products, which are generally close to the docks or picking areas, while the random system is used for other products and reserve areas.

The management of spaces, mainly in the specific systems, is in keeping with productivity criteria through the optimisation of routes, particularly those for preparing orders.

In addition to choosing the appropriate criterion, it is vital to have a WMS suitable for each case.

1.9.4 What functions does a WMS perform?

Although the flow analysis and the decision as to the type of location to use in the warehouse will determine the specific form and configuration of the management software, there are basic functions that are fundamental for any WMS to perform, such as the management of goods received and locations, stock control, and the dispatch of goods.

The **management of goods entering the warehouse** involves what are called receipt processes, which manage the entry of goods coming into the warehouse from different sources, such as purchases from suppliers, the transfer of goods between warehouses, manufacturing orders, and returns from customers.

Goods are received through the receipt process, during which the diversity, quantity, characteristics, and condition or quality of goods entering the warehouse (and which, therefore, will become part of its stock) are closely monitored. As a result, the information gathered is checked against the order received from the ERP system, which integrates internal and external management information across the organization.

Location management involves what are called location processes. These processes carry out orders for the placement of goods in the warehouse, determining their best position according to their type, characteristics, dimensions, etc. To do this, it uses previously specified rules and strategies.

Stock management is one of the most important tools in the WMS because it is used to obtain, in real time, the status, quantity, and characteristics of stock stored in the warehouse.

Last, but not least, are the dispatch processes. These processes create the orders sent to customers, transfers to other warehouses, and returns to suppliers. In short, they are responsible for the exit and removal of stock from the warehouse, through operations such as picking, the issue of complete containers, the consolidation of orders, and the dispatch of orders to the distribution vehicle.

The following sections contain a summary of the operations that must be performed by the WMS for each of these basic functions.

Chapter 1 - Concepts common to all warehouses

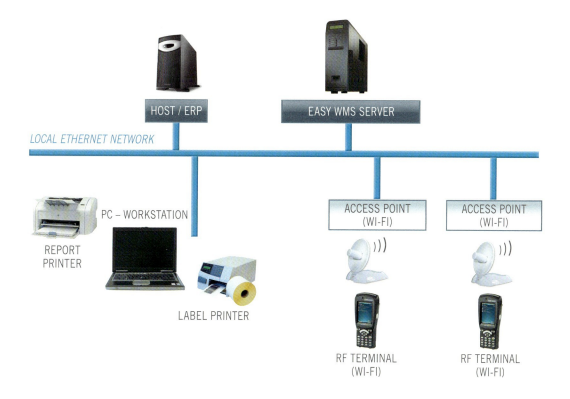

Entry functions

Within this group there are three main operations that can be managed through the WMS: receipt, capturing logistical data, and labelling containers and goods.

In terms of **receipt,** items are at times received not palletized. These need to be consolidated into different containers as their characteristics and logistics attributes are recorded, before being located within the warehouse.

Sometimes goods arriving are already palletised, which means that there is no need for consolidation and it is only necessary to validate their logistics attributes and the quality of goods received before locating them in the warehouse.

The third type of basic receipt is that of returns. While this is similar to the types of receipt mentioned above, it does involve specific features, such as applying statuses and blocks when the items enter the facilities. These statuses and blocks can indicate, for example, the need to pass the items through quality control, remain pending inspection, etc. These must then be located in the warehouse in specific areas established for this type of goods.

The second main function when goods enter is to **capture logistics data**. These data include information such as the batch to which the load belongs, its best before date, weight, temperature, serial number, etc. Capturing these data during receipt provides the stock with a degree of traceability.

Logistics attributes, such as the batch or serial number, tell us a posteriori which goods have been used by each specific client.

The third function when goods enter is complementary to the above. A WMS must be able to generate barcode labels for all containers and goods stored. Thanks to this, all processes and operations carried out within the warehouse will be accurately validated by reading these codes, eliminating the possibility of errors or confusion that can arise when handling the goods.

Each item received can also be labelled with a barcode so that processes when the goods leave the warehouse are quicker and more efficient.

Receipt documentation can also be used to prepare reports that show the differences between the goods forecast and those actually received, as well as other aspects, such as compliance with time slots for receiving goods.

The role of the WMS does not end with these activities. Through an interface, it **transmits the completion of receipt to the company's ERP**, stating the exact number of units that have entered the warehouse. The ERP can then carry out the administrative procedures with the suppliers.

<u>Location functions</u>
This type of operation involves the following three important processes: location through rules and strategies, cross-docking, and restocking and consolidation.

The first of these processes, **managing the location through rules and strategies**, means finding the ideal location within the warehouse for a specific good. To determine this, the software takes into account parameters such as the rotation of items (A, B, or C), the types of containers used for the consolidation of goods, the families or types of products being handled, the hazardousness or incompatibility of different products so that they are not stored close to each other, the features and volume of items, etc.

The use of **cross-docking reduces the number of movements** with the load. If there is a live order but a lack of stock, when the relevant product arrives in the warehouse it is taken directly from the receipt area and housed in the order preparation area. Once the necessary items have been prepared for dispatch, the remainder are located within the warehouse.

The third function, the **management of restocking and consolidation**, is also designed to reduce the movement of goods within the warehouse. As with cross-docking, it is applied before the load is placed in its final position. This function is carried out in centres with picking positions. If there is little of the product left in these positions, the latter must be restocked with the goods that have just arrived, ensuring that there is sufficient stock to fulfil orders. The load that remains after this operation is then located within the warehouse.

Stock control functions

When managing the goods stored, the WMS must be able to provide complete and useful information about the stock. To do this, it uses several features.

The most intuitive of these is the **display of a map of the warehouse**. This provides access, on a screen, to a graphical representation of the facilities showing each of the locations and their composition, both in terms of the containers and the goods themselves.

Location management is another tool that must be offered by a WMS. With this tool, the user can obtain and edit information about the positions, such as the type of location, the blocks applied, its dimensions, its characteristics, the storage areas to which it belongs, etc.

It must also be possible to manage the status of stock, in order to check and change data relating to quarantines, breakage, losses, blocks, reserves, etc.

The WMS can also perform operations that help with stock management. One of these is the **calculation of item rotation**. Using movements over a specified period of time, the system can determine and report on the ideal rotation for an article and compare this with the relevant information in the article master. With this tool, the A B C rotation can be recalculated and the classification assigned to the item changed where this is considered more efficient or helpful.

There is a final vital feature relating to stock, which is the **recount and inventory**. With these programmable tasks, a recount and inventory can be taken of everything from the entire warehouse to a specific article, location, or particular area. Any discrepancies in stock are automatically reported to the ERP.

Exit functions

In addition to managing the receipt and location of goods, the management system also monitors the dispatch of goods.

The main functions for this storage phase start **with managing the preparation of the load** leaving the warehouse. This includes grouping and assigning orders, among other aspects, and allows for control over how orders are filled and who is responsible for them: assigning dispatch docks, the operators to complete the preparation, the way of grouping orders and the time slot in which it occurs, etc.

As part of the preparation, the WMS can manage operations that need to be carried out, such as **picking processes**, at a very detailed level. In this regard, the system determines and guides the routes of personnel assigned to this task, as well as the presentation of items.

One of the most important advantages of having a WMS control picking is that the system is capable of optimising the process so that it is completed in the shortest time possible and using the least number of movements necessary, while simultaneously respecting the parameters specified for the order sent by the ERP.

Another part of preparing goods is the labelling of dispatches, through which order items are identified. The same procedures as labelling on receipt are used.

Dispatches are documented upon exit, which helps with the generation of documents such as the packing list (list of articles included in the order), documentation for the transport company, and reports that reflect any discrepancies found.

After these operations, the WMS manages the process of loading the good for dispatch onto the vehicles. Thanks to this function, the quality of the dispatch is controlled and errors such as the dispatching of a material not requested by the client are avoided.

The WMS can manage everything up to the final phases of the issuing operations, such as communicating the final dispatch to the ERP using through the interface between the two systems. With this function, the company's resource manager is informed of how many units of each item have been included in the dispatch, as well as which items are dispatched in each of the issue orders completed. With this information, the ERP can manage administrative processes with the customers.

Functions in complex warehouses

On occasions, facilities consist of interrelated areas or warehouses. For example, it may be necessary to manage an area of conventional pallet racking, an automated warehouse with stacker cranes, an automated horizontal carousel (explained later in this manual), etc. There are endless combinations that can create highly complex centres. A single WMS must be able to manage all of these different types of area with different operations for the receipt, location, and issuing processes globally and in a coordinated manner.

The software must be capable of managing **order preparation systems that use pick to light and put to light solutions**. This type of facility, which is described in another section of this manual, helps provide greater fluidity and speed in order preparation.

Picking can also be sped up through the use of other technology, such as voice picking. With this system, which must be managed by the WMS, the operator does not have to use his or her hands to operate the terminal or other controls, but receives the orders over a voice system and can also give instructions to the system verbally. This allows for greater manoeuvrability with goods that have to be handled using two hands. This solution is excellent for warehouses of frozen products, since it allows communication without having to use the terminals while wearing gloves and speeds up work (where times are monitored) within the chambers.

The management system must also be able to **manage the stackability** of goods when preparing orders. This allows items to be prepared in an optimal manner following determined parameters. In other words, it is ensured that, for example, on a single pallet or in a single container the goods are prepared starting with the most solid and ending with the least solid.

There are another three functions that are essential for integrating the facilities into the rest of the company or logistics centre. The first is the **management of the flows of goods (receipt and dispatch) to production lines**. With this feature, the optimal flow of goods to or from the production or manufacturing lines is achieved, which obviously facilitates internal processes.

The second function relates to the administration of various warehouses with a single WMS (**multi-warehouse management**). With this feature, a company can manage all of its warehouses with a single global system and, as a result, optimise resources as well as IT systems. This also helps the processes of transferring goods between different warehouses.

Thirdly, and at a higher level to the above, we have multi-organisation management which, as the name suggests, means that various organisations can be managed by the same WMS.

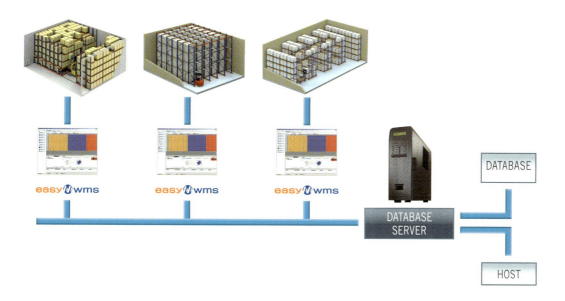

Lastly, for some projects **developments that are specifically adapted to the customer are required**. Certain operations carried out by some companies may not be included a priori in the software, so a specific development is required which takes as its starting point the existing WMS. As a result, the management system must be sufficiently versatile and open to allow for the programming of these customised features.

1.9.5 The importance of radio frequency

When performing tasks controlled by the WMS, one aspect of great importance is communication between the management system and the operators carrying out the orders assigned to them and from whom the system also receives information, such as information on receipt of an item.

Operators must be given instructions for tasks and the order in which these are to be carried out. This can be done verbally, in a written document (such as a delivery note), or through radio frequency terminals (RF).

The use of radio frequency technology has many advantages. There is no need for paper, since the orders are sent to the IT terminals that operators carry with them or are fixed to the handling machines. Communication between the IT server and these devices takes place without the need for cables, using radio waves emitted and received by the aerial equipment strategically positioned around the warehouse.

Using the terminal's keyboard (now this can also be done through voice), personnel in the warehouse confirm each operation and immediately receive a new order. The system is very fast, and avoids the need for operators to ask about or contemplate every action, as they only need to carry out the orders. The result is very high performance and almost error-free operations.

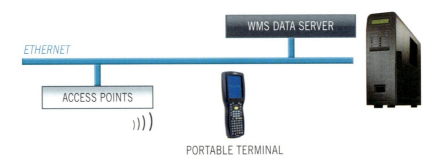

The use of radiofrequency means working in real time. In other words, the management system automatically knows at all times where the goods are, what quantity there is, under what circumstances or in which processes, etc.

As set out in the section on the operations when goods arrive, to be able to work with radio frequency goods and locations must be encoded, allowing the automatic confirmation of data.

1.9.6 Automatic identification systems

The application of technology to the warehouse is not limited to the management of the facilities and goods or to communication with the operators. It is also used to identify the items being handled.

Chapter 1 - Concepts common to all warehouses

Source: Mecalux.

At present, the vast majority of products have a recorded or printed barcode or integrated RFID chip (an identifier that uses radio frequency to transmit data). These systems allow each unit to be managed in the warehouse using laser or radio readers, respectively.

These codes follow rigorous standardised rules on general use, which allow details such as the product in question, its manufacturer, its traceability, its logistical data, and its specific features to be ascertained.

Understanding how these identifications work is essential to understanding how some operations in modern warehouses work.

Barcodes

This type of identification system consists of printing bars on labels (which are then affixed to the items) or on the packaging itself. These bars are generated in accordance with approved encoding standards (currently EAN-13 and EAN-128).

Example of an EAN-13 barcode label that identifies the product.

Example of an EAN-128 barcode label that identifies the pallet, the product it contains and the characteristics of said product.

Chapter 1 - Concepts common to all warehouses

In the foreground, the P&D station for an automated warehouse. In the background, conventional storage.
Source: Mecalux.

When barcodes are scanned (read) with a laser terminal, the terminal interprets the data and reports them to the management system.

In addition to identifying items, this labelling system is used to identify locations on racks, as well as pallets and containers.

All automated systems for management and movement must have these codes to so that data about the load being handled can be communicated at any time.

<u>RFID encoding</u>
This type of identification of products by radio frequency, which involves attaching a chip to the product, has been gradually introduced over the last few years. When this label is within the action radius of a special aerial, the information contained in the chip is automatically read.

The great advantage of this system is the speed of reading since, among other things, there is no need for the label to be facing a reading system in a specific position.

In terms of storage, the main benefit comes from the ease it provides in identifying the positions of units stored in their locations.

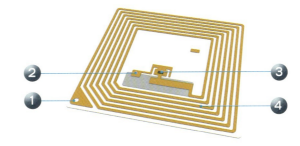

1. **Contact**
2. **Condenser**
3. **Microchip.** Device that stores information on the product.
4. **Transmission aerial.** This can be low frequency, emitting radio waves of up to 2 m (on average) or high frequency, whose transmission capacity can reach up to 100 m.

CHAPTER 2
THE LOAD UNIT, IN DEPTH

In the previous chapter, we mentioned load units and defined them in general terms. We will now go into more detail about this element, which is fundamental for the operation of the warehouse.

Load unit is the term given to a number of small products grouped together to make it easier to handle them in logistics processes. The number of items in a group depends on their nature and size and on financial aspects of their management, for both production functions and distribution.

When making decisions about storage, one of the most important factors is to choose the most appropriate size and weight for the load unit.

2.1 GROUPING PRODUCTS INTO LARGER LOAD UNITS

Some products are not subject to physical limitations for handling purposes (such as items supplied in bulk), and can therefore be grouped into a wide variety of load units of all sizes. As a result, their handling costs are lower.

Given that one of the main objectives when it comes to managing goods is to limit the number of movements to an absolute minimum, it is convenient and desirable to generate the largest load unit possible.

The problem that can arise is that while these products are often produced on a mass scale or in large batches and are supplied in the largest load units that can be handled, their distribution may be subject to different needs when it comes to the most appropriate size of the loads.

Chapter 2 - The load unit

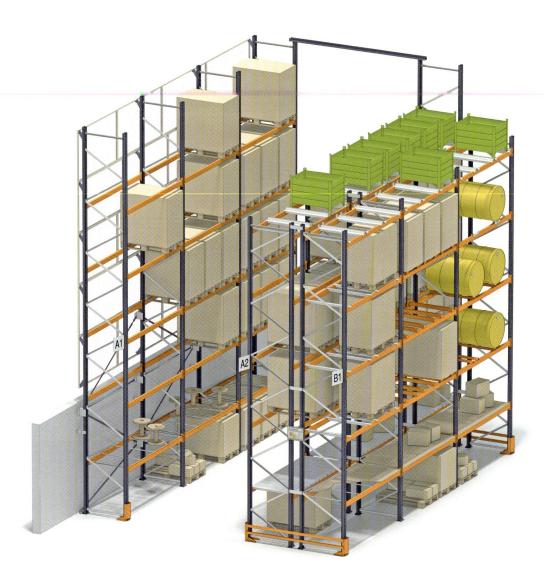

There is no doubt that in the vast majority of cases, handling large loads makes storage easier. However, it is common for products that entered a warehouse in a specific load size to leave it in much smaller units.

One way of combining both criteria is to generate a small load unit, one that can be handled individually but which is also suitable for being handled once grouped, thereby reducing costs.

In view of these issues, all elements in a materials handling system must be considered as a whole. Therefore, the first step is to analyse the strength and stability of the loads in more detail.

Pallet | Container

2.2 PALLETS AND CONTAINERS: GENERAL ISSUES

When it comes to load units, one of the fundamental issues is what in many cases constitutes the support structure in which the items to be stored are grouped.

Support structures consisting of a platform onto which the goods are deposited are called pallets, while recipients or packages into which the load is placed are called containers. Both are auxiliary equipment used to create, move, and store load units and products.

It is essential to pay particular attention to these elements, since their shapes, dimensions, and strengths and the materials used to manufacture them are not always suitable for all different storage systems, or may require complementary tools or accessories to help position them on racking units. Furthermore, their characteristics also affect the handling equipment and methods used.

This manual reviews the most common types of pallets and containers. However, when planning the facility, there are specific models the details of which it is necessary to know in advance, such as their shape, dimensions, materials, etc.

2.3 PALLETS

Pallets can be made of wood, metal, or plastic. The following is a review of the models and characteristics following this classification according to material.

2.3.1 Wooden pallets

Platforms made of wood are the most commonly used, and in the main are manufactured in accordance with the five models set out below.

TYPE 1

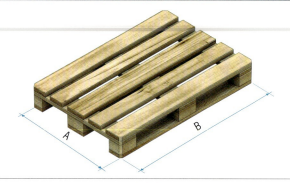

LENGTH (B)	DEPTH (A)
	800
1200	1000
	1200

Nominal dimensions in mm.

This is the most commonly used model and is the only one that can be used interchangeably in all storage systems, as long as its skids (the lower supports bearing the flat platform where the load will rest) are perpendicular to the beams of the racking units, the support rails or the roller conveyors, as shown in the following illustration:

 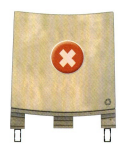

In each case they must be handled using the side which makes this possible (see the illustration above):
Side A: Storage in a conventional racking unit, by gravity and with roller push-back.
Side B: Storage in drive-in pallet racking units, trolley push-back and radio-shuttle systems. Cross ties for pallets are required in conventional racking units.

Any type of forklift or pallet handling element can easily handle these pallets.
They are ideal for automated warehouses.
The only precaution to be taken when using them is to ensure they are of the appropriate quality.
There is a European standard which specifies how they are produced. Pallets that meet these specifications are called europallets (see below).
Not all 800mm x 1200mm pallets are europallets. Europallets are identified by a circular logo with the letters EUR inside.
1000mm x 1200mm and 1200mm x 1200mm pallets produced in accordance with europallet specifications and quality are called "europallet type".

TYPE 2

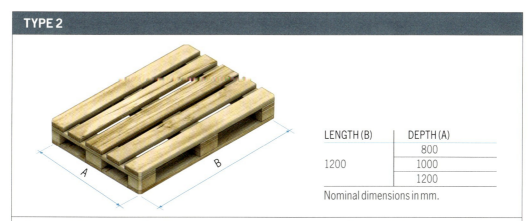

LENGTH (B)	DEPTH (A)
	800
1200	1000
	1200

Nominal dimensions in mm.

The use of these pallets is quite widespread in some countries (mostly 1000mm x 1200mm).
They can be stored on conventional, drive-in pallet, trolley push-back, and radio-shuttle racking units.
They can cause problems in systems operated by gravity and in roller push-back systems.
They are not ideal for use with stacker cranes or bilateral forklifts, except when lifted by the lower part (the bases that link the skids).
They are not suitable for handling with stackers.
They are not the most suitable type to be used with automated roller conveyors; it is advisable to use automated chain conveyors instead.

TYPES 3 AND 4

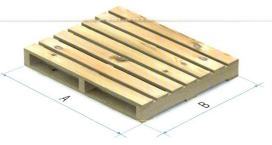

TYPE 3

LENGTH (B)	DEPTH (A)
1200	1000
	1200

Nominal dimensions in mm.

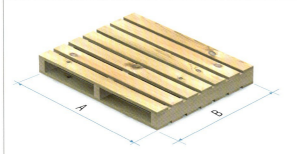

TYPE 4

LENGTH (B)	DEPTH (A)
1200	1000
	1200

Nominal dimensions in mm.

These can be stored on conventional or drive-in pallet, trolley push-back, and radio-shuttle racking units. They cannot be used in systems with gravity or roller push-back systems. When they are stored on conventional racking units care must be taken with the edges, as the two scenarios described below could come to pass. These two situations are entirely unacceptable, since they put the safety and integrity of the facility and the load at risk.

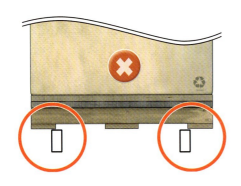

The pallet is not well supported by the beam, so it could fall.

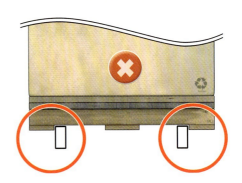

The beam is very close to the lower board so the forklift, on picking up the pallet, could push it and deform the beam.

TYPES 5A AND 5B

TYPE 5A

LENGTH (B)	DEPTH (A)
800	600

Nominal dimensions in mm.

TYPE 5B

LENGTH (B)	DEPTH (A)
600	800

Nominal dimensions in mm.

These platforms are also called half-pallets, as their measurements are half those of a 1200mm x 800mm pallet.
These pallets are frequently used in the distribution sector for mass-market products, since they facilitate distribution of the most appropriate quantities for sale. In addition, thanks to their size, they are ideal for being handled at a point of sale (such as in supermarkets).
Equivalent to half a europallet.
To store these in conventional racking units, cross ties or a support surface must be placed on the beams.
Only pallet 5A can be stored in live pallet racking units, although with some restrictions.
For other uses, they must be positioned in pairs on normal 1200mm x 800mm europallets (when used in this way, these lower pallets are called slave pallets).
Any type of forklift can be used to handle them without restrictions, although it is necessary to take into account the measurements of the forks.
Unless used with slave pallets, automated conveyors must be specifically designed if these pallets are to be moved. They must either have more rollers than conventional automated conveyors or have four chains.

OTHER PALLETS

The five types of wooden pallet discussed above are the most frequently used, but not the only ones.

There are different standards whereby attempts have been made to establish internationally recognised criteria for production in terms of dimensions, shapes, types of wood, nails, etc. The europallet is the result of such standardisation, as will be discussed later.

However, there are other pallets that do not comply with this standard, such as those illustrated below. Although they have external measurements similar to those of the europallet, they are not produced to the same specifications and, as a result, may not be strong enough nor have the expected strength.

There is a wide variety of formats available other than those of types 1, 2 and 3 (as regards both measurements and construction). All of these cause problems when stored on racking units or when handled using handling elements. This means that specific handling is required and complementary pieces must be fitted to the racking units.

Particular care must be taken with platforms described as "single use" or disposable pallets. Although these are of standard measurements, the wood used may be of a thickness and quality which makes them unsuitable for storing directly on racking units.

These are examples of pallets which could cause difficulties.

Chipboard.	Two openings, double-sided, reversible.	Four openings, double-sided, reversible.
Four openings, double-sided, not reversible (single use).	Two openings, double-sided, not reversible.	Four openings, double-sided, not reversible.
Two openings, single-sided, not reversible.	Four openings, double-sided, reversible.	

2.3.2 Metal pallets

In addition to those made from wood, pallets can also be produced from other materials, such as metal.

Metal pallets are most commonly used in the automotive sector and metal industry. As a result, their upper parts can be adapted to transport pre-assembled components.

They are normally produced following the specifications and measurements for wooden europallets. In this case, they are used in the same way.

Metal pallets produced using specifications other than those for the europallet will require specific treatment. The possible deformation of support beams must also be taken into account.

Given their rigidity and the possibility of deformation, care must be taken when using metal pallets with live pallet roller racking units.

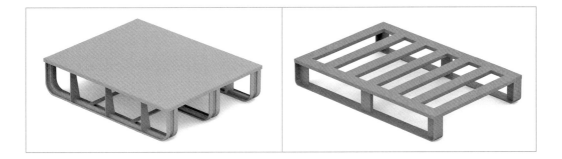

2.3.3 Plastic pallets

The third material used to produce this type of support structure is injection moulded plastic. At present plastic pallets are not widely used, despite the fact that, a priori, they offer certain advantages over wooden or metal pallets.

First, plastic pallets are around half the weight of wooden pallets with the same characteristics.

A second advantage is that they are the easiest type to clean, something that is highly valued in the food industry in particular. However, it should be borne in mind that plastic pallets with a complex design require mechanised and exhaustive cleaning, since they have many corners that are difficult to access in which dirt can very easily accumulate.

Plastic pallets can be coloured, and therefore personalised for each user to make them easier to locate and control. They are also more durable, lasting approximately ten times longer than wooden equivalents, and do not suffer as much from the inevitable blows that occur during handling.

However, plastic pallets are not without disadvantages. To start with, they are more likely to become deformed under an excessive load. At the time of publishing this manual, they were also more expensive than wooden ones.

Another disadvantage is that when this type of pallet is damp there is a risk that they will slip on the forks of forklifts, live pallet racking units, or on mobile racking units, with the associated risks of falling or sliding.

Lastly, particular care must be taken in relation to their strength. The type of plastic, the thicknesses and ribs used, the mould construction system, and the injection will all have a bearing on their strength and rigidity.

As regards use, plastic pallets normally adhere to the production and dimension specifications of wooden europallets (types 1, 2 and 3). In these cases, their application is the same.

Some examples:

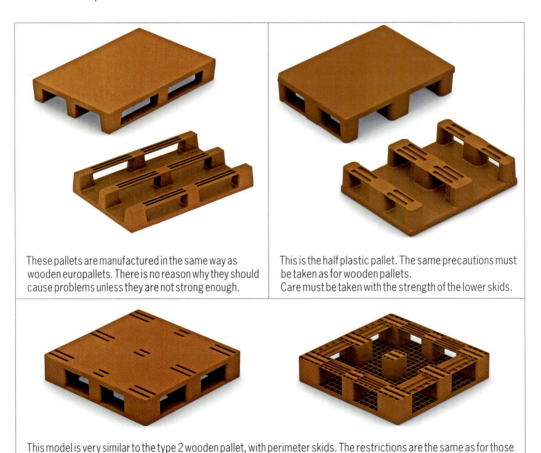

These pallets are manufactured in the same way as wooden europallets. There is no reason why they should cause problems unless they are not strong enough.

This is the half plastic pallet. The same precautions must be taken as for wooden pallets.
Care must be taken with the strength of the lower skids.

This model is very similar to the type 2 wooden pallet, with perimeter skids. The restrictions are the same as for those pallets.

2.3.4 Other plastic pallets

There are other types of plastic pallet that require specific handling if used in the different storage systems, and which will require special attention if chosen for use in the warehouse. Some examples of this type of pallet are shown below.

Image provided by Disset.

2.4 CONTAINERS

The second type of load support structure, though not used as widely as the pallet, is the container. Containers can also be made of wood, metal or plastic and come in various shapes, sizes, and types of construction.

2.4.1 Wooden containers

These are normally produced using a wooden europallet as the base, onto which two or more side panels of metal mesh or wood are placed.

Image provided by Embalajes Cantabria.

Image provided by Embalajes Bercalsa.

If the base is a europallet, the container can be used in all the applications already listed for type 1 pallets. Specific handling will be required for other container models.

Care must be taken when choosing a container. It is vital that all of its characteristics, as well as how it will be used, be taken into account.

For example, the containers shown below can cause problems in terms of strength, depending on the load and how they are used.

The lower skids on wooden containers may be weak, since they are generally used for a single delivery with no return.

2.4.2 Metal containers

A wide variety of metal containers is available, and can be purchased in different sizes. Their use can be limited when used in storage systems with racking units, as explained below.

METAL CONTAINERS WITHOUT SKIDS. TYPE 1
To store these on conventional racking units, specific supports for containers or platforms must be placed on the beams.
They can be placed on drive-in pallet racking units, although this is not advisable due to possible local deformation of the rails.
They are not suitable for use in push-back or radio-shuttle systems, or in live pallet racking units.
Nor are they valid for use in automated warehouses.
They cannot be used on roller or chain conveyors.
Measurement "B" is normally greater than "A" (see image) and care must be taken with clearances.
They are mainly developed to be stacked on top of each other.

Chapter 2 - The load unit

METAL CONTAINERS WITHOUT SKIDS. TYPE 2
Depending on measurement "A" (see image), these can be placed on conventional racking units without a container support, although the installation of such a support is advised.
These metal containers can be stored on drive-in pallet racking units, while in push-back systems with trolleys their use depends on measurement "A" and the number of trolleys.
They are not suitable for live pallet racking units, roller push-back, or radio-shuttle systems.
They are, however, suitable for automated warehouses, taking into account the dimensions of the legs.
They are not ideal for use with roller conveyors. The use of chain conveyors is advised.

METAL CONTAINERS WITH SKIDS
These are suitable for use with any storage system and can be used with any handling element.
It should be remembered that for clearances, measurement "B" is greater than "A" on both sides.
Care must be taken with rigidity and possible deformations of the lower skid, as these could prevent live pallet racking units from functioning correctly.
The dimensions and shape of the lower skids must be checked to prevent local deformations in the support beams or rollers.

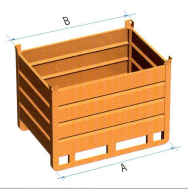

Chapter 2 - The load unit

OTHER METAL CONTAINERS
These require specific handling if they are to be stored on racking units.
Special care must be taken with large containers – those exceeding 1200mm at the front – and clearances increased.

Image provided by Tatoma.   Image provided by Tatoma.   Image provided by Plastipol.

2.4.3 Plastic containers

The base of a plastic container is normally made in the same way as plastic pallets.

Those produced with a base that meets europallet specifications can be used under the same conditions as type 1 pallets, with specific considerations for plastic pallets.

Image provided by Plastipol.

Chapter 2 - The load unit

Where the base of the container does not comply with Europallet requirements, specific handling is required (the following images show two examples of this type of container).

Image provided by Plastipol.

2.4.4 Box type containers

These are smaller containers than those previously discussed (maximum dimensions 800mm x 600mm), and are mainly designed to store small loose or unstable products.

These containers are normally placed on pallets using automatic conveyors for boxes (see below) or miniload stacker cranes (also explained in the next chapter), manually or statically on racking units.

The measurements of the most commonly used boxes are submultiples of the europallet. They are called euroboxes. Some models are shown below.

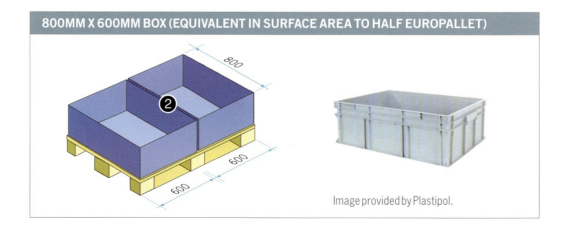

800MM X 600MM BOX (EQUIVALENT IN SURFACE AREA TO HALF EUROPALLET)

Image provided by Plastipol.

Chapter 2 - The load unit

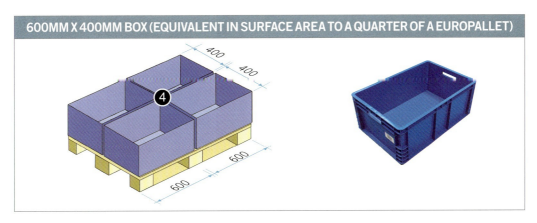

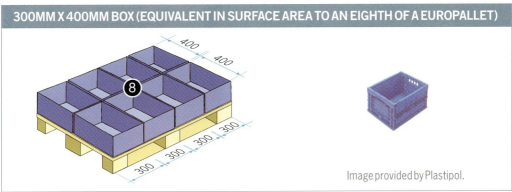

Image provided by Plastipol.

Of the three models described the most commonly used is the 600mm x 400 mm box, followed by the 800mm x 600mm box.

The above boxes can be subdivided to contain various items without mixing.

Some models include a folding lid.

The base can be reinforced depending on the weight the box contains and the handling system used.

When handling the boxes, a series of factors must be taken into account depending on their use within the warehouse. For example, when resting on pallets they are handled in the same manner as these pallets.

When using automatic conveyors for boxes, four factors must be considered: the width of the conveyors; the weight of the box; the rigidity of the base of the box; and the stability of the product inside the container. These are the same factors that must be evaluated for the use of boxes in miniloads.

In facilities where boxes are handled manually, it is essential to take into account their dimensions, ergonomics, and weight. If they are static and housed on racking units, they serve as pigeonholes holes and, therefore, provision will have to be made for the necessary space or method of accessing the product.

Chapter 2 - The load unit

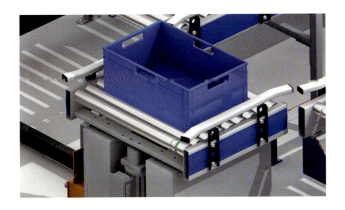

Industrial supplies company. Source: Mecalux.

Other types of boxes

In addition to the previous models, which are the most commonly used, there are other types of boxes with other dimensions and other production systems that will require specific handling in each case. Some examples are shown here.

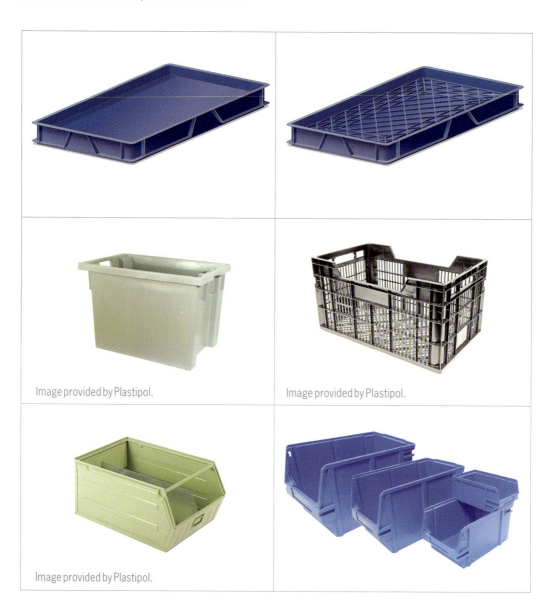

Image provided by Plastipol.

Image provided by Plastipol.

Image provided by Plastipol.

The standardisation of pallets arose from the need to optimise their use and make the best possible use of space.

In Europe, the UNE-EN 13698-1 standard includes the production specifications for pallets and, as a result, the 1200mm x 800mm europallet was adopted.

There are many advantages associated with using this pallet. It can be used in any storage system, but above all it is ideal for automated warehouses. It can be handled, without restrictions, by any type of forklift or handling equipment. In addition, the dimensions (1200mm x 800mm) are multiples of standard plastic boxes, which makes it easier to group goods and products.

As explained earlier, the dimensions of the most commonly used plastic and cardboard boxes

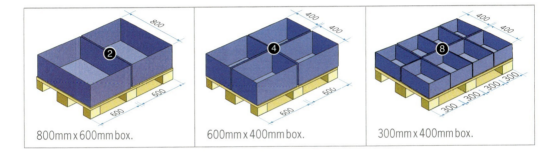

| 800mm x 600mm box. | 600mm x 400mm box. | 300mm x 400mm box. |

are submultiples of 1200mm x 800mm.

Standardisation has also resulted in spaces in trucks and shipping containers being made more uniform.

The platforms used by trailer-type trucks can fit 33 of the 800mm x 1200mm pallets, positioned as shown in the images below.

Shipping containers have a smaller pallet capacity, as their internal dimensions are 2300mm.

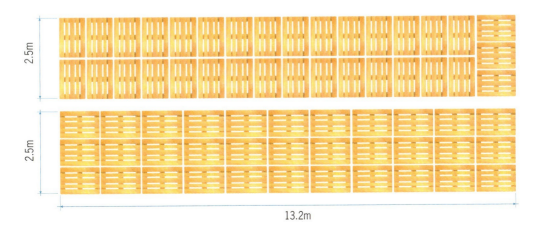

Shipping containers have a smaller pallet capacity, as their internal dimensions are 2300mm.

While the advantages are clear, what specifications must be met for a pallet to be classified as a europallet?

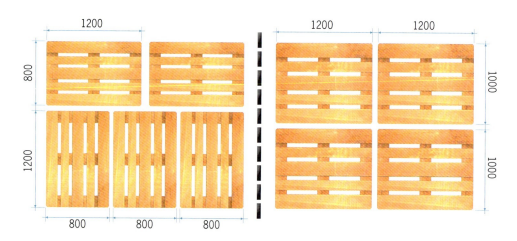

Layout of pallets in a shipping container. Dimensions in mm.

Europallets are type 1 pallets that measure 800mm x 1200mm and are produced according to specific quality specifications. The different parts of the pallet and the dimensions are shown on the next page.

One important detail about europallets is that they have chamfers on the four corners and bevelled upper edges on the skids to assist their extraction.

Block

Skid

CONSTRUCTION OF EUROPALLETS

Longitudinal view. Dimensions in mm.

Cross-section view. Dimensions in mm.

Top view. Dimensions in mm.

Bottom view. Dimensions in mm.

TABLE OF PALLET PARTS

No.	No. of parts	Name of the parts	Measurements (in mm)
1	2	Lower opening	1200 x 100 x 22
2	2	Upper opening	1200 x 145 x 22
3	1	Central board	1200 x 145 x 22
4	3	Tie bar	800 x 145 x 22
5	1	Central board	1200 x 145 x 22
6	2	Intermediate board	1200 x 100 x 22
7	6	Block	145 x 100 x 78
8	3	Block	145 x 145 x 78
9	42	Threaded countersunk wood screw or threaded nail	M 5.5 x 90
10	18	Threaded countersunk wood screw or threaded nail	M 5.5 x 38

2.6 STACKING GOODS ON PALLETS

The standardisation of pallets and containers has advantages when it comes optimising how load units are created, since boxes can be stacked on top of each other, taking full advantage of the space available.

The correct stacking of boxes on pallets is fundamental for guaranteeing the stability of the whole structure.

For this reason, the trend is towards the production of cardboard boxes that are submultiples of 1200mm x 800mm (the measurements of a europallet) to make the best possible use of the surface area of the pallets.

Boxes are normally stacked on pallets in one of the two ways illustrated below.

Staggered boxes.   Stacked boxes

In the first example a 400mm x 200mm box has been chosen, while in the second example the box is 400mm x 300mm. Both measurements are submultiples of 1200mm x 800mm, so full advantage is taken of the space. The first approach is more stable as the boxes are stacked in staggered fashion.

When the boxes are staggered, it is recommended that they be strapped or shrink-wrapped. This is essential if the boxes are stacked.

It must be remembered that the layers may have a chimney-like empty space, depending on the dimensions of the boxes.

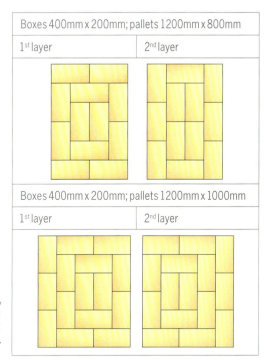

Examples of load unit layouts, using staggered layers of boxes that are submultiples of the pallet dimensions.

Even when the goods are shrink-wrapped, it is still fairly common for packages to shift due to movements during transportation and handling of the pallets. As a result, there is an increase in the dimensions of the load unit, generally in the upper part. Some examples are as follows:

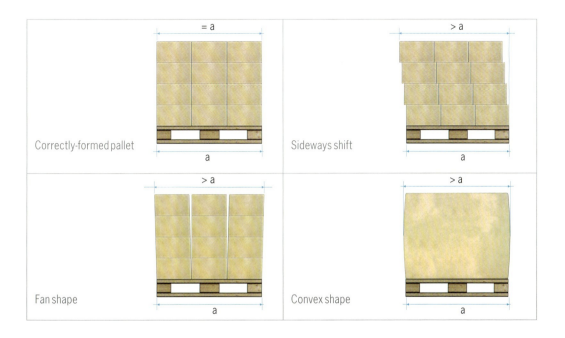

Chapter 2 - The load unit

When the measurements of the boxes used are not multiples of the dimensions of the pallet on which they are stacked, two situations can arise.

The first is that the storage capacity of the pallet is reduced, as can be seen in the following example:

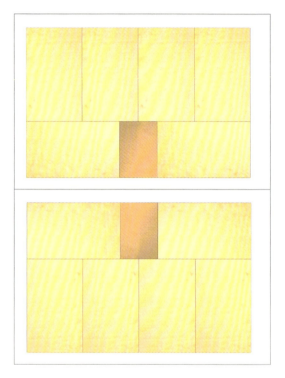

The second is that the layer of boxes is wider than the pallet. In this case, this particular feature must be taken into account and storage positions must be designed to allow a sufficiently wide space.

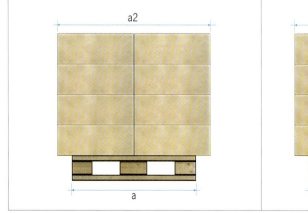

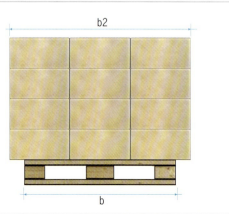

2.7 CONCLUSION

The construction, dimensions, and quality of pallets and containers, as well as the measurements of the load, how it is stacked, etc. are factors that have a direct impact on the solution proposed when planning a warehouse.

A correct evaluation of data relating to the load unit (in this case, the pallet or container) is essential to achieving the ideal logistics solution which will both meet the specific needs of the client at all levels and operate smoothly.

CHAPTER 3
HANDLING EQUIPMENT

Within warehouses, goods need to be moved from the reception point to their storage position and, from there, to their point of dispatch. This is done with the help of handling equipment. The use of this equipment determines the distribution, performance, and number of operators required in the warehouse. Therefore, it is essential to know what types of machines are available, how they work, what they are used for, and what their basic features are.

The great variety of warehouses and operations has also resulted in a wide range of handling equipment available, from simple forklift trucks that carry out all tasks (loading and unloading, internal transport, and storing on the racking units) to groups of specific pieces of equipment, such as pallet trucks, automated conveyors, reach trucks, VNA trucks, stacker cranes, etc., each with a specific function.

This chapter contains an overview of both non-lifting – or minimal lifting – equipment, used only for transport, and other equipment that can lift and position goods in locations at a certain height.

The cost of these machines, the storage capacity they provide, the use to which they are put, and the personnel required to operate them, among other aspects, will have a direct bearing on the facility's investment and running costs. As a result, these elements are crucial when assessing the return on investment.

Certain basic features of handling equipment influence the layout of a warehouse, such as the types of machines used, their dimensions, the manoeuvring aisles they require to operate, the maximum lifting height for goods reached, and the volume of goods handled. A warehouse's capacity will to a large extent depend on these features, particularly on the manoeuvring aisle and the height to which loads can be lifted.

The following is a summary of the basic features of this handling equipment. To make comparisons easier, they have been grouped into conventional systems with manual controls and totally automated systems.

Chapter 3 - Handling equipment

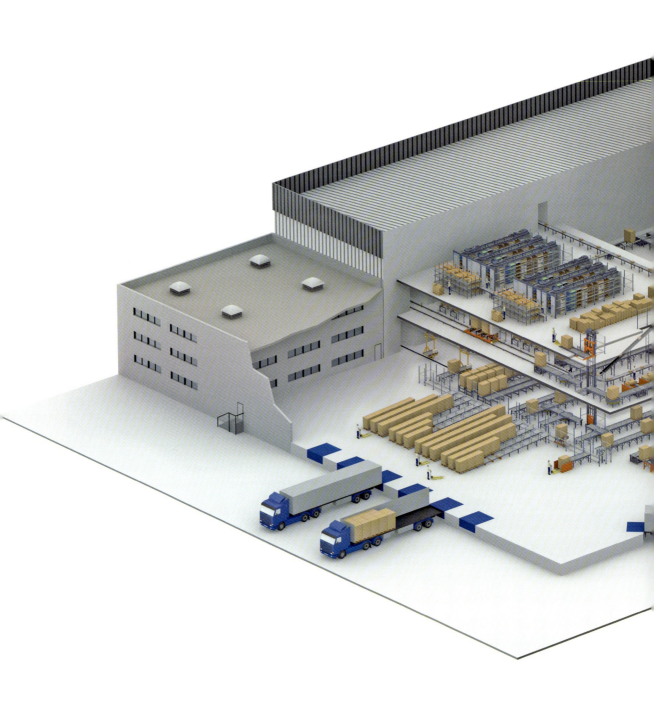

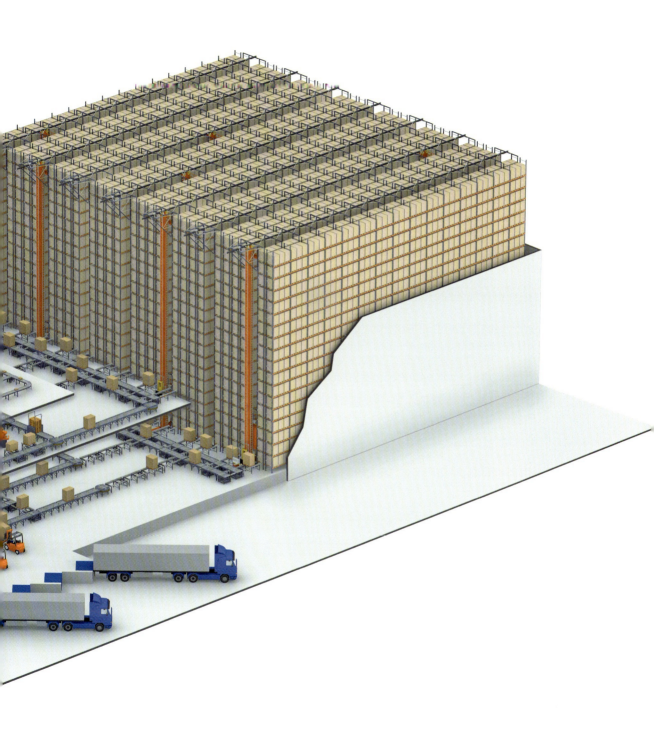

3.1 CONVENTIONALLY OPERATED SYSTEMS

These systems are operated by people who either move along with them on foot or control them standing on platforms or sitting in cabins. They are usually operated with electric batteries, so a space must be set aside in the facility where they can be recharged.

3.1.1 Pallet trucks

In modern warehouses, the simplest and most widely used piece of equipment is the pallet truck. This equipment is for transporting, not lifting, and in most cases tends to be manually operated.

These machines are highly versatile and can be used to perform a number of tasks, such as loading and unloading lorries and transferring pallets and containers over short distances, and as auxiliary support equipment for picking operations. They are also employed as auxiliary equipment to supply the intake areas, positions within the warehouse where the unit loads are placed so that they can be collected by all types of forklifts (including counterbalanced, reach, VNA, and even stacker cranes) and placed in the corresponding spaces.

In general, pallet trucks, but particularly manual ones, are essential low-cost elements that can be used to resolve situations (at times difficult ones) in all warehousing activities.

Pallet trucks can be manual or electric. Manual ones are controlled by an operator who must be on foot, while electric ones enable the person to use them on foot or ride on them, depending on the model. Both types are described below.

<u>Hand pallet trucks</u>

These do not have any electrical devices, and so have to be moved manually. Their skids (the parallel platforms that sustain loads) can be raised slightly to lift the pallet off the ground, making it easier to move the pallet. They are very widely used in most warehouses, particularly for auxiliary tasks.

Chapter 3 - Handling equipment

Electric pedestrian pallet trucks
These pallet trucks have motors that allow them to move and lift the pallet slightly off the ground. The operator accompanies the pallet truck on foot and handles it by using the controls.

Image provided by Toyota.

Electric rider pallet trucks
These are similar to the pedestrian variety, but operators ride on a folding platform (bottom left picture) or on a seat (bottom right picture).

Image provided by Toyota.   Image provided by Toyota.

Image provided by Toyota.

3.1.2 Stackers

When a fork truck is equipped with a lifting element it becomes a stacker. The lower skids (in yellow in the top left picture on the next page) are inserted below the pallets, which explains why the lower pallet boards must always go in the direction of penetration and never crosswise. Otherwise, they would break on lifting.

Stackers are electric. In the market, you can find both foot-operated models operated and rider models, which are ridden by the operator seated or standing on a platform.

Chapter 3 - Handling equipment

Foot-operated stackers.

Rider stackers.

Comments about stackers

Like forklift trucks, stackers are versatile. However, it is important to be very clear about their limitations.

Stackers are only the best option when the number of movements is very limited. It should be remembered that the lifting height of these handling elements does not exceed 3m for the pedestrian type, and 6m for the ridden type.

Certain stacker types include side stabilisers that open when the forks are raised above a certain height.

Another important issue is that the lower legs go under the pallets and the forks fit into these lower skids. Some stackers have these open and the pallets stay inside, but during use with racking units this tends to cause problems even if the first location level has been raised, since the skids can coincide with the uprights of the racking units, making it impossible to approach the space.

In addition to these factors, it should be remembered that with stackers, the mast (the vertical part along which the forks move up and down) is rigid. Therefore, contingencies must be made for adjustments to certain racking units, such as those with gravity flow (which must have split rollers), so that they are compatible with the operations of these machines.

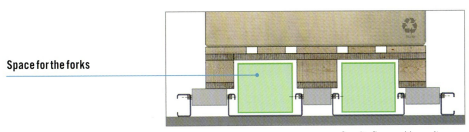

Space for the forks

Gravity flow racking unit.

3.1.3 Order pickers

These are a further development of the forklift trucks and electric stackers. They are specially designed to help with the preparation of orders, allowing the operator to access the machine's controls from one side and the pallet or load from the other, speeding up the process of collecting the goods.

Some pickers work at ground level and others can rise. Both types have three basic characteristics.

First, the pallet truck must be capable of housing the operator, so the body of the machine is separated from the load forks. A small platform on which the driver can stand opens up in this space.

Second, the operator must access the controls from this position, so the configuration of the shaft has been changed, turning it 180° with respect to how this element is assembled on standard pallet trucks and stackers.

Finally, for the most common use for these machines, it is helpful, but not essential, to use the versions with extra-long forks (1600mm to 2400mm), since this allows two or three orders to be prepared at the same time.

There is a wide variety of machines available on the market with very different characteristics. However, they can be grouped into three main types.

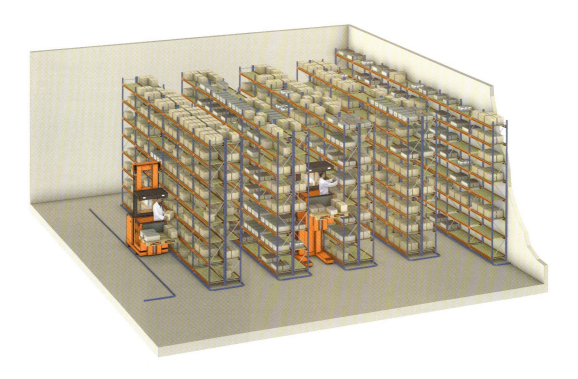

GROUND LEVEL PICKERS

The most basic type of picker is that which works with loads at ground level. Although these can only pick items on the first level (racking unit, on the ground, etc.), some models have a small platform on which the operator can stand to access higher spaces. The machine has space for a driver and can transport one or two pallets. Pickers with extra long forks can manage two or three pallets at the same time.

LOW-LEVEL PICKERS

The second type of picker is that which works at a low level. Given the need for operators to be able to access higher levels, these machines have been developed using those working at ground level as their starting point.

There are two options for this type of machine. The simpler option has a non-slip platform at the top of its structure. Since this is usually fairly high up, a small intermediate ladder must be installed between the operator's platform and the upper platform. This ladder can be either fixed or foldable.

Another, more expensive option consists of adding an electro-hydraulic lifting system to the platform where the operator is, so that the operator can be raised as required.

MID- AND HIGH-LEVEL PICKERS

This type of picker can reach medium and high levels.
Mid- and high-level pickers consist of a body with a traction motor, a hydraulic pump, a battery, and control devices.
This body is connected at its base to two support legs mounted on small wheels. A lifting mast is also attached to the body, and the cabin in which the operator stands moves up and down this mast.

Two forks can be welded to the cabin; in this case, the lifting height is limited to that which is reached by the floor of the operator's cabin. Another option is for the forks to be mounted on a trolley on a second lifting mast incorporated into the cabin, so that the operator can raise and lower the load to the most convenient working height.

The aisle width required to operate these machines can be ±1150mm when using pallets facing forward, and ±1500mm when using pallets facing sideways.

The maximum lifting height that can be reached by the highest pickers is 10m or 11m.

One alternative to this type of machine is the combi type VNA truck (see Section 3.1.7), which has a maximum lifting height of over 12m.

3.1.4 Conventional forklift trucks (counterbalanced)

Counterbalanced forklift trucks get their name from the large iron counterbalance they carry at the rear. They are of the cantilever loader type, which means that they carry the load in front of their support point. They operate according to the first degree lever principle, in which a weight, called the effort, can lift another weight, called the resistance (the load), supporting itself on an intermediate point called the fulcrum.

Image provided by Toyota.

In counterbalanced forklift trucks, the effort weight consists of the entire machine including the chassis, which in turn contains the motor, transmission, hydraulic pump, and other control devices. The counterbalance, normally screwed into the back of the chassis, and the axles (the front one being for driving and the rear one for steering, so that the machine is easier to manoeuvre) are also part of the effort weight. While part of the forklift truck, the mast, fork carriage, and forks are included in the resistance weight since they are in front of the centre of the front axle, which acts as the support point or fulcrum. The resistance weight consists of all elements in front of the support point, such as the load that needs to be transported.

Why is it so important to understand the role of each element in this lever system? Because the dimensions of the machine, its weight, the counterbalance, and other elements will define the nominal load that the forklift can handle and lift.

Furthermore, the distance from the mast to the centre of gravity of the load will also influence its nominal capacity. The greater the distance, the lower the load capacity.

In terms of their use, apart from being very fast, counterbalanced forklift trucks are ideal for working both inside and outside the warehouse, although due to their construction and design they are particularly good when operating outside. They are also ideal machines for loading lorries, as only the forks stick out in front.

When using them in a warehouse, it is important to bear in mind that the lifting height of these forklifts is usually limited to 7.50m and that the normal working aisle adapted to these elements must provide 3200mm to 3500mm of free space.

Chapter 3 - Handling equipment

Image provided by Toyota.

The aisle can vary considerably with this type of machine, depending on the load and on its construction, so in some cases aisles of over 4000mm may be required. It is therefore important to choose the most appropriate machine for each facility.

In addition to the features already discussed, one of the main differences between the models found on the market is how they are powered. Some machines are battery-powered, while others are thermal or powered by gas or diesel.

Similarly, there may be differences in the types of mast included. Masts are built based on the lifting height provided and can be: double, with two telescopic bodies that extend when lifting begins; double with totally free lifting, in which, unlike for the previous type, the telescopic mast does not extend until the fork has been completed raised; and triple, with three telescopic bodies.

One final feature which can vary from model to model is the type of forks used. Some machines use forks that move sideways and oscillate to make it easier to pick up and deposit pallets.

3.1.5 Reach trucks

This type of machine is an electric forklift that moves and performs turning and lifting manoeuvres by retracting the mast, which moves it toward the machine's centre of gravity.

Thanks to this feature, these have an advantage over counterbalanced forklift trucks in that they weigh less, can operate in narrower manoeuvring aisles (± 2700mm free), and perform better.

On the other hand, although the masts and forks are similar to those for counterbalanced trucks, to deposit or pick up pallets from the racking unit the machine is centred in front of the unit load and the mast moves outwards, which makes manoeuvres easier.

Some forklifts can lift loads over 10m. Support devices can be fitted to help with manoeuvres at the highest levels.

As a result of all these advantages, reach trucks are currently the most commonly-used machines for warehouses.

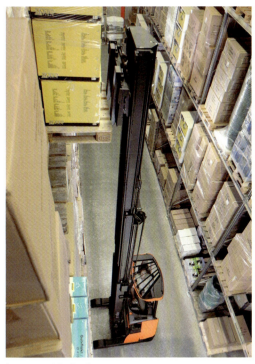
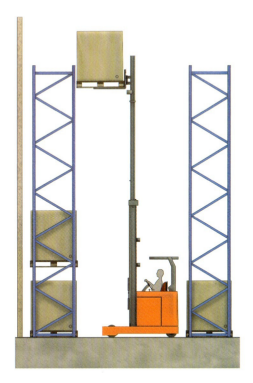

Image provided by Toyota.

Chapter 3 - Handling equipment

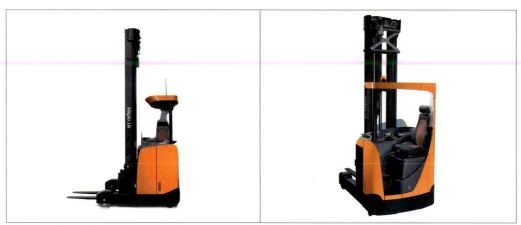

Images provided by Toyota.

Reach trucks have lower beams in which the front wheels are housed. 800mm x 1200mm pallets, which are picked up by the 800mm side, fit between the two beams so no height needs to be lost in the racking units.

Reach truck with the pallet inside the chassis.

When the pallets are wider or handled by their longer side, they must be transported positioned on top of the wheels. To do this, the options are to have wider aisles, which will not result in a loss of capacity in the racking units, or to increase the margins between the upper part of the pallet on the ground and the first beam of the racking unit (to avoid hitting it), which would mean a loss of height in the location space. All of these factors must be taken into account when planning the warehouse.

Chapter 3 - Handling equipment

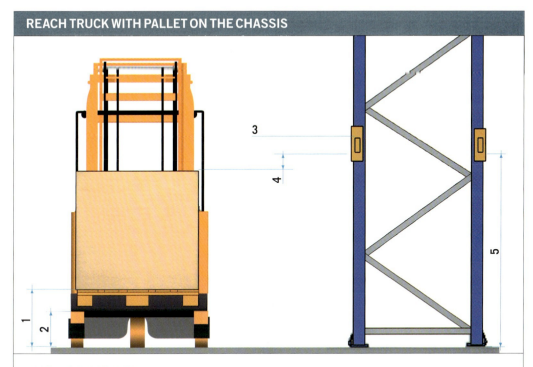

REACH TRUCK WITH PALLET ON THE CHASSIS

1. Chassis height + 200mm
2. Chassis height
3. First load level
4. Minimum margin of 50mm
5. Pallet height + chassis height + 100mm minimum margin

There is a version of the reach truck in which the mast remains fixed (does not retract) and the forks extend to the position required to pick up or deposit the load using a system similar to a pantograph.

While these are less often found in warehouses, they too are a valid option and are used in a similar manner to reach forklifts.

Image provided by Crown.

Chapter 3 - Handling equipment

Image of a double-reach truck used in a warehouse for mass-market food products
Source: Mecalux.

Image of a side-loading reach truck in a warehouse for metal sections.
Source: Mecalux.

Chapter 3 - Handling equipment

Double-reach truck

Also available in the market are reach trucks that can operate with double-deep racking units. In addition to a moveable mast these models have moveable forks, which make it possible to access the second line of pallets.

Using double-reach trucks can significantly increase storage capacity.

Their disadvantages include loss of accessibility and limitations in terms of the load they can handle and the lifting height they can reach.

3.1.6 Side-loading reach trucks

This is a variation on the conventional reach truck, which has been fitted with a system that allows the wheels to turn 90°. The result is that sideways movement is possible, as well as the standard backward and forward movements.

Although they can handle pallets, they are ideal for longer loads such as larger pallets and items, sections, tubes, etc.

Images provided by Toyota.

Pharmaceutical industry logistics warehouse using VNA trucks. Source: Mecalux.

3.1.7 Turret trucks (for narrow aisles)

Used when operating in narrow aisles (from 1500mm to 1800mm), these forklift trucks can increase storage capacity considerably and reach lifting heights of over 14m.

Turret trucks have certain limitations which must be taken into consideration. First, they require a very even floor in the warehouse on which to move. They must also be guided using rails placed on both sides of the aisle or be wire-guided or even laser-guided in the same way as LGVs, as will be explained later in this chapter.

Furthermore, they do not turn in the aisle. Rather, it is the forks that make the movements needed to pick up or deposit the pallets. This is why these machines are designed for working within warehouse aisles. Manoeuvres outside this space are slow, and must therefore be minimised.

It is common to use other lift trucks or conveyors as auxiliary elements, and these pick up or deposit the pallets in the P&D stations from the racking units, meaning that turret trucks do not have to leave the aisle.

These forklifts can be divided into two groups, according to the type of forks they use: trilaterals and bilaterals.

With trilateral forklifts, the head that supports the forks can rotate and can pick up and deposit loads on one side of the aisle or the other, as well as in front. They can also deposit pallets directly on the ground.

With bilateral forklifts, the forks are telescopic and assembled on what is called a cradle. Unlike trilaterals, these machines can neither deposit pallets on the ground nor place them in front. Yet they do have the advantage that they can operate in even narrower aisles and can complete a greater number of cycles.

Chapter 3 - Handling equipment

Trilateral turret truck.

Bilateral turret truck.

The turret type truck has a space, a cabin, where the operator driving the truck can sit. When this cabin is fixed to the body of the machine it is called a man-down type. If, on the other hand, it rises along with the forks (and therefore with the load), it is called a man-up cabin. This second system is also called combi, as it enables the operator to combine pallet handling operations with order preparation operations.

Man-down (simple). Source: Mecalux.

Man-up (combi). Source: Mecalux.

108

Warehouse for construction machinery and tools. Source: Mecalux.

Combi VNA trucks

These have a very similar configuration to that just described for mid- and high-level pickers. The only difference is that instead of using simple forks incorporated into a board that runs along the secondary mast, they have a rotating head with genuine load forks.

With this head with these forks, the machine can pick up and deposit pallets on both sides of the racking unit. It can thus perform a double function: to prepare orders and store or reposition complete unit loads. VNA combi trucks have an advantage over pickers in that they can reach heights of up to 14m.

Guidance systems

When we started discussing turret trucks, we mentioned the need for these handling elements to be guided using rails (mechanical guidance) or wires. The following are the most common options.

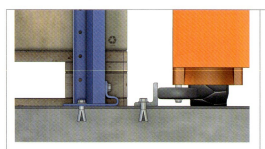

Guided with LPN 50 rail
The pallets sit directly on the floor. An "L" shaped rail attached to the floor acts as the guide.

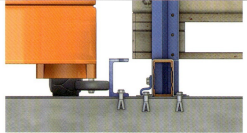

Guided with UPN 100 rail
The pallets sit on rails placed on the ground or on beams. A "U" shaped rail attached to the floor acts as the guide.

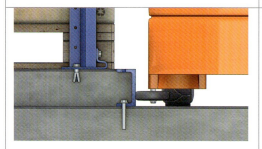

Guided with UPN 100 rail forming an island
The space between the guides for the aisles is filled with concrete, forming an island on which the racking units sit.

In the entrance of the aisles with mechanical guidance, entry rails with mouths have been put in place to help centre the machines.

Wire-guided
A wire buried in the ground produces a magnetic field which the machine detects and follows as a guide.
When the guidance system is laser-guided, there is no buried wire and it is the position of the reflectors that helps it to move safely.

3.2 MANUAL PICKING STACKER CRANES

These are half-height stacker cranes (up to 10m or 12m) designed to carry a person onboard, which allows them to pick from the full height of the racking unit.

This type of machine is now rarely used, as it has been replaced by automatic picking stacker units, in which the goods-to-man principle is used, and by picking robots.

Warehouse for components. Source: Mecalux.

3.3 OBSERVATIONS ABOUT THE USE OF FORKLIFT TRUCKS WHEN PLANNING A WAREHOUSE

When non-automated systems such as the ones discussed up to this point are used, a series of measures must be considered so as to carry out the work in the safest, most efficient way possible (for people, machines and racking units). The following section goes over the factors related to the use of these machines that should be borne in mind when designing a warehouse.

3.3.1 Technical specifications of the forklift

All forklift truck manufacturers provide technical specifications with data on each type and model of machine they sell. These can be used to obtain the data necessary for the design of the facility. The key data are the width of the aisle required to operate the machine, the lifting height for the load, and the height of the retracted mast. These specifications also provide information on load capacity.

Chapter 3 - Handling equipment

2005		TECHNICAL CHARACTERISTICS				VDI 2198			
CHARACTERISTICS	1.1	Manufacturer				NUOVA DETAS Spa		NUOVA DETAS Spa	NUOVA DETAS Spa
	1.2	Model				SE 163	SE 163 L	SE 183	SE 183 L	SE 203 L
	1.3	Propulsion unit: electric, diesel, LPG				Electric		Electric	Electric
	1.4	Operation station				Seated		Seated	Seated
WEIGHTS	1.5	Rated capacity	Q	(t)		1,6		1,8	2,0
	1.6	Load centre	c	(mm)		500		500	500
	1.8	Load distance from front axle centre	x	(mm)		366		366	366
	1.9	Wheelbase	y	(mm)		1300	1435	1300	1435	1435
	2.1	Truck weight without load		Kg		3289	3425	3415	3493	3508
	2.2	Load on axles with load front / rear		Kg		4214 / 675	4144 / 881	4646 / 569	4571 / 722	4904 / 604
	2.3	Load on axles without load front / rear		Kg		1571 / 1718	1599 / 1826	1647 / 1768	1684 / 1809	1697 / 1811
TYRES	3.1	Tyres PN/SE				SE / CU		SE / CU	SE / CU
	3.2	Tyres front size				18x7 - 8 / 457x178		18x7 - 8 / 457x178	200 / 50 - 10 / 457x203
	3.3	Tyres rear size				15x4 1/2 - 8		15x4 1/2 - 8	15x4 1/2 - 8
	3.5	Tyres, number front / rear (x=driven)				2x / 2		2x / 2	2x / 2
	3.6	Tread front wheel centre	b10	(mm)		893		893	913
	3.7	Tread rear wheel centre	b11	(mm)		170		170	170
DIMENSIONS	4.1	Mast tilting forward / backward	α/β	(°)		5 / 7		5 / 7	5 / 7
	4.2	Height with lowered mast	h1	(mm)		2170		2170	2170
	4.3	Normal free lift	h2	(mm)		60		60	60
	4.4	Standard lifting	h3	(mm)		3170		3170	3170
	4.5	Height with extended mast	h4	(mm)		3750		3750	3750
	4.7	Overhead guard height	h6	(mm)		2100		2100	2100
	4.8	Seat height	h7	(mm)		1050		1050	1050
	4.12	Height of coupler	h10	(mm)		525		525	525
	4.19	Total length	l1	(mm)		2845	2982	2864	3001	3001
	4.20	Length including fork back	l2	(mm)		1845	1982	1864	2001	2001
	4.21	Total width	b1/b2	(mm)		1053		1053	1120
	4.22	Standard forks: thickness / width / length		(mm)		35x100x1000	35x100x1000	35x130x1000	35x130x1000	35x130x1000
	4.23	Fork bearing plate FEM denomination	FEM			2A		2A	2A
	4.24	Width of bearing plate	b3	(mm)		1000		1000	1000
	4.31	Ground clearance at centre of wheelbase	m1	(mm)		90		90	90
	4.32	Ground clearance at lowest point with load	m2	(mm)		100		100	100
	4.33	Aisle width with pallet bxa pallets = 1000x1200	Ast	(mm)		3190	3327	3190	3327	3327
	4.34	Aisle width with pallet axb pallets = 800x1200	Ast	(mm)		3314	3451	3314	3451	3451
	4.35	External steering radius	Wa	(mm)		1498	1635	1498	1635	1635
	4.36	Minimum between the centres of rotation distance	b13	(mm)		0	0	0	0	0
PERFORMANCE DATA	5.1	Speed of travelling with/without load		Km/h		15,2 / 16,0		15,2 / 16,0	15,2 / 16,0
	5.2	Speed of lifting with/without load		m/s		0,42 / 0,50		0,40 / 0,50	0,36 / 0,50
	5.3	Speed of lowering with / without load		m/s		0,52 / 0,42		0,52 / 0,42	0,52 / 0,42
	5.5	Tractive force with / without load		N		3050 / 3520	3010 / 3480	2920 / 3450	2900 / 3430	2840 / 3420
	5.6	Max tractive force with / without load		N		11280 / 9320	11240 / 9710	11100 / 9770	11075 / 10230	11010 / 10300
	5.7	Gradeability with / without load		%		6,8 / 11,8	6,5 / 11,6	5,8 / 10,3	5,5 / 10,1	5,2 / 10,0
	5.8	Max gradeability with / without load		%		24,3 / 25,8	23,5 / 25,7	22,3 / 26,0	22,0 / 26,6	21,0 / 27,0
	5.9	Acceleration time with / without load		s		4,9 / 4,4		5,0 / 4,5	5,1 / 4,5
	5.10	Service brake				Hydr. + electr.		Hydr. + electr.	Hydr. + electr.
DRIVE	6.1	Drive motor S2 60 min rating		KW		4,5x2		4,5x2	4,5x2
	6.2	Hoist motor S3 15% rating		KW		10		10	10
	6.3	Standard battery				DIN 43531 A		DIN 43531 A	DIN 43531 A
	6.4	Voltage/capacity		V/Ah		48 / 420-620	48 / 525-775	48 / 500-620	48 / 525-775	48 / 525-775
	6.5	Minimum weight std battery		Kg		800	950	940	950	950
	6.6	Battery consumption		KW/h					
OTHER	8.1	System of transmission				Microprocessor AC		Microprocessor AC	Microprocessor AC
	8.2	Working pressure for equipment		bar		175		175	175
	8.3	Quantity of oil for equipment		l/min		-		-	-
	8.4	Noise level at operation station		dB(A)		70		70	70
	8.5	Type of coupler				-		-	-

All information and descriptions are indicative only, and are in no way binding for the manufacturer

Example of a technical specifications sheet. Image provided by Nuova Detas.

3.3.2 Lifting height

One piece of information in the technical specifications requiring particular attention is the lifting height, which is the distance between the ground and the upper part of the fork.

To calculate the maximum height of the top level of the racking unit, one must take into account the fact that as the forks pass between the pallet legs, part of the pallet is positioned under the fork. This means that the support rail for the top level must be at least 200mm below the maximum lifting height.

This ensures that when the mast is fully extended vertically, the pallet is lifted to the height needed for its skids to avoid the beam and not hit it.

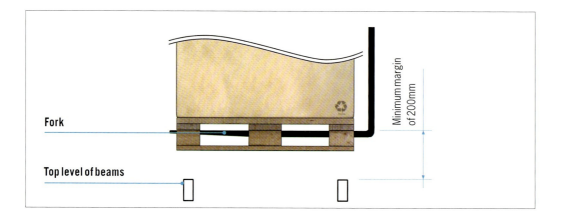

The height of the retracted mast must also be calculated, as this will determine the height of the doors and lower passageways between racking units, ceilings (if circulating below mezzanine floors), etc. The distance between the retracted mast and the ceiling or beams on top of the passageway must not be less than 500mm.

Chapter 3 - Handling equipment

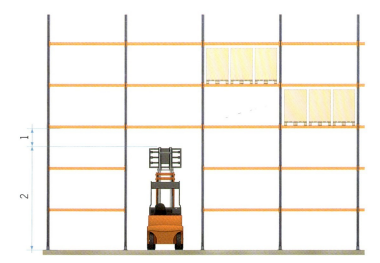

1. Height with mast retracted
2. Minimum margin of 500mm

Logistics warehouse. Source: Mecalux.

Chapter 3 - Handling equipment

Warehouse/cold chamber for storing meat and other food products. Source: Mecalux.

3.3.3 Issues related to the use of forklifts with drive-in pallet racking

With a drive-in pallet storage system (explained in depth in the next chapter) trucks have to enter the aisles with the load lifted, which slows return manoeuvres.

To speed operations up and make them safer, it is recommended that guides be placed on the floor. One must take into account the width of the machine, leaving a minimum clearance of 50mm (25mm per side) between it and the guides. If the forklift includes centring wheels, the clearance can be reduced to 10mm.

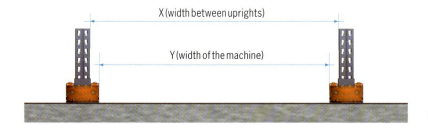

116

When using forklift trucks with drive-in pallet racking, one must bear in mind that the first raised level of the racking unit could be below the roof of the forklift.

Should this occur, this protection may need to be modified depending on the dimensions and the system used to protect the machine, as shown in the image below.

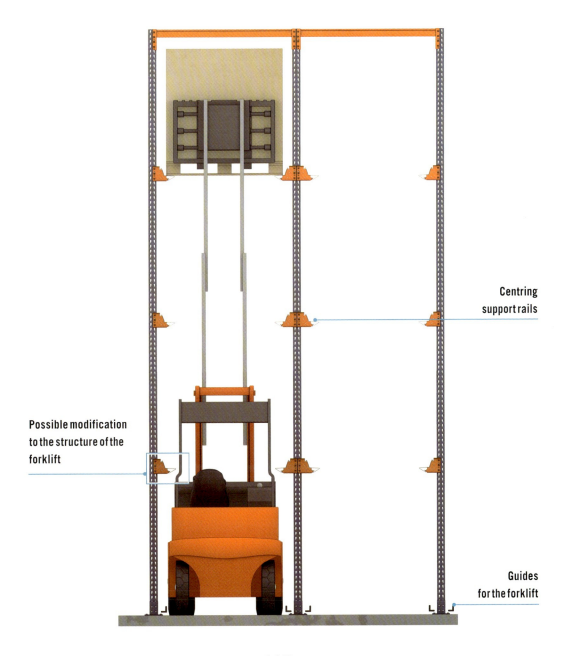

3.3.4 Clearances required with conventional pallet racking units for each type of forklift truck

The following is a table of clearance distances which must be left in the spaces or compartments of the racking units in accordance with standard EN 15620, which has been in force since January 2009. The machine classes mentioned are the 400 (counterbalanced and reach truck types), the 300A (VNA trucks with the operator on board) (the operator accompanies the load, man-up) and the 300B (VNA trucks with the operator on the ground (man-down), in which the driver remains at ground level). The X and Y measurements are explained in the diagram accompanying the table.

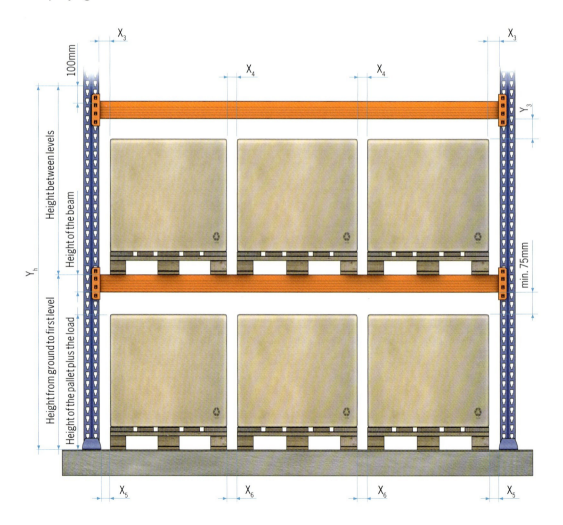

	MACHINES					
For levels between:	Class 400		Class 300A		Class 300B	
	$X_{3,4,5,6}$	Y_3	$X_{3,4,5,6}$	Y_3	$X_{3,4,5,6}$	Y_3
0 and 3000mm	75	75	75	75	75	75
3000mm and 6000mm	75	100	75	75	75	100
6000mm and 9000mm	75	125	75	75	75	125
9000mm and 12,000mm	100	150	75	75	100	150
12,000mm and 13,000mm	100	150	75	75	100	175
13,000mm and 15,000mm	–	–	75	75	100	175

Figures in mm.

3.3.5 Clearances in the aisles along which the forklift trucks move

As mentioned earlier in this chapter, one must consider the height data of the forklift truck's mast when this is retracted to ensure the appropriateness of the height of the aisles through which the forklift truck is going to move when it goes under load levels or other structures, such as mezzanine floors.

This is not the only safety measure to be met when planning aisles in a warehouse: it is but one of a number of specific standards that define the characteristics the facility in question must possess. These standards have been developed to guarantee the safety of manoeuvres carried out with forklift trucks when these do not have guides inside the aisles.

Each country may have its own standards in relation to the issues in this section which must be taken into account. The measurements set out in this section are those in force in Spain, as set out in the technical safety notes number 852 concerning storage on metal racking units.

In the technical notes, it is specified that the external side frames must extend at least 500mm over the top load level and the internal ones, 100mm. These extensions can be provided by using structural accessories suitable for this purpose.

If upper transverse beams are used in the aisles, they must be located in the upper part so that the clearance or vertical distance between them and the load or mast of the handling equipment is at least 150mm.

The dimensions of the working aisles must be established based on the largest forklift truck that will move along them and the likelihood of people passing by.

Chapter 3 - Handling equipment

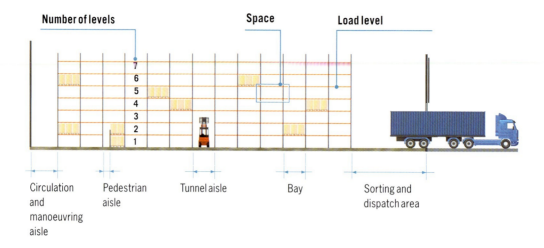

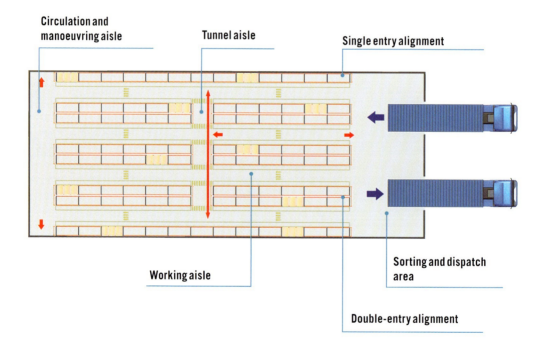

The width of single circulation aisles must be no less than either that of the forklifts (or vehicles moved by them) or that of the largest-sized loads plus at least 600mm, except when using turret type trucks. If pedestrians must also use these aisles, a minimum width of 1m must be retained and reserved for pedestrians only. The same rule applies to double circulation aisles, but the space added to the dimensions of the largest-sized loads must be at least 900mm.

Chapter 3 - Handling equipment

When underpasses are used by forklift trucks, there must be parallel but separate passageways reserved solely for pedestrians. In terms of the width of the tunnels, the same measures apply as for aisles. Since they are tunnels, there will inevitably be upper elements that can also be struck if planning is inadequate, so an additional rule is applied which specifies that clearance will be the minimum passing height necessary, leaving 500mm, either with the mast folded (retracted) without a load or with a load that vertically exceeds the folded mast.

For more information about this design, refer to standards EN15512 and EN15620.

1. Guard mesh
2. Upper crossbeam
3. Safety catch
4. Spacer
5. Frame extension 100mm (min.)
6. Sideguard 500mm (min.)
7. Upright guard
8. Double sideguard
9. Plate of racking unit specifications
10. Working area
11. Working aisle
12. Sorting and dispatch aisle
13. Pedestrian aisle
14. Pedestrian crossing
15. Pedestrian tunnel

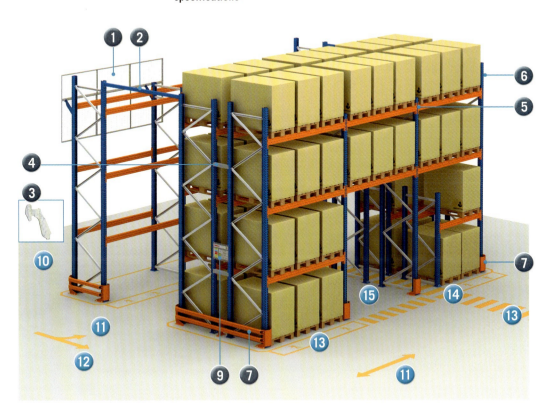

Stacker cranes for pallets.

Warehouse for company specialising in the manufacture and distribution of healthcare technology. Source: Mecalux.

3.4 AUTOMATED OPERATING SYSTEMS

While the equipment discussed up to this point must be operated with someone at the controls, with automated systems all operations are managed through a control and management software application. Communication and safety devices are handled through electronic components.

In addition to not requiring operators to guide them, these automated machines are also independent in terms of their electricity supply, since they take the current directly from specific lines installed for this purpose. The exception to this rule are guided vehicles (AGV and LGV, explained in this chapter), which use electric batteries.

The rest of the chapter will provide a detailed overview of all types of this automated equipment which has revolutionised how the most innovative warehouses are managed today.

3.4.1 Stacker cranes for pallets

The real stars of the automated pallet warehouse are stacker cranes.

These indispensable elements can be built to be more than 40m high and operate in aisles just 1.50m or 1.60m wide. This gives an idea of the load capacity they can provide in a warehouse, compared with traditional systems.

Stacker cranes are guided by their upper and lower parts (some models have only lower guides) and are designed to operate exclusively within the aisles. As a result, conveyors are needed in the P&D stations for the racking units, which move pallets to or from a position that can be reached by the stacker cranes. An alternative is to use consoles (platforms), which the cranes can also access and on which the load can be deposited and picked up using manually operated machines.

There are stacker cranes that can carry one (the most common) or two pallets. Some can handle sections, tubes, or large packages.

In general terms, a stacker crane consists of a body that includes, among other elements, electronic controls, lifting and displacement motors, and the displacement kit (with the wheels). Attached to this body is one mast (or column) or two (double-column stacker crane), depending on the dimensions of the load being handled or the speed at which the machine is to be operated.

Using a system of cables with pulleys connected to a lifting motor, the element called the cradle, which contains forks and is what supports the pallets, slides up and down the mast. The entire vehicle moves along lower guides and is usually stabilised by using another upper guide in contact with the top of the mast.

The fork, which is generally telescopic, is mounted onto the cradle. It can transfer the unit load between the stacker crane and the spaces on the racking units available on both sides of the aisle (the lowest level must be raised off the ground so that it can also access this).

The forks can be single-deep (the system just described) or double-deep, and can deposit and pick up loads from a second racking unit connected to the one nearest the aisle. As a result, a stacker unit can be used for four racking units at the same time (two on each side of the aisle).

Detail of a fork. Source: Mecalux.

If the cradle has a shuttle added to the storage system rather than telescopic forks, it is called a radio-shuttle system.

The shuttle moves with the pallet, sideways, inside the racking units (which have rails for this purpose) until it reaches the first empty position. This is a high-capacity drive-in pallet storage system.

Detail of a radio-shuttle.
Source: Mecalux.

Source: Mecalux.

When a stacker crane is used for more than one aisle, the lower wheels enable the machine to turn and change aisles (as can be seen in the detailed images below). Alternatively, the machine enters what is called the crane bridge, which is waiting at one end of the warehouse and is responsible for taking the stacker crane and moving it to another aisle, as can be seen in the above images.

Crane bridge in an automated warehouse. Source: Mecalux.

Turning bend system, which allows the stacker cranes to change aisles. Source: Mecalux.

3.4.2 Stacker cranes for boxes: miniload

The version of the stacker crane for pallets designed for boxes is called the miniload. Its basic functions are the same as those of its larger counterparts, the difference being that the type of unit load handled is a box (generally measuring 600mm x 400mm or 800mm x 600mm).

The elements that comprise a miniload are very similar to those of the stacker cranes for pallets, and, like these, can work in single deep or double-deep and transport one unit, two units or – and this where it differs from the large versions – up to four boxes at the same time.

Their maximum height is also somewhat lower than that of the pallet version. Even so, they reach the not inconsiderable height of 20m. In terms of aisle width, it is 800mm for boxes of 600mm x 400mm and greater when handling larger boxes or more units.

Just like the stacker cranes for pallets, miniloads work exclusively inside the aisles and need roller, chain or belt conveyers to transport loads between the location in the racking unit and the point of entry or exit, which is generally located at the end of the aisle.

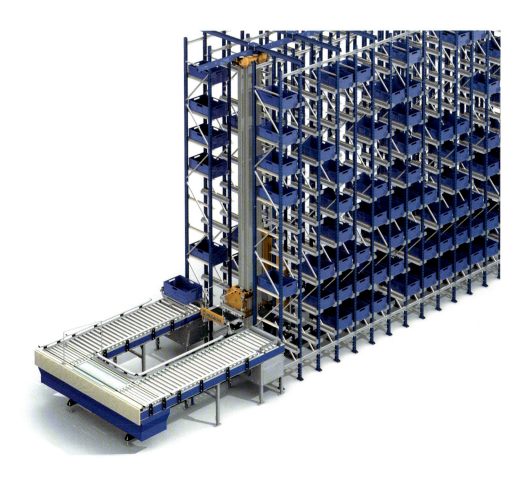

Chapter 3 - Handling equipment

Above: Electrical components warehouse.
Left: Image of a single-mast stacker crane for boxes.

The versatility of stacker cranes for boxes is reflected in the variety of forks and extraction systems that can be implemented: some allow for handling plastic boxes, while others are suitable for use with cardboard boxes and some can handle metal trays. The right choice of forks is vital for the proper functioning of the entire system.

The different extraction systems are shown here.

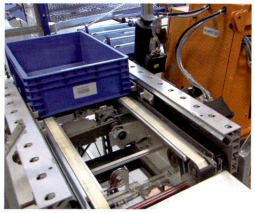

Miniloads can have one or two extraction systems in their cradle, as shown in the above images.

Furthermore, depending on the lifting height required and the weight to be handled, these stacker cranes can include a single mast (single-mast miniload) or two (double-mast miniload).

Usually one machine is installed per aisle but, as with the pallet version, these stacker cranes also have systems that enable them to work in more than one aisle.

Chapter 3 - Handling equipment

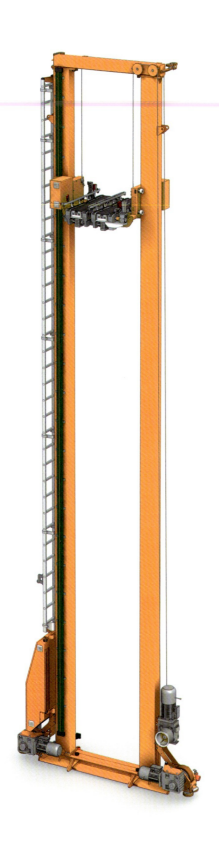

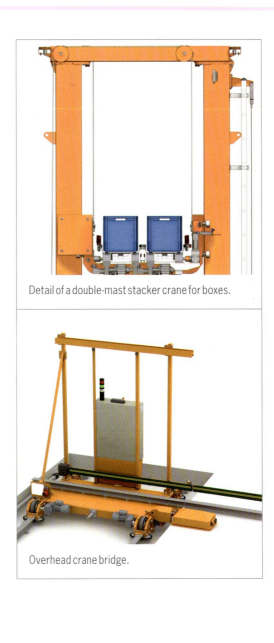

Detail of a double-mast stacker crane for boxes.

Overhead crane bridge.

When goods do not have very high rotation but the volume of storage space is significant, there is no need to have one stacker crane per aisle. Instead, an overhead crane bridge can be used to move the stacker crane between aisles.

With this system to move the stacker crane, the miniload operates inside the aisle exactly as it would if it were to remain in one aisle at all times, i.e. at full capacity. However, efficiency can be reduced by the need to switch the miniload between aisles of racking units. The answer to this problem is appropriate management through the WMS, anticipating the movements required sufficiently in advance and planning these to minimise the number of transfers.

Thus, the use of a system for changing aisles first requires an exhaustive study of the factors that determine the operation to be carried out in the facilities.

On the other hand, transfer and lifting speeds can vary based on the type of machine chosen and the estimated level of performance it must achieve.

Depending on the number of boxes to be handled, miniloads are classified into average performance, high performance, and very high performance systems. Technical specifications can vary substantially from one machine to another based on these differences in performance.

3.4.3. Automatic guided and laser guided vehicles (AGV/LGV)

AGVs and LGVs are transport machines, similar to forklifts, which move automatically following a route that has been set out or programmed in advance.

They are guided using one of two possible systems. Vehicles capable of following the route assigned to them using a wire-guided system are called automatic guided vehicles (AGV). The warehouse floor has a wire built into it which emits a magnetic field that is picked up by the machine. The wire establishes the route and the AGV follows this.

The second system is laser guided. Machines with this feature are known as laser guided vehicles (LGV). These emit a laser signal, which bounces off deflectors positioned at points close to the route and this signal is read, on its return, by the machine. The time difference between emitting the laser and the return beam being picked up is calculated by a processor in the machine, which tells it at all times how far it is from the control points, thus enabling it to deduce its position. With this information, the vehicle on its own can perform the corrections required to follow the specified route. From a technical perspective, programming and modifying the routes is very easy.

There are machines that lift and different types of forks for handling pallets or items. The market also offers AGV and LGV models specifically designed to transport pallets, boxes, reels, and large loads.

These vehicles are very convenient when moving between distant points at a moderate speed without obstacles. One must also remember that at stopping points (points for picking up and depositing goods) roller or chain conveyors or another type of device that can transfer the load and act as a link with the rest of the facility must be used.

Image provided by Asti.

Image provided by Artisteril.

Image provided by Artisteril.

Logistics and handling centre for fish.
Source: Mecalux.

Warehouse specialising in the manufacture of products for the home and personal care. Source: Mecalux.

3.4.4 Roller and chain conveyors and shuttles for pallets

Conveyors and shuttles are the automated transport systems most commonly used in warehouses, since they can be used to form different circuits (occupying little space) accumulate, turn and lift pallets, as well as to form manual or automated working areas.

They are also compatible with both stacker cranes and forklifts and can be combined with other transport and lifting systems, such as the AGV and LGV systems, shuttles, electrified monorails, stacker cranes, etc.

Current automated transport systems include different devices to ensure that automatic displacements are safe. These machines usually operate at a speed of 10m to 20m/minute.

Chapter 3 - Handling equipment

1. Roller conveyor
2. Chain conveyor
3. Cross-tables
4. Turntables
5. Lift conveyor
6. Picking lift conveyor
7. Lift station
8. Single shuttle
9. Double shuttle
10. Ground level roller conveyor
11. Gravity conveyor
12. Overhead electrified monorail system

Chapter 3 - Handling equipment

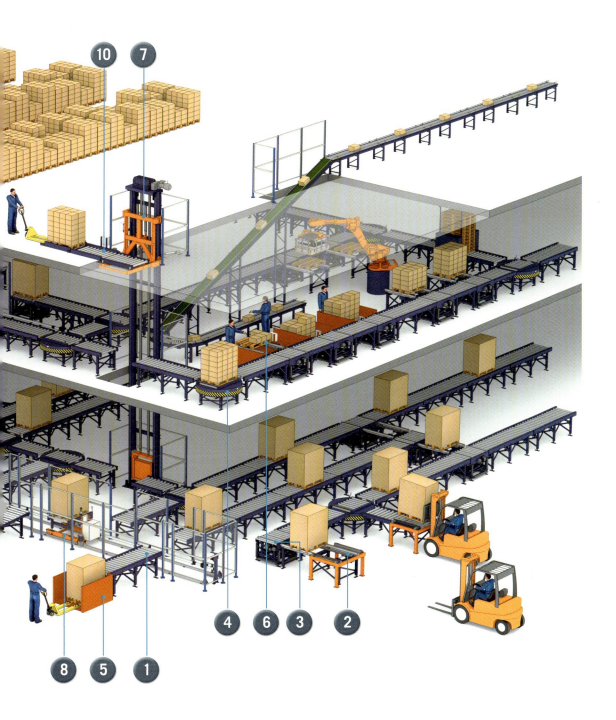

An automated transport system can consist of various different elements that are grouped together or distributed across different areas of the warehouse. As a result, unit loads can be handled in the greatest possible number of ways, as shown in the image below.

The following is a summary of the different basic transport elements that can be found.

ROLLER CONVEYOR
The roller conveyor allows pallets to be moved in the longitudinal direction of the skids.
It is the most commonly used element in internal transport systems for pallets, owing to its simplicity and the variety of ways in which it can be manufactured to cover long distances.
It can be used simply for transport or to gather pallets (for example, leaving them waiting, as a support for creating buffers, etc.).

CHAIN CONVEYOR

The chain conveyor can be used to transfer pallets in the transverse direction to the skids. It is the perfect complement to the roller conveyor, given that the combination of the two allows for the creation of 90° turns.

This makes it possible to create recirculation routes and conveyor circuits, useful for certain requirements. These conveyors can have two chain sections (at the ends) or three (at the ends, plus one between both), depending on the characteristics of the load.

Detail of a chain conveyor.

MIXED ROLLER AND CHAIN CONVEYOR

This is a conveyor with rollers and chains that allows for a 90° change in direction. The rollers are fixed to a bedplate and the chains are placed on an eccentric lifting frame, passing the pallet from rollers to chains, or vice versa, without turning the pallet.

TURNING ROLLER AND CHAIN CONVEYOR

With this conveyor, the rollers or chains have been arranged to create a turntable, which makes it possible to transfer the unit loads between the non-aligned conveyors (such as those in the image) at any angle in which they are positioned with respect to others.

LEVEL 0 ROLLER CONVEYOR

These elements can be used to transport pallets up to a height of 80mm off the ground, which then enables them to be lifted to the conveyor level.

Positioned in the inbound and outbound positions, these conveyors render forklifts essential and make it possible to work with stacker cranes alone.

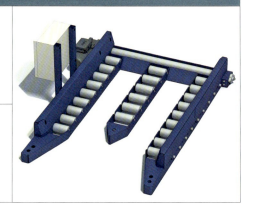

LEVEL 0 ROLLER CONVEYOR WITH LIFTING

Allows pallets to be deposited on and picked up from the ground and lifted to the conveyor height.

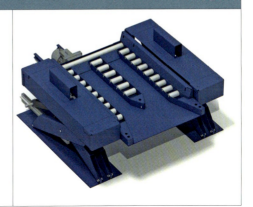

PALLET LIFT

Its purpose is to raise or lower pallets between conveyors at different heights. It is similar to a lift, moving pallets vertically by means of a counterbalance and lifting motor. Thanks to these elements a vertical recirculation is made possible.

ENTRY INSPECTION POST

This is a price of control equipment for the transport system. Its purpose is to check at the entrances that the dimensions of the unit loads comply with the specifications of the facility.

Given that this is the first control device in the conveyor system, it includes a barcode reader or RFID to identify the product and later record it in the warehouse management system (WMS).

This is essential when pallets are going to be stored in an automated warehouse.

SHUTTLE CAR

This machine belongs to non-continuous unit load category of conveyor systems.
It allows loads from different transport routes to be deposited or picked up. For example, it can be used so that from a single departure of pallets, these pallets can be distributed over different routes, with each intended to serve a loading dock.

It is suitable for use when the live pallet requirements are not high.
It always includes another conveyor element, such as rollers or chains, which allows the load to be transferred between sections.

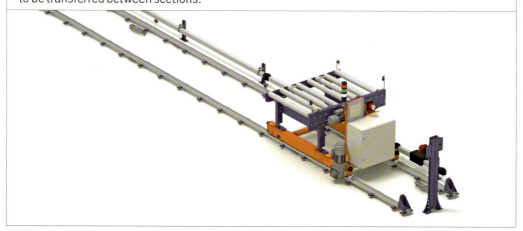

SINGLE OR DOUBLE SHUTTLE

Similar in function to the shuttle car, but faster. It can be single (for one pallet) or double (for two pallets at the same time, which improves performance).

RADIO-SHUTTLE

Allows for the transfer of radio-shuttles when working within the channels of drive-in pallet storage racking units.

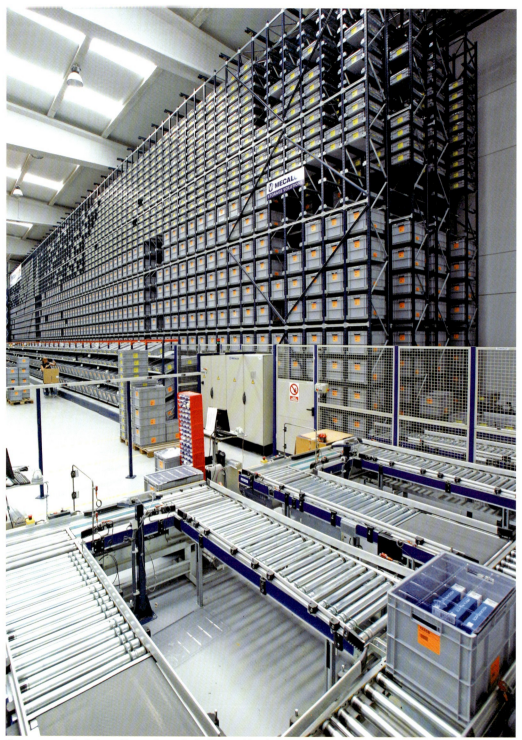
Company manufacturing orthopaedic products. Source: Mecalux.

3.4.5 Roller, belt, and band conveyors for boxes

As with conveyors used for pallets, conveyors for boxes can be used to form very diverse circuits, with straight, curved, and inclined sections and with changes in level.

They can supply unit loads to storage or handling (picking, component assembly, etc.) areas and supply automated robots, create re-routing and classification areas, provide boxes, accumulate them, and manage them.

Company selling cosmetic products. Source: Mecalux.

The following illustration shows different examples of circuits that can be designed with these elements.

1. Straight roller conveyor
2. Accumulation roller conveyor
3. Roller conveyor with 180° curve
4. Roller conveyor with 90° curve
5. Roller conveyor with 45° curve
6. Mixed conveyor
7. Roller conveyor at 45°
8. Roller conveyor with lift and wait feature
9. Motorised conveyor
10. Diverter
11. Continuous band conveyor
12. Inclined band conveyor
13. Lift station
14. Shuttle car

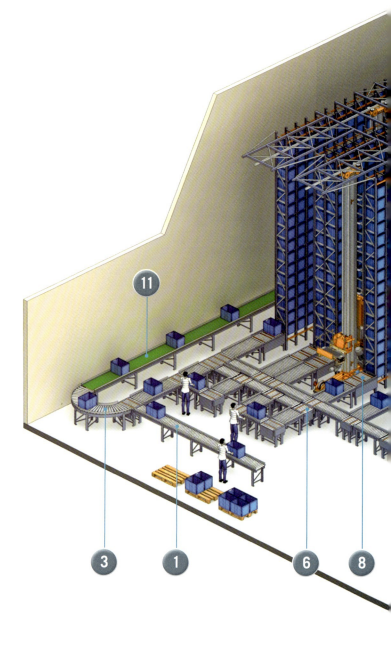

Chapter 3 - Handling equipment

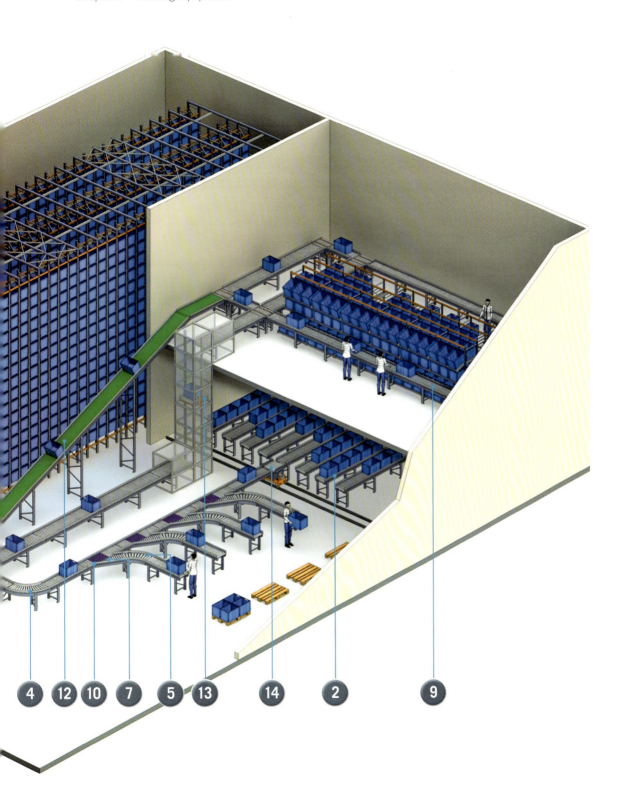

145

As can be seen from the circuits illustrated, the composition of all these conveyors can vary greatly, from a single, short, straight section to systems involving different working areas and different plants.

The basic components that can form part of a system for conveying boxes are shown below. Their use is similar to that for the elements employed for pallets already described in this chapter, although their technical characteristics and components differ.

Straight roller conveyor.

Accumulation roller conveyor.

Roller conveyor with 180° curve.

Roller conveyor with 90° curve.

Roller conveyor with 45° curve.

Mixed conveyor.

Chapter 3 - Handling equipment

Distribution centre for all types of products for wholesalers and shopping centres. Source: Mecalux.

Source: Mecalux.

Frozen products factory warehouse.
Source: Mecalux.

3.4.6 Electrified monorail systems

These are automated systems for transporting pallets, and are ideal when connecting distant fixed points at a speed which can exceed 100m/minute. They consist of rails fitted overhead in the roof or supported from the ground, along which the shuttles move. These shuttles have rollers or chains to facilitate the entry and exit of pallets. The rails have an electric current to power the motors that drive the mobile elements.

The drawing shows the different types of rails that can be combined to configure the widest range of circuits, with straight, curved and inclined sections, turn-offs, maintenance and classification areas, etc.

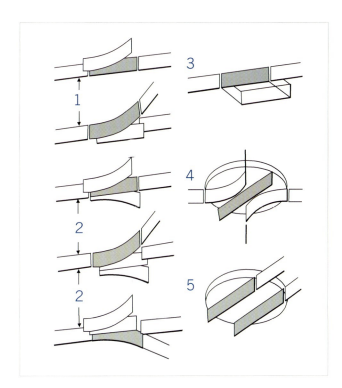

1. Entry and exit turn-off
2. Switch between three rails
3. Parallel switch
4. Turn-round
5. Turn-round of two rails

Roller or chain conveyors are required at stopping points, as these complement the circuit and facilitate the transfer of loads between the electric monorails and the rest of the transport elements in the warehouse.

3.4.7 Other transport systems

In addition to those set out above, there are also other transport systems. These can be either general or specific, since some of them have limited uses. These are discussed briefly below.

MANUAL TROLLEY

Generally used to transport boxes or items or as complements to the order pickers.

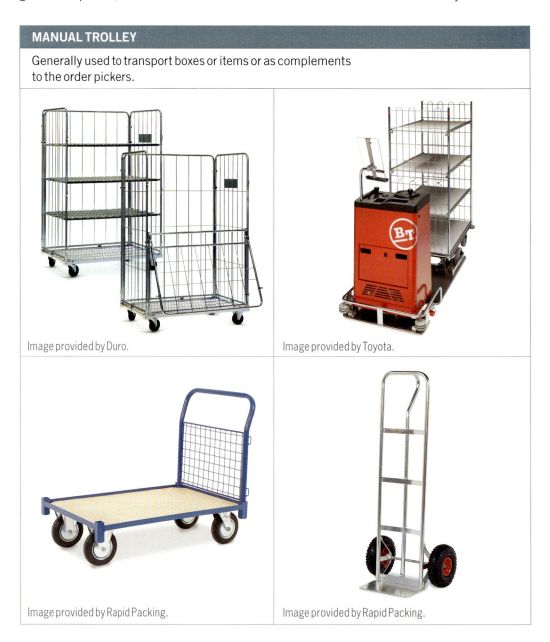

Image provided by Duro.

Image provided by Toyota.

Image provided by Rapid Packing.

Image provided by Rapid Packing.

OVERHEAD CHAIN CONVEYORS

These conveyors use continuously moving chains that cover a specified circuit. Suspended from these are different support points that can be used to carry different products (boxes, clothing on hangers, components, etc.).
Here are two examples.

Solution for boxes.

Solution for clothing on hangers.

OVERHEAD CRANES OR HOISTS

These are transport and lifting systems that consist of one or two beams with a drive motor, thanks to which there is longitudinal movement supported on raised beams, located at the ends by way of a rail. On these beams is a shuttle with a transverse drive motor and a motor for lifting, which operates some cables to which a safety hook is attached.

The goods or object requiring transportation must have some sort of hook system or have been fitted with slings that go fully around it and allow it to be attached to the hook on the overhead crane. The movement takes place in the air, and there must be no obstacle to prevent this movement. These machines are ideal for transporting very wide loads, such as sections, but cannot be used with racking units unless the appropriate devices are installed.

Image provided by GH.

Chapter 3 - Handling equipment

VNA type truck. Source: Mecalux.

3.5 COMPARISON TABLE FOR PALLET CONVEYOR AND LIFTING MACHINES

TYPE		MAX. LIFTING HEIGHT	MINIMUM FREE AISLE	OPERATING SYSTEM	STORAGE SYSTEM
Stackers		3.00m-6.50m	2.10m-2.20m	Manual	Conventional[1] Live pallet[2]
Conventional forklifts (counterbalanced)		7.50m	3.20m-4.00m	Manual	Conventional Drive-in pallet Live pallet Push-back Movirack
Forklifts Reach trucks	Normal	8.50m	2.70m-2.80m	Manual	Conventional[6] Drive-in pallet Live pallet Push-back Movirack
	High	10.50m	2.90m-3.00m	Manual	
Turret type trilateral		>12.00m	1.70m-1.80m	Manual	Conventional[3] Live pallet[2]
Turret type bilateral		>12.00m	1.50m-1.60m	Manual	Conventional[3][4] Live pallet[2]
Stacker cranes		>40.00m	1.50m-1.60m	Automatic	Conventional[4][5] Drive-in pallet[7] Live pallet[2]

The aisle measurements are established for use with europallets handled by their narrow side. Figures are approximate.

Notes

(1) Pallets must be handled by the open side, without lower boards.

(2) Can be used in the live pallet system, adapting the entry and exit areas of the racking units using split rollers.

(3) These forklifts must be guided, either mechanically (rail located on the floor), or wire guided (wire buried in the ground).

(4) Pallets cannot be picked up directly from the ground. Another conventional or reach forklift is required to place or remove the pallet at the aisle entrance, or a mechanical transfer and positioning system can be used (roller conveyor, drag chains, shuttles, etc.).

(5) Guided at the top and bottom. Some machines are guided only at the bottom.

(6) When the pallets are moved sideways or are wider than the distance between the front skids of the forklift, the movement must be with these on said skids, having to increase the clearance between the ground and the first load level to the height of the chassis plus 20cm.

(7) By satellite car or radio-shuttle.

Drinks warehouse. Source: Mecalux.

CHAPTER 4
STORAGE SYSTEMS

This manual examines the different storage systems that can be used with products that form load units, either individual or in combination, or products that are in themselves sales units. Not included within the scope of this book (and therefore not dealt with here) is the handling of bulk products, which require specific systems and transportation, as well as any storage by stacking or overlaying unit loads (as used in some facilities), where the homogeneity of the product and its ability to be stacked allow for this.

This point having been clarified, this chapter examines the characteristics of four groups of storage systems: palletised on racks; individual boxes and loose products; mixed systems; and, lastly, specific systems.

4.1 PALLETISED ON RACKING STORAGE

These are systems in which pallets containing goods are placed onto racks using forklift trucks or lifting machines.

This storage system has three essential elements: the racks, the pallets, and the forklift trucks or handling equipment. Each of these is chosen based on the product to be handled, storage requirements, working and positioning systems, and the management used in the facilities.

Palletising on racking can be arranged in two different ways: with direct access to pallets, or through compacting.

Direct access provides great efficiency when it comes to managing the pallets being stored. However, depending on the design of the system and the forklift truck or handling equipment used, the storage capacity obtained in the facility may not be optimal.

With compacting systems, however, the storage capacity obtained is normally greater, but it is more difficult to access some pallets.

Chapter 4 - Storage systems

Central warehouse of a company in the ceramics sector. Source: Mecalux.

Chapter 4 - Storage systems

The following is an analysis of each of these options, so that the most appropriate one can be chosen in each case.

4.1.1 Storage systems offering direct access to pallets

Only conventional racking, as shown in the picture below, provides direct access to each of the pallets stored. This racking can be static (when placed on the floor) or mobile (when placed on a motorised base).

Conventional static racking is placed on each side of the working aisles used by the forklift trucks or handling equipment. As discussed in Chapter 3, the width of the aisles will be determined by the type of machine used. Each aisle will serve two single racks.

Conventional racks can be mounted onto mobile bases instead of directly onto the floor. These mobile bases move around on rails embedded into the floor. This system is known as mobile racking, or Movirack.

Nowadays the control and protection devices used for this type of system are automated, guaranteeing smooth and safe movement.

They can be operated manually, by pressing a button at the P&D station for the rack, or by radio control (illustrated on the next page).

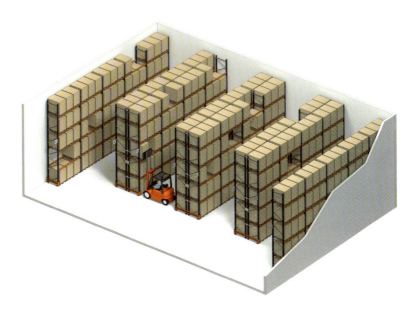

Chapter 4 - Storage systems

Storage and distribution of frozen products. Source: Mecalux.

The Movirack system allows for direct access to each pallet and helps compact space, so that a single working aisle can be used to access various racks.

Rail for mobile racking.

Guide rail for mobile racking.

1. Radio control aerial
2. Mounted box
3. Control panel
4. Main box
5. Radio control remote controller

Remote radio control system for mobile racking.

158

Depending on the space available at the facilities, the number of working aisles created, and the forklift truck used, this mobile system can increase storage capacity by between 80% and 120% compared to static racking, but at the cost of creating a less flexible system.

When should conventional static racking be installed?
This is the most versatile system in any warehouse, although its storage capacity can be less than other alternatives.

Thanks to its versatility, the use of conventional static racking is recommended for multi-client warehouses, since when it comes to planning the use of the facilities the logistics operator cannot anticipate exactly what products its clients are going to send it.

Its flexibility makes it the ideal system for storing pallets of different sizes. Similarly, it is suitable for warehouses with operations that involve picking directly from the racks and for facilities that store bulky products.

Warehouse for a logistics operator. Source: Mecalux.

Chapter 4 - Storage systems

Above: Logistics warehouse for the distribution of food products.

Left: A cross tie for pallets.
Source: Mecalux.

In terms of rotation, this type of storage solution is suitable for installations where many items are handled but the number of pallets of each item is low, as well as those with a rapid movement of goods. This racking is also appropriate for small warehouses where high rotation products (A) do not account for a large proportion of the pallets. In addition, when combined with other systems, this type of storage is ideal for storing medium and low rotation products (B and C).

In all these cases, rotation can be very easily controlled using a warehouse management program. With WMS, one can work on the basis of empty spaces (chaotic system), leaving the program to decide and record positions. This can provide an effective capacity of over 90% (as explained in section 4.1.3 below).

When handling pallets with this type of system, they have to be picked up from the narrow side, parallel to the entry skids. If they are handled from the wide side, cross ties must be placed in the load levels.

When should mobile bases (Movirack systems) be used?

When one or more of the recommendations we have just seen for conventional static racking apply, it may be appropriate to use mobile bases. They should also be used when there is a need to increase the capacity of the warehouse.

However, there is one exception. This solution is not appropriate if pallets are to be frequently moved. Therefore, it is better to use it for operations that require a minimal number of forklift trucks.

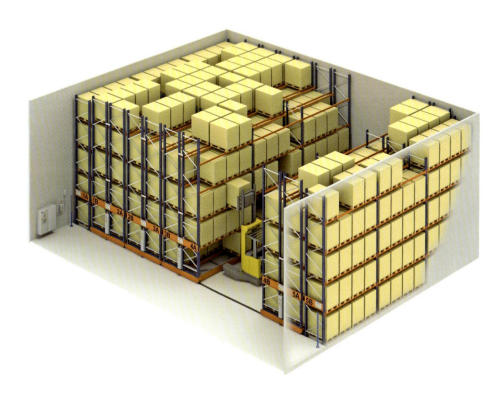

Chapter 4 - Storage systems

Warehouse/cold chamber for the storage and distribution of frozen products. Source: Mecalux.

It is also very useful as a complement to an automated warehouse (specifically, for storing irregular pallets).

It is best used when storing low rotation products (C), products that require some time without movement (in quarantine), or products that are pending quality testing.

Meanwhile, thanks to advantages such as the more efficient use of space, direct access to pallets, and the ability to store load units of different sizes, Movirack racking is particularly useful for small and medium-sized cold chambers no more than 11m in height. This system provides notable and ongoing energy savings, since the volume of space that needs to be cooled is half that required with conventional static racking. This benefit, in turn, affects the return on the investment.

Elevated installations

Nowadays it is possible to manufacture extremely high conventional racking that can reach heights of more than 40m, although this determines the type of handling equipment required to manage the load in these facilities. Specifically, VNA trucks can be used for racking of up to 14m, while for higher racking stacker cranes operated through automated systems must be used.

Tall racking is a good way of optimising available space, in that it offers a greater capacity in a limited space without losing the advantages of having direct access to any pallet. This is the ideal situation in any warehouse.

If the building has already been constructed, its height will determine the maximum dimensions of the racking used. If it has not yet been built, the facilities can be designed to allow for the required height and a self-supporting solution may be chosen (an excellent option particularly for buildings over 15m tall).

Self-supporting warehouses are buildings in which the structure is formed by the racks themselves, which, in addition to housing the goods, also support the walls and roof.

These are integrated and very strong buildings, given that the forces they have to bear from wind, snow, and earthquakes are calculated at the time of their construction. This type of structure is examined in more detail in Chapter 6.

Above: Self-supporting warehouse for the manufacture and distribution of health technology products.

Right: Inside an industrial building for the production and sale of ceramic products for construction.
Source: Mecalux.

Chapter 4 - Storage systems

The double deep option

Conventional racking can be installed in a double-deep configuration. This provides access to two pallets from the same side of the aisle, with one placed behind the other towards the back of the rack (the illustrations below will give you a better idea of how the load units are arranged).

Although the main advantage of the double-deep system (i.e., the ability to save space due to the need for fewer aisles to access loads) is clear, we should also be aware of its limitations and requirements.

One such limitation is that there is only direct access to the front pallet. To reach the second unit, the first pallet has to be moved, either to its destination (the dispatch area, for example) or to another empty space (in other words, relocate it).

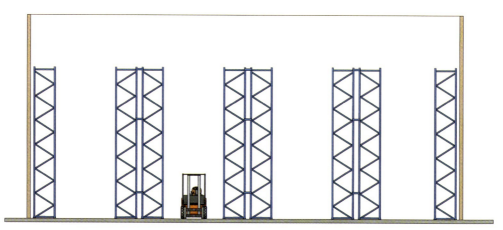

Standard racking distribution.

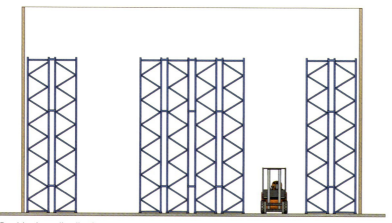

Double-deep distribution.

Chapter 4 - Storage systems

Logistics operator. Source: Mecalux.

Where goods are handled using forklift trucks, some models of forklift trucks have telescopic forks or pantographs which allow access to the second depth, as described in Chapter 3. In automated warehouses, double-deep configurations can also be established thanks to the use of stacker cranes with telescopic forks.

To use double-deep racking, one must anticipate the number of pallets for each item. This method of racking is appropriate if the pallet that is going to be at the back contains the same item as the one in front of it, and perfect rotation is not required.

For facilities with automated machines, the problem of access caused by the use of the double-deep configuration is resolved by the management program and its corresponding relocation module. To determine position, this software takes into account the rotation of the item (A, B, or C) and the quantity of the item in question. The result of this is that although the racking is double-deep, access is almost as good as for single-deep but without losing the benefit of a considerable increase in capacity.

Single-deep racking in a company in the sector providing ceramics for construction. Source: Mecalux.

Double-deep racking in the warehouse of a pharmaceuticals company. Source: Mecalux.

Conventional racking with automated systems

Conventional racking is ideal for use with automated systems, in both its single-deep and double depth modes.

Single-deep racking provides direct access to any pallet, since all load units are positioned along the aisle. This system is recommended when there are many different items and a very large number of cycles are required (entry, exit, or combined entry and exit movements).

With double-deep racking, capacity is increased considerably. It is particularly useful when there are several pallets of the same item.

The relocation program available with this type of system guarantees the rotation of all units.

For both single-deep and double-deep modes, automated warehouses are built to heights that generally exceed 8m, and can even exceed 40m. As a result, they can be used for many configurations. In addition, the wide range of stacking cranes and handling equipment available allows them to be used for most warehousing requirements that arise. For example, there are stacking cranes for the two different depth modes mentioned, double cradle stacker cranes for single-deep racking, with a crane bridge, with turning bends, for cold chambers, etc.

With automated warehouse systems, pallets are transported from the reception area into the warehouse on automated conveyors, generally with rollers and belts, that carry loads to the P&D stations for each aisle. An entry conveyor and an exit conveyor are installed there, at the sides of the aisle. The stacker crane picks up and stores the pallets, normally combining both movements. Thus, for exam-

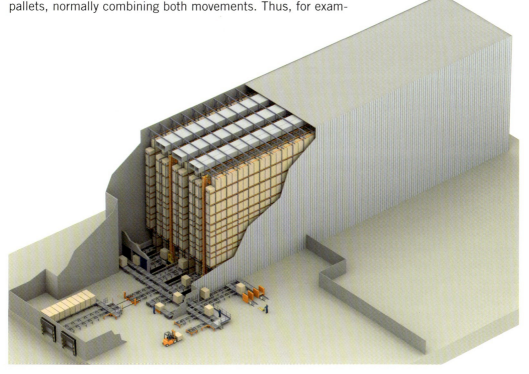

Automated warehouse/cold chamber for the manufacture of frozen products. Source: Mecalux.

ple, it places a pallet onto the racking and takes advantage of the fact that it is already halfway up the aisle to collect another unit and leave it at the P&D station. From there it goes to collect another pallet to be stored on the rack, and a new cycle begins.

The automated conveyors are also used to take the goods to the dispatch docks or to other working areas, such as the picking or production areas.

Warehouse management and control systems automatically move and manage all these processes. Software also optimise movements, so that as little time as possible is required to complete each cycle and each movement of a load. This saves time in performing operations and reduces energy consumption, for example. These are just some of the advantages of an automated warehouse, but there are others and these are discussed below.

Among the main benefits of a system of this type are **improved productivity and high availability.** Compared to other storage methods, productivity is improved in processes for the receipt and dispatch of goods and it offers better features, such as greater availability in the movement of goods without having to adhere to timetables, more efficient maintenance, etc. With the use of an automated system, there is also the option to establish continuous flows.

Similarly, with automated management, the WMS identifies and controls the goods at all times, enabling a facility of this type to have an **real time inventory.** The software can also provide complete product traceability, while also generating a historical record and controlling all movements of units.

Automated warehouse/refrigerated chamber Source: Mecalux.

Thirdly, although the installation of an automated warehouse requires a degree of financial investment, there are various factors that help reduce costs and provide a return on this investment, such as less need for forklift truck operators, preparers and administrative staff, as well as a reduction in handling items. Similarly, it offers lower maintenance costs, a reduced impact on structures, goods and machines, the elimination of waste produced by the incorrect use of the facilities, less demanding technical requirements for flooring, structures, etc.

These cost reductions do not affect safety. Quite the contrary: in an automated warehouse **goods are absolutely safe**, since there is no access to them. Goods remain on the racks until the stacker crane moves them, eliminating what are known as "unknown losses" of products. The load is therefore always in perfect condition, and breakage due to incorrect handling is avoided. Lastly, the number of and need for intermediate controls is reduced.

Automated systems are not only the **safest for goods**; they are also the **safest for personnel**. These systems are designed for use with minimal human intervention, with integrated safety devices and ergonomic dimensions for workstations. There is also constant general protection for professionals that have to interact with or move around the warehouse.

Finally, as explained later in this chapter, with an automated system full use is made of the warehouse space available. This is due to the ability to use much narrower aisles than with other conventional systems, which results in a larger area being available for racking (greater storage capacity) or in the need for a smaller warehouse (cost reduction).

In addition, the height of the **warehouse is more effectively used** due to the fact that the stacker cranes can achieve must more elevation than manual handling machines. The characteristics of an automated facility also result in the need for less space and greater flexibility and scalability.

4.1.2 Compact systems

As established at the beginning of this chapter, the other important group of systems used for storage (apart from those allowing direct access to each pallet (seen in earlier sections) is compact systems.

This group includes solutions with drive-in, push-back, radio-shuttle, and live storage racking units. Although each of these systems naturally has its own unique features, they do share a number of common characteristics.

The fact that they are compact systems means they make better use of space. However, they are best used though when there are a large number of pallets with the same SKU and rotation is not a priority. Only live racking enables FIFO flows (first in, first out) to allow for perfect rotation.

These storage systems do not provide access to any pallet at any time. Rather, if the unit load is in an internal position, the pallets in front of it must first be moved in order to gain access to it.

Image of a drive-in pallet system. Source: Mecalux.

Image of the push-back system. Source: Mecalux.

Unit loads must be handled by the wide side, perpendicularly to the lower skids. The exception is for live and Push-pack racking units with rollers, in which the pallet must be loaded and unloaded from its narrow side.

Each lane (in compact systems) or each level of a lane (push-back, radio-shuttle, and live racking units) must have only a single SKU. As a result, there can be a big difference between physical and effective capacities. The fewer the lanes or levels used for a single SKU, the greater the difference between these capacities will be.

Furthermore, with these systems, having a management system does not always automatically mean an increase in effective capacity. This is because when each lane is assigned to a single SKU, in a normal working flow it is considered half full and its effective capacity is 50% of its physical capacity. However, when there is more than one lane this differential is reduced.

Finally, there are two important issues relating to the height of the racking units. These systems tend to be used with counterbalanced and retractable trucks, which limits the maximum construction height. In addition, the higher the racking units the more difficult it is to handle the pallets.

Live storage pallet racking. Company manufacturing frozen dough. Source: Mecalux.

Radio-shuttle system installed in a company in the decorative wrapping paper sector. Source: Mecalux.

Drive-in racking units

Now that the basic issues common to all compact storage systems have been clarified, we shall analyse the individual features of each of these.

The simplest, most economical system in the compact family is the drive-in racking unit. This consists of a set of structures which form internal lanes with support rails for the pallets.

Provided that they are of the appropriate dimensions, these racking units can be used to store pallets not classified as europallets. However, different sized models should not be used simultaneously.

Forklift trucks are used with this type of racking unit. To place or remove pallets, these trucks enter each loading lane with the forks raised to the height required to perform the operation. This operating method means that the manoeuvres in these facilities are slower than other options.

For the same reason, the deeper the lane, the greater the capacity obtained but the more time is required to handle the pallets.

With this compact storage system, every level of each lane must have the same SKU. As a result, it is ideal for storing multiple pallets with the same SKU (high consumption products). However, each manoeuvre will take longer than it would using systems that provide direct access to the pallets.

It is also a perfect solution for temporary storage, acting as a buffer for dispatches or manufacturing, prepared orders, etc.

With these racking units, the system for placing and removing the pallets is generally known as drive-in (single-sided entry). With this system, the first pallet positioned on each level of each lane is the last to be removed, as shown in the diagram below.

There is another way of placing and removing pallets, called drive-through (double-sided entry), in which the pallets are entered on one side of the racking unit and removed from the other side. This tends to be used when the racking unit acts as an intermediate warehouse between two points of the production process.

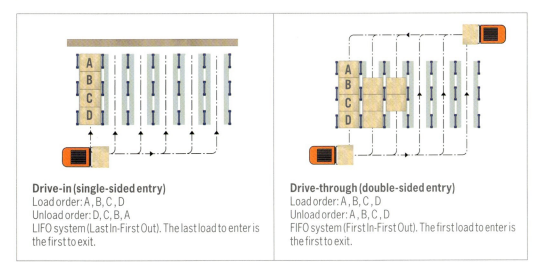

Drive-in (single-sided entry)
Load order: A , B, C , D
Unload order: D, C, B, A
LIFO system (Last In-First Out). The last load to enter is the first to exit.

Drive-through (double-sided entry)
Load order: A , B, C , D
Unload order: A , B, C , D
FIFO system (First In-First Out). The first load to enter is the first to exit.

Push-back racking units

In this type of compact system, each level of each lane is independent and so can contain a different SKU. This differs from the drive-in racking unit system, in which all pallets in the same lane (on all levels) must contain the same SKU.

Another difference between this system and drive-in racking units is that handling times are faster, since the forklifts do not have to enter the storage lanes.

The most logical application of this system is for storing average consumption products. Given that it allows for quicker manoeuvres, it can also be used for high consumption products.

This system is based on a racking unit in which each level of the lanes has a strip of rollers or trolleys that move on rails. The pallets slide along these, between the front and back of the racking unit (as shown with a double-headed arrow in the illustration).

The first pallet is placed in the first position of a level (the one closest to the aisle), on a trolley or on the strip of rollers. The second pallet is used to push the first and so on, until the level is full.

The strips are arranged so that they slope downwards toward the front of the racking unit, thus taking advantage of gravity. Thus, when the pallet closest to the front (to the aisle) is removed, the rest slide forward, making a new unit load available for removal.

Levels of up to four pallets deep can be installed using trolleys. With rollers, six pallets can be stored (depending on their weight).

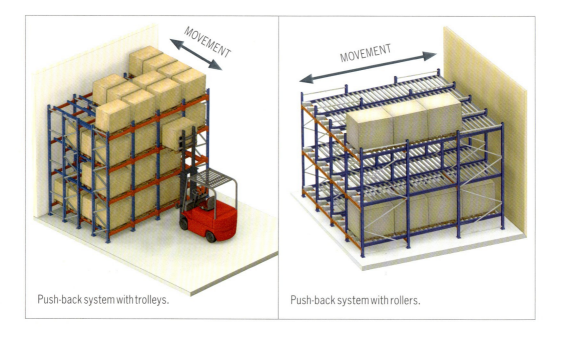

Push-back system with trolleys. | Push-back system with rollers.

When forklift trucks are used to handle equipment, if a trolley system is used the pallets must be handled by their wide side, perpendicular to the skids.

If rollers are used, pallets must be handled by the narrow side so that the skids slide perpendicular to the rollers.

Irrespective of whether rollers or trolleys are used, the pallets are placed and removed on the same side of the racking unit (at the front). This must be taken into account for product rotation, since the last pallet in is the first one out (LIFO).

Racking units with radio-shuttle

A more sophisticated version of the push-back racking unit is the drive-in racking unit with radio-shuttle. It is used for the same purposes as push-back systems, since each level must house a single SKU, but some features of the two systems differ.

To understand how this system differs from the push-back system, one must first understand how it works. The system is semi-automatic, with a robot used to position the pallets along the lane, but the loads are placed at the front of the racks with the help of a forklift.

The procedure is as follows: the forklift places a radio-shuttle (an automatic shuttle or trolley) at the start of the lane level where the goods are to be placed. A pallet is then dropped onto the trolley and, while this trolley is carrying the pallet to the first empty position it finds and returns to the start of the lane, the forklift is collecting the next pallet (thus reducing the time needed for manoeuvres and improving performance).

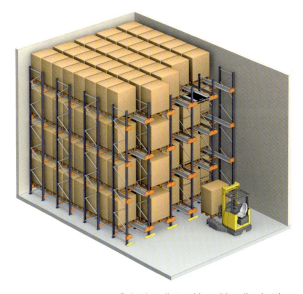

Drive-in pallet racking with radio-shuttle.

Detail of a radio-shuttle.

Before placing the last pallet on the level, the forklift removes the automatic shuttle so that it can be used on another level or in another lane. The system for removing pallets is similar but in reverse.

With the radio-shuttle system there is no limit to the depth of the lanes. As a result, this solution is perfect for deep racking units, with the entry and exit of the same product on a massive scale, although operability is lost when continually changing lanes.

On the other hand, these racking units can be loaded on one of the two sides and unloaded on the other (drive-through), but this option is not very practical unless the unloading operation is for the entire lane in one go. For the same reason, it is not advisable for the compact radio-shuttle system to be used as a replacement for continuous flow live storage pallet racking (explained below), since this system involves continually repositioning the pallets, moving them closer to the removal position, which is not very practical.

Live storage pallet racking
This is the ideal compact system, offering all the advantages of the systems described above.

It is a straightforward system. Each level of each lane is used for a single SKU and has a strip of slightly inclined rollers.

The pallets are placed on one side of the strip and gravity moves them over the rollers until they reach the other end of the strip (which is why they are also called gravity systems). The goods are removed from this far side. The forklifts do not have to move inside the lanes.

With this method, the first pallet that enters the level is the first to exit (FIFO system), which makes for perfect product rotation.

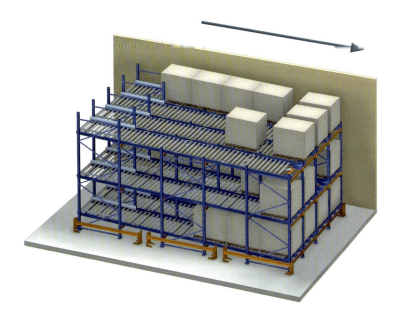

Lanes more than 20m deep can be installed. However, the pallets used must be in good condition pallets and have to be of good quality and weight.

This type of solution is best used for storing high rotation perishable goods and continuous flow high consumption products (constant entry and exit).

Two factors must be taken into account when considering this storage system. The first is that, since the pallets are positioned on a slant, it requires more height than the other compact options, which in some cases can mean the loss of a load level. Furthermore, greater depth requires greater height. The second observation is that, depending on the size of the warehouse, this can be the most expensive compact system.

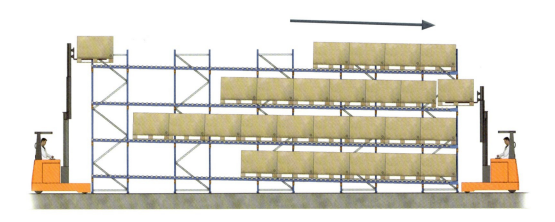

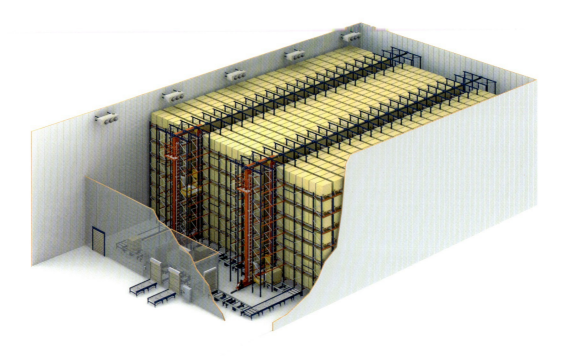

Compact system with automated handling and management

Compact racking units can also be automated, although only radio-shuttle and live storage (by gravity) systems can operate in this automated way, in which the supply takes place using stacker cranes or shuttles. Automated compact systems have all the advantages of the standard automated systems, but provide greater capacity.

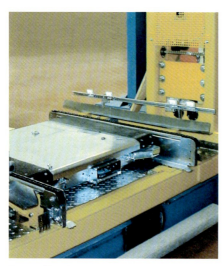

Source: Mecalux.

Warehouse/cold chamber for the packing and distribution of fish and seafood. Source: Mecalux.

In automated radio shuttle solutions, the stacker crane or shuttle carries a trolley in its cradle. This trolley placed on the levels of the storage lanes and automatically positions each pallet in the deepest available space.

When a stacker crane is used as the basic handling equipment, it serves all positions of a single lane across its full height.

When shuttles are the basic handling equipment used, each level is served by a shuttle that accesses all lanes on that level. Lifts are installed at the ends of the location positions to raise and lower the goods and drop them off on, or pick them up from, the shuttles.

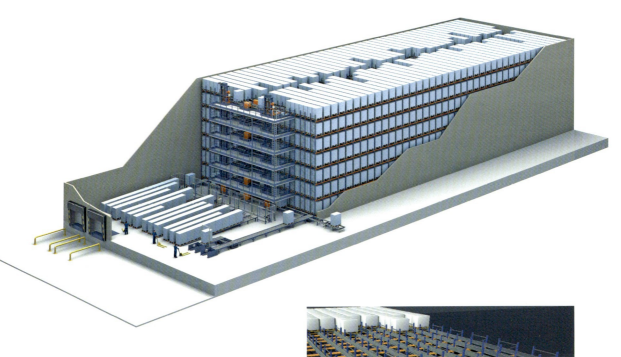

Simulation of the combined movement of a radio-shuttle and a shuttle.

The combination of a radio-shuttle and a shuttle on each level makes for a significant increase in the number of cycles, since the shuttle moves through the lanes at a certain level, supplying the pallets to the radio-shuttle, which then takes them to their positions in the storage lane.

In these systems, the height limit is determined by the local regulations in force. However, these systems can exceed 40m if this is permitted and the project so requires.

Warehouse for the manufacture of disposable tableware and articles. Source: Mecalux.

Automated live storage racking units have one stacker crane installed on the entry side (which supplies the racking unit) and another on the exit side (which unloads the racking unit). An intermediate version is to supply the live storage lanes automatically and unload them using conventional methods, such as forklifts.

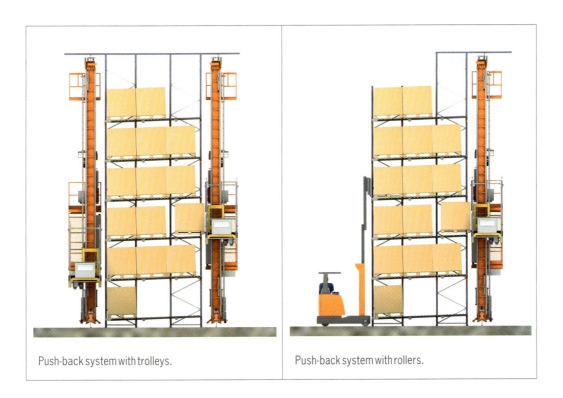

Push-back system with trolleys. Push-back system with rollers.

Automated systems with live storage are ideal for high consumption products, products produced on a constant basis, and products for which rotation and cycles are very important. It is also perfect as an intermediate buffer between production and dispatch.

The importance of the need to monitor and ensure the quality of the pallets used in live storage racking units has already been mentioned. This is even more important in facilities of greater height and when using automated systems.

4.1.3 Capacity differences between systems

The information in this chapter can be used to identify the most appropriate system to provide the best physical capacity ratio. However, physical capacity is not the only criterion to be taken into consideration when planning a warehouse. There are other equally essential factors, such as the speed of handling the pallets with one specific configuration or another.

On the other hand, the physical capacity of a warehouse (the maximum number of pallets that can be stored at one time) is not always the same as its effective capacity, which is merely that which can be obtained in a normal working cycle, in accordance with the maximums and minimums for the SKUs and the space required for each. Here, the positioning system used is vital.

The specific positioning system requires a certain number of spaces to be reserved for each SKU, except for those that can share positions with others. When goods enter the warehouse, all available spaces are filled but are then emptied as the orders are prepared. Given that these are reserved and cannot be filled with other SKUs, the effective capacity will be lower than the physical capacity. Specifically, the effective capacity will be the minimum stock plus half of the difference between said minimum stock and the number of spaces assigned to that SKU. Effective capacity with these specific positioning systems is between 55% and 65% of real capacity.

When working with random positions, the management system assigns positions to the pallets, which will be stored at random in any empty space. The WMS records the position and provides it to the operator when necessary. In this case there are almost no empty spaces, so the effective and physical capacities will be very similar (between 80% and 92%).

Unless these differences are taken into account, the solution chosen for the warehouse may not be the correct one. While any system can operate with the two positioning types mentioned, compact storage systems, for example, are inflexible and, while they can provide greater physical capacity than other systems, they may actually provide lower effective capacity.

To illustrate the differences that can arise in facilities when using one storage system or another, the following is a hypothetical example of a warehouse with specific measurements and a particular unit load. Different solutions (configurations and handling equipment) are offered for this hypothetical case and the results of using each method are shown.

Capacity is calculated on the basis of the surface area and defined for a storage level, since height is a variable that depends on the building itself and the lifting height of the forklift. To help with the comparison, the space required for the reception and dispatch areas has not been taken into account either. The unit load chosen is a 1200mm x 800mm pallet (europallet), which in the conventional pallet system means that up to three of these pallets can be stored in each space 2700mm wide.

Load unit:
1200 x 800 mm pallet

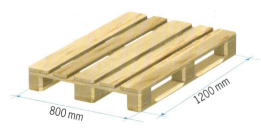

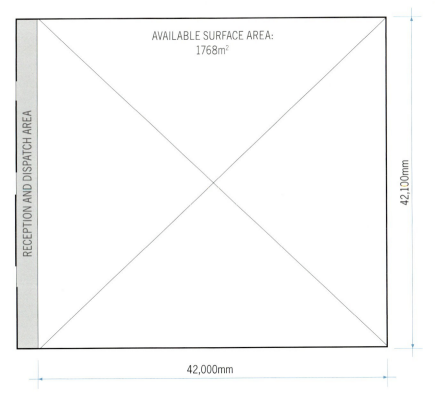

AVAILABLE SURFACE AREA:
1768m²

RECEPTION AND DISPATCH AREA

42,100mm

42,000mm

EXAMPLE 1. Conventional pallet racking with counterbalanced forklift truck.
594 pallets per level

System: Conventional pallet racking.
Aisle: 3500mm. A minimum of 3600mm between racking units.
Handling: Electric counterbalanced forklift.

Capacity obtained: 594 pallets per level.

Distribution company warehouse.
Source: Mecalux.

Dimensions in mm.

EXAMPLE 2. Conventional pallet racking with reach truck. 678 pallets per level

System: Conventional pallet racking.
Handling: Reach truck.
Aisle: 2750mm. A minimum of 2850mm between racking units.

Capacity obtained: 678 pallets per level.

Logistics warehouse.
Source: Mecalux.

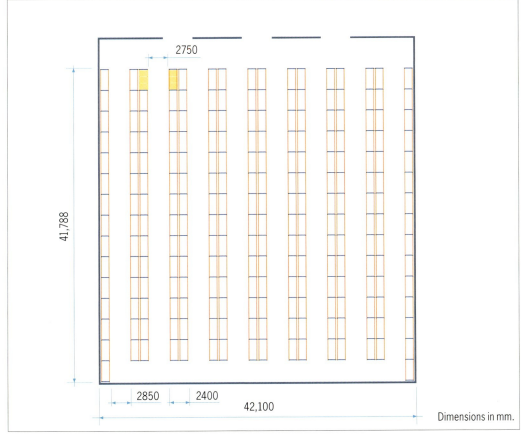

Dimensions in mm.

EXAMPLE 3. Conventional pallet racking with trilateral turret-type forklift or stacker crane. 840 pallets per level

System: Conventional pallet racking.
Handling: Trilateral turret-type forklift or stacker crane.
Aisle: 1700mm. A minimum of 1800mm between racking units.

Capacity obtained: 840 pallets per level.

Note: A stacker crane can work in an aisle of 1500mm wide between loads, so the width of the space available in the example can be 40,000mm instead of 42,100mm to obtain the same result.

Turret truck warehouse. Source: Mecalux.

Automated paper reel warehouse. Source: Mecalux.

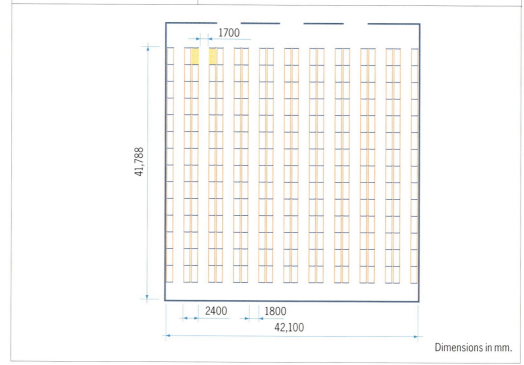
Dimensions in mm.

EXAMPLE 4. Double-deep conventional pallet racking with stacker crane.
1008 pallets per level

System: Double-deep conventional pallet racking.
Handling: Stacker crane.
Aisle: 1500mm. At least 1600mm between racking units.

Capacity obtained: 1008 pallets per level.

Note: As in example 3, for this facility the warehouse can be 40,000mm wide instead of 42,000mm.

Warehouse for high consumption products. Source: Mecalux.

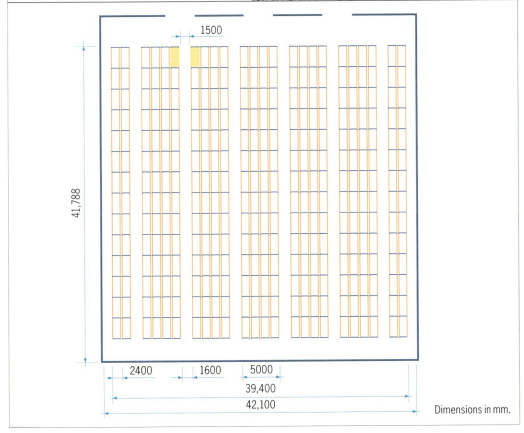

Dimensions in mm.

EXAMPLE 5. Conventional pallet racking on mobile bases.
1144 pallets per level

System: Conventional pallet racking on mobile bases.
Handling: Forklifts.
Aisles: Two of 3750mm each.
Two forklift trucks can pass in these (maintaining the appropriate margins).

Capacity obtained: 1144 pallets per level.

Frozen meat warehouse.
Source: Mecalux.

Dimensions in mm.

Chapter 4 - Storage systems

EXAMPLE 6. Drive-in pallet racking. 960 pallets per level

System: Drive-in pallet racking.
Handling: Forklifts.
Aisle: 3500mm, with enough space for two forklifts to pass each other.

Capacity obtained: 960 pallets per level.

Source: Mecalux.

Dimensions in mm.

EXAMPLE 7. Push-back with trolleys. 848 pallets per level

System: Push-back with trolleys.
Handling: Forklifts.
Aisle: At least 3500mm.

Capacity obtained: 848 pallets per level.

Source: Mecalux.

Dimensions in mm.

Chapter 4 - Storage systems

EXAMPLE 8. Push-back with rollers. 893 pallets per level

System: Push-back with rollers.
Handling: Forklifts.
Aisle: At least 3400mm.

Capacity obtained: 893 pallets per level.

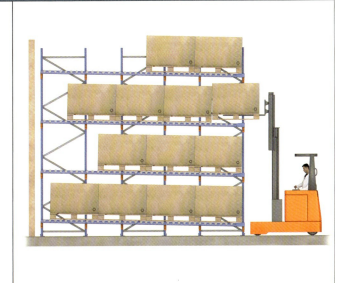

Dimensions in mm.

Chapter 4 - Storage systems

EXAMPLE 9. Pallet racking with radio-shuttle. 1080 pallets per level

System: Pallet racking with radio-shuttle.
Handling: Forklifts.
Aisle: At least 3500mm (space for two forklifts to pass each other).

Capacity obtained: 1080 pallets per level.

Furniture kit company.
Source: Mecalux.

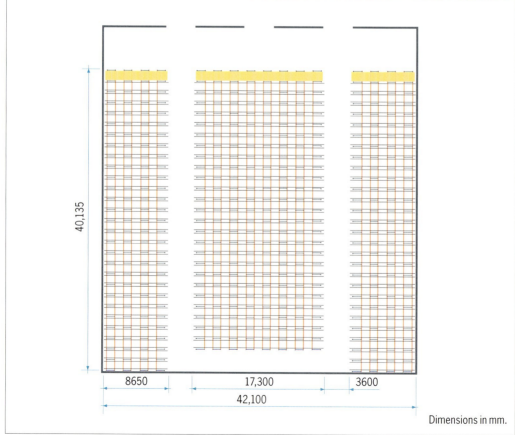

Dimensions in mm.

Chapter 4 - Storage systems

EXAMPLE 10. Live pallet storage racking unit. 910 pallets per level

System: Live pallet storage racking unit.
Handling: Forklifts.
Aisle: At least 3400mm.

Capacity obtained: 910 pallets per level.

Juice manufacturing company.
Source: Mecalux.

Dimensions in mm.

SUMMARY TABLE COMPARING PHYSICAL CAPACITY AVAILABLE SURFACE AREA: 1768m²			
Storage system	Pallets per level	Surface area for pallets	Ratio (proportion of premises occupied by pallets)
Conventional warehouse with counterbalanced forklift	594	570m²	32.2%
Conventional warehouse with reach truck	678	651m²	39.2%
Conventional warehouse with trilateral turret truck or stacker crane	840	806m²	45.7%
Conventional double-deep warehouse with stacker crane	1008	968m²	54.9%
Conventional warehouse with mobile bases	1144	1098m²	62.2%
Drive-in warehouse with reach truck	960	922m²	53.8%
Push-back with trolleys	848	814m²	46.0%
Push-back with rollers	893	857m²	48.0%
Pallet racking with radio-shuttle	1080	1037m²	58.8%
Live storage racking unit	910	874m²	47.6%

Capacity by volume is not linear because other factors come into play, such as the useful height of the warehouse and pallet height optimisation. Another determining factor is the construction system, since live storage racking units involve a loss of height due to the slope used by this system; and in double-deep facilities with stacker cranes more separation between levels is required. In other cases, support sections and a specific height for the first level are required.

This table is for illustrative purposes only and refers to physical capacity, as opposed to effective capacity.

<u>Comments on capacity differences between the various systems</u>
The above examples have been put forward based on the assumption that the warehouse is of average width. If the warehouse is larger, the capacity ratio may be significantly different. If, on the other hand, the warehouse is smaller, the differences between storage systems could increase but not in a linear manner, since each adapts to smaller spaces in its own individual way. In short, the examples in this chapter have been provided merely to show the differences that may exist between the various systems. However, different values will be obtained from each specific configuration of space.

To demonstrate these variations as a function of available space, below are several examples applied for comparative purposes to two different warehouses. To differentiate between them, the warehouse 21m wide and with a surface area of 882m² is called warehouse B, while the warehouse 18m wide with an available surface area of 756m² is called warehouse C. The examples are only for conventional direct access racking units, which can have the most extreme variations. These differences are not usually as great with compact systems.

Chapter 4 - Storage systems

EXAMPLE 1-B
CONVENTIONAL PALLET RACKING UNIT WITH COUNTERBALANCED FORKLIFT

Capacity: 258 pallets per level (the same as for options 1-C and 2-C).
Ratio: 28%

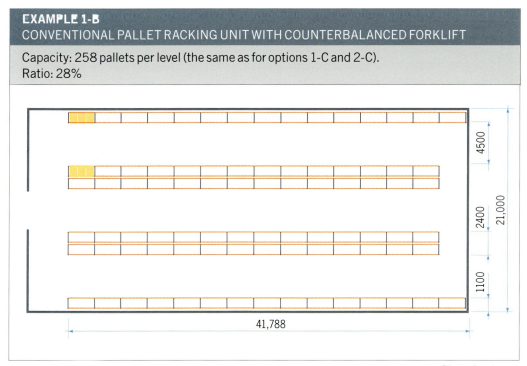

Dimensions in mm.

EXAMPLE 1-B (WITH REDUCED AISLE)
CONVENTIONAL PALLET RACKING UNIT WITH COUNTERBALANCED FORKLIFT

Capacity: 353 pallets per level.
Ratio: 38.4%

This example is similar to the previous one but with a smaller aisle, which allows a compact system to be used (in this case, drive-in racking units). This variation would be of interest for products suitable for storage on a racking unit of this type.

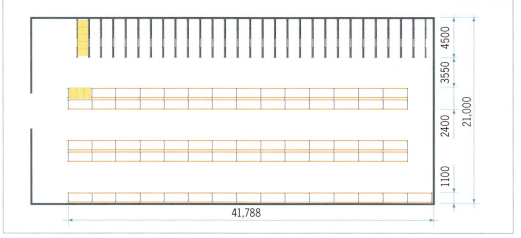

Dimensions in mm.

EXAMPLE 2-B
CONVENTIONAL PALLET RACKING UNIT WITH REACH TRUCK

Capacity: 342 pallets per level.
Ratio: 37.2%

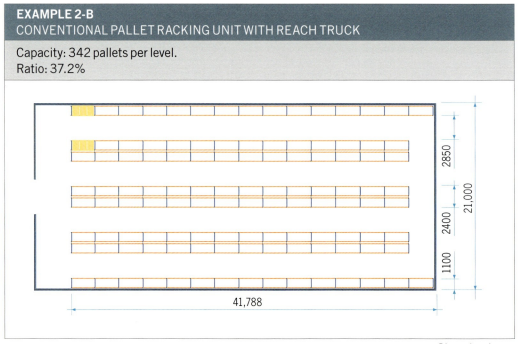

Dimensions in mm.

Chapter 4 - Storage systems

EXAMPLE 3-B
CONVENTIONAL PALLET RACKING UNIT WITH TRILATERAL TURRET-TYPE TRUCK OR STACKER CRANE

Capacity: 420 pallets per level.
Ratio: 45.7%

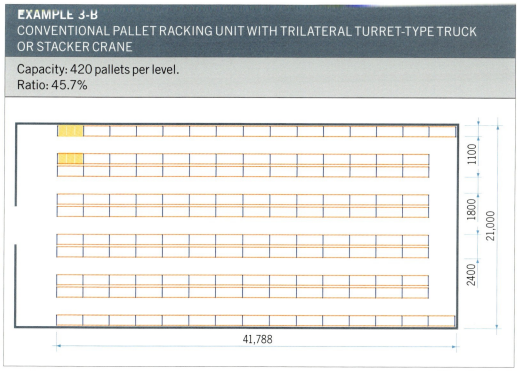

Dimensions in mm.

EXAMPLE 1-C
CONVENTIONAL PALLET RACKING UNIT WITH COUNTERBALANCED FORKLIFT

Capacity: 258 pallets per level (same as for options 1-B and 2-C).
Ratio: 32.8%

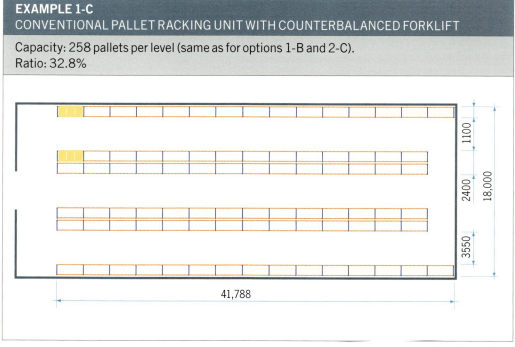

Dimensions in mm.

Chapter 4 - Storage systems

EXAMPLE-C
CONVENTIONAL PALLET RACKING UNIT WITH REACH TRUCK

Capacity: 258 pallets per level (same as for options 1-B and 1-C).
Ratio: 32.8%

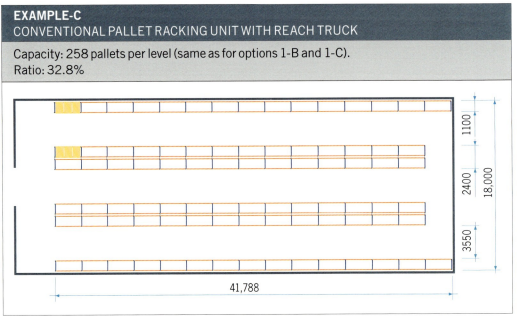

Dimensions in mm.

EXAMPLE 2-C (WITH REDUCED AISLE)
CONVENTIONAL PALLET RACKING UNIT WITH REACH TRUCK

Capacity: 297 pallets per level.
Ratio: 37.7%

This solution is similar to the previous example, but the aisle has been reduced to the space strictly necessary. This enables part of the plant to be used for the compact system, which in this case is a compact push-back system with trolleys. This variation would be advisable for products suitable for storage in push-back racking units.

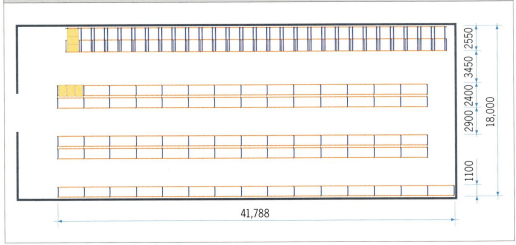

Dimensions in mm.

EXAMPLE 3-C
CONVENTIONAL PALLET RACKING UNIT WITH TRILATERAL TURRET-TYPE TRUCK OR STACKER CRANE

Capacity: 336 pallets per level.
Ratio: 42.7%

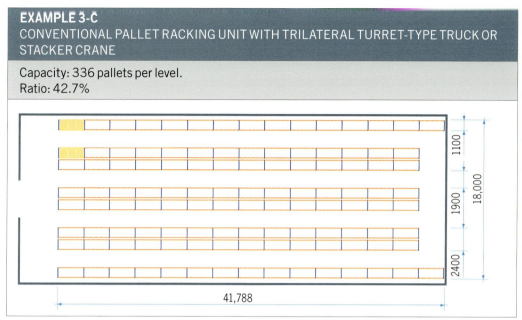

Dimensions in mm.

TABLE COMPARING THE OCCUPATION OF PALLETS (PERCENTAGE)

Storage system			
Conventional pallet racking units with counterbalanced forklift	Example 1(*)	Example 1B	Example 1C
	34.3%	28%	32.8%
Conventional pallet racking units with reach truck	Example 2(*)	Example 2B	Example 2C
	39.2%	37.2%	32.8%
Conventional single-deep pallet warehouse with trilateral turret truck or stacker crane	Example 3(*)	Example 3B	Example 3C
	45.7%	45.7%	42.7%
Mixed conventional/drive-in		Example 1B (with variation)	Example 2C (with variation)
	–	38.4%	37.7%

(*) Examples 1, 2 and 3 are those seen in the previous table (comparing all storage systems).

As can be seen, the greatest differences occur in systems that need a wider aisle. On the other hand, each storage system has its own way of adapting to the space available. The greatest differences occur when varying the width of that space.

In any event, these data are for illustrative purposes only and provided here to show the differences that can exist between three hypothetical scenarios. In practice, each specific warehouse will provide its own ratios depending on the storage system used.

4.2 STORAGE OF INDIVIDUAL BOXES AND SMALL PRODUCTS

Now that we have examined the options available for pallet storage, we can turn our attention to those used for smaller units, such as individual boxes and loose products (products removed from boxes). The handling of these two types of units is based at all times on the need to help with the picking operations, meaning that for the most part they are used for preparing an order.

As mentioned earlier, the picking operation is the warehouse operation with the greatest impact on the product cost. Given the high cost of designing a picking operation, the first thing to analyse is how to move goods inside the facility so as to perform the task of selecting and removing units.

1. Classic light duty racking unit
2. Classic light duty racking unit with walkways
3. Classic light duty racking unit on mobile bases
4. Racking units with pickers for loose boxes
5. Racking units with pickers for pallets
6. Pallet racking unit with turret-type forklift trucks
7. Live picking racking units
8. Live picking racking units with pick to light systems
9. Automated storage with miniload stacker crane

The first method is called man-to-goods, in which the operator carrying out the picking has to move around the warehouse to the position of each of the units to be picked for each of the lines requiring preparation.

The second method is called goods-to-man, in which the operator remains at the picking post and a machine moves the goods to that position, leaving them within the reach of the operator.

The third system is mixed. In a warehouse several storage systems with different operating principles can be put in place, each for a specific type of product. The image on the previous page shows different ways of carrying out the picking; all of these can be combined in the one warehouse.

Other systems can also be added to those already mentioned, such as vertical lift modules and horizontal carousels, such as those shown below, which will be discussed later in this chapter.

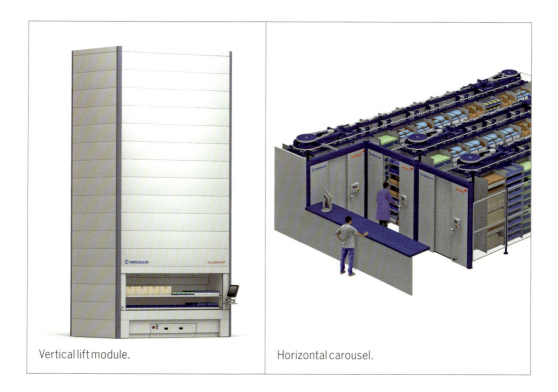

Vertical lift module.   Horizontal carousel.

4.2.1 Man-to-goods solutions

Traditional racking units: M3, slotted angle, and Simplos
The simplest and most traditional man-to-goods system is that based on simple racking units that provide direct access to boxes and loose items. These racking units consist of vertical struts

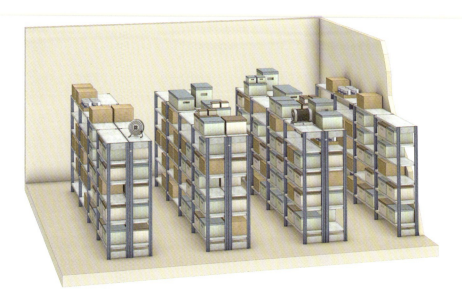

and shelves, and are very widely used in small warehouses with varied and small to medium-sized goods. Their main advantages are simplicity, versatility, and the low initial cost of installation.

Given that loads are normally accessed manually by operators, these racking units are not usually more than 2.5m high, since a person cannot comfortably access products more 2m above the ground. The trays used to hold the boxes and units tend to be no more than 1400mm long and 600mm deep, and generally hold up to 200kg of goods.

Racking units come in different models, with or without screws, and can be adapted to the specific needs of each storage environment.

These structures also come with a large number of accessories suitable for each product, as shown in the accompanying images.

Adjustable pigeonholes, levels for cylindrical elements, mesh shelves, drawers, doors, etc. can also be added.

The major drawback to this type of racking unit is that it makes little use of the available surface area and height. Nonetheless, certain strategies can help ensure better use of height.

With the use of the appropriate picker machines, such as those seen in Chapter 3, it is possible to access and pick from racking units up to 8m high. Another possible option for putting the height of the building to good use is to add intermediate walkways between the racking units, which act as aisles and can be accessed by staircases.

Chapter 4 - Storage systems

Warehouse for a company specialising in the manufacture of electronic equipment. Source: Mecalux.

Warehouse for a company specialising in the distribution and supply of components for cars, industrial vehicles and railways. Source: Mecalux.

Medium-duty racking units (M7)

Medium-duty racking units work in a similar way to the classic racking units discussed above. The main difference is that their spaces can be larger than in the classic ones, and they can hold more weight.

Given these features, they are most appropriate for storing medium-sized products or units packed in boxes.

Like classic racking units, they are very versatile, in that they can also be used with different accessories and complements, and thus be adapted to meet the widest range of needs. As a result, they can be used to store boxes, cylinders, clothing on hangers, etc.

Strategies for taking advantage of the building's height can also be used with medium-duty racking units, with the installation of intermediate walkways accessed by stairs. The construction height can exceed 12m. Similarly, they are the most commonly used racking units when working with high level pickers.

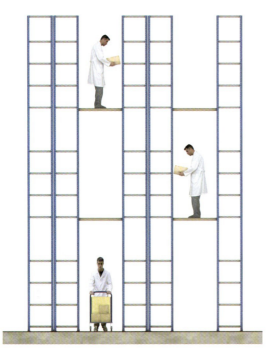

Top left image: Example of a picking system with walkways for clothing on hangers.

Top right image: Racking units for picking with component pickers.

Source: Mecalux.

Medium-duty racking units are usually installed in a warehouse by adding two single-deep structures per aisle. This means that between two aisles there will be two racking units attached to each other, forming a double one (as shown below). This option is the most versatile, as it allows for the height of the levels to be adjusted with ease.

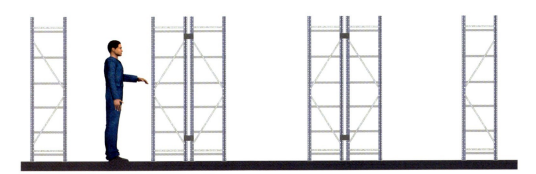

Another possible configuration consists of creating a double racking unit using a wider structure, as shown in the image below. This option is appropriate when the load is light and the levels do not need to be set independently for each aisle.

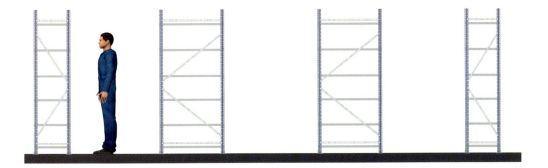

Chapter 4 - Storage systems

Traditional and medium-duty racking units on mobile bases (Movibloc)

As we have seen, static racking units are laid out by placing a structure on each side of an aisle. A large amount of space is therefore required for these access points.

The solution to this problem is similar to that for pallet racking units: place them on mobile bases. In this way all but one of the aisles can be removed, considerably increasing storage capacity or reducing the space required to store the same load.

The mobile bases move along guides installed in the floor. They can be moved manually, using cranks and flywheels, or electrically.

Three examples of the Movibloc system. Source: Mecalux.

These Movibloc racking units or cupboards can incorporate the same accessories and complements as static models, which means they can be used to store any small or medium-sized products, and can therefore be adapted to any needs that may arise. The following image shows the parts of a structure of this type, as well as the various configuration options available.

1. Mobile racking unit
2. Fixed racking unit
3. Sheet metal side panel
4. Melamine-covered wooden side panel
5. Open side panel
6. Metal mesh side panel
7. Handle with option to add a lock
8. Vertical dividers
9. Plastic drawers
10. Cross bracing set
11. Load retaining frontpiece
12. Panel
13. Guide rail
14. Mobile base set
15. Chain guard set
16. Rail stop

Intermediate walkways can also be used with mobile racking units, increasing storage capacity by maximising the available height, as seen in the image below.

In addition to the great benefit of offering increased storage capacity, these systems on their own can also be used to form closed restricted access storage areas, for which key interlocks are fitted.

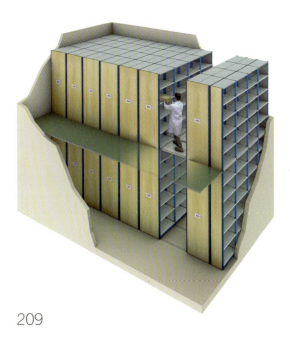

Boxes and loose units on pallet racking units

Storing small and medium-sized goods that will be picked does not always have to involve racking units designed specifically for this task, such as those described above. More often than not, orders are prepared by picking the product directly from the pallets.

If this option is used for the lower levels of pallet racking units, trolleys, stacker cranes, or low level pickers are used. If used for higher levels, then mid-high reach pickers or combi type VNA trucks (in which the cabin, where the operator sits, rises along with the load) must be used.

These solutions are appropriate when each pallet contains a single SKU. They are also suitable if high consumption products are picked from low levels medium to low consumption products are picked from high levels. They are also suitable when the number of lines that can be prepared is not a priority.

Warehouse for ground level pallet picking. Source: Mecalux.

Warehouse for loose boxes on racking units with pickers. Source: Mecalux.

Warehouse for high level pallet picking. Source: Mecalux.

Mixed warehouse. Source: Mecalux.

Preparing orders directly from the pallet racking units has certain limitations that must also be taken into account.

Emptied pallets must be replaced by others stored in the reserve area. In some warehouses, the higher levels are used for storing these reserve units, which replace the lower units used for picking.

For high consumption products, it is advisable to place two pallets of each SKU at the picking levels, to avoid delays in replenishing stock (while one is being replaced, the other contains the product).

Furthermore, to increase the number of lines, storage and replacement aisles must alternate with those for preparing orders.

Levels with are often fit with racking at the bottom of the pallet racking units to facilitate picking. With this type of solution, high rotation products can be stored on pallets placed directly on the ground.

As a safety precaution, to prevent accidents forklifts must not enter aisles where an operator is carrying out the picking, unless under the control of that same operator.

Source: Mecalux.

Source: Mecalux.

Chapter 4 - Storage systems

Source: Mecalux.

Live picking racking units

Live racking units are unbeatable assets when managing SKUs with high rotation volume and a large number of units. These structures have platforms on a slight slope fitted with pulley wheels or rollers. Goods are dropped off on the higher side of the platform and slide to the other side (the exit aisle) under the force of gravity.

All boxes positioned in a single row have the same SKU. The product is removed from the first of these boxes, while the ones behind it are reserves. When the box closest to the picking aisle is removed (to pick it as a complete unit or because it is empty), the entire row slides forward and the position is automatically filled.

This solution can be used for a large number of SKU in a single bay. In the bottom left-hand image is an example in which three levels have been created with four channels (rows) in each. A single bay like this can have 12 different SKUs. The bottom right-hand image is another example of how boxes of different sizes are used, allowing up to 18 SKUs to be stored.

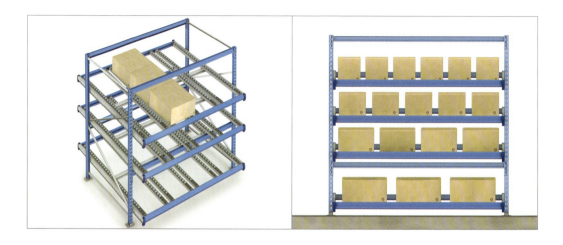

Live picking racking units really speed up the preparation of orders, both for entire boxes and for items inside them. These structures can be combined with roller conveyors, placed across them, making it very easy to move the prepared goods (see illustration).

The ergonomic design of the levels, as shown in the images below, also facilitates product access and removal.

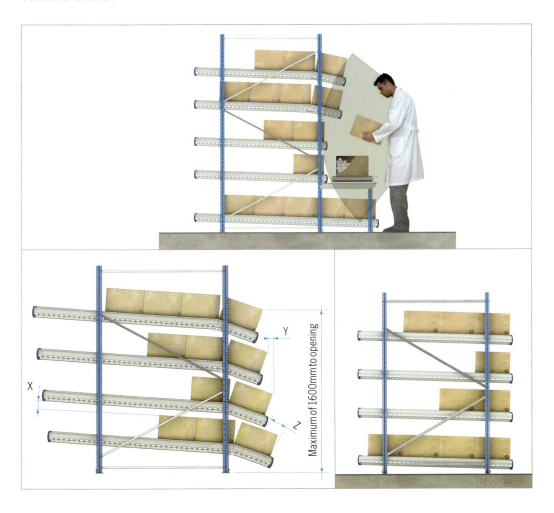

Live picking units are a very compact solution that considerably reduces the distance operators need to cover to prepare orders (all SKUs can be accessed from a single aisle) and makes better use of space. The following is an example comparing the surface area occupied by a traditional picking solution and that required by a live shelving picking system.

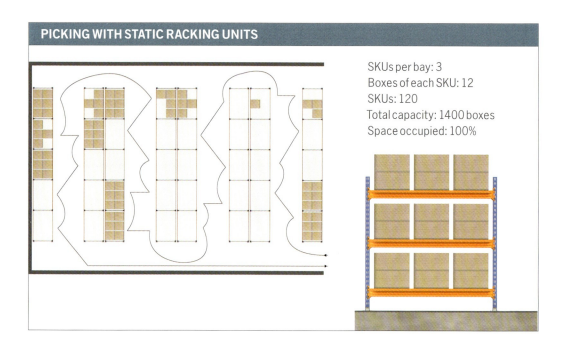

PICKING WITH STATIC RACKING UNITS

SKUs per bay: 3
Boxes of each SKU: 12
SKUs: 120
Total capacity: 1400 boxes
Space occupied: 100%

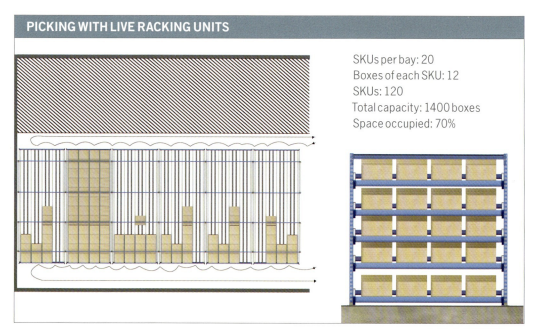

PICKING WITH LIVE RACKING UNITS

SKUs per bay: 20
Boxes of each SKU: 12
SKUs: 120
Total capacity: 1400 boxes
Space occupied: 70%

While the surface area of the premises is the same in both examples, in the second example the load layout is more compact so the space taken up by the longitudinal access aisles is made available. This reduces the surface area used for storage by 30%, which can be reused for preparation, storing more goods, etc.

Due to these features, the live picking racking system is the fastest for picking orders when the product is removed from inside boxes.

It is the perfect choice when picking small and high rotation products (A). It is not ideal for medium and low rotation products (B and C).

As can be seen from the following examples, the facility can be fitted with devices such as pick to light (explained in the following section "Live racking units with the pick to light system") and roller conveyors to move or transport boxes with goods already prepared or in progress.

These racking units can also be combined with pallet racking units, either to remove orders from full pallets or to store those that will then be fed into the picking channels. In the photo on the right, for example, high rotation products are stored in pallets positioned on live racking units. The top two levels are live picking levels, each with the pick to light system.

Source: Mecalux.

Detail of the pick to light system. Source: Mecalux.

Live racking units are one of the most versatile storage elements for small and medium-sized items. They can be combined with accessories, with other racking units, and with manual or automated handling equipment, creating solutions adapted to the needs of each facility. Here are some examples of possible configurations.

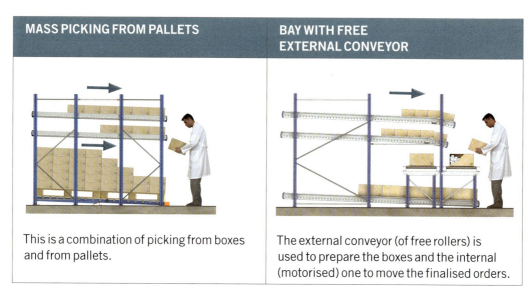

MASS PICKING FROM PALLETS

This is a combination of picking from boxes and from pallets.

BAY WITH FREE EXTERNAL CONVEYOR

The external conveyor (of free rollers) is used to prepare the boxes and the internal (motorised) one to move the finalised orders.

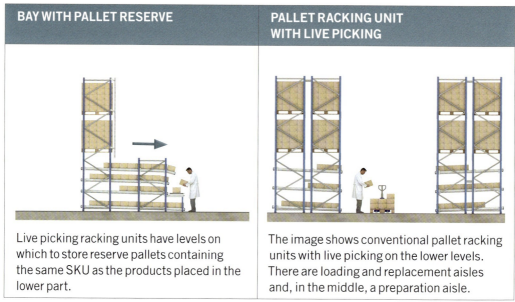

BAY WITH PALLET RESERVE

Live picking racking units have levels on which to store reserve pallets containing the same SKU as the products placed in the lower part.

PALLET RACKING UNIT WITH LIVE PICKING

The image shows conventional pallet racking units with live picking on the lower levels. There are loading and replacement aisles and, in the middle, a preparation aisle.

BAY WITH RESERVE PALLETS ON PUSH-BACK LEVELS

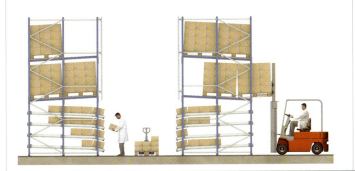

With this solution, the space over the live racking units is used to store reserve pallets on levels with rollers (push-back). Pallets are placed and removed on the opposite side to the preparation aisle.

PUSH-BACK PALLET RACKING UNIT WITH ROLLERS

In this case, the space above the preparation aisles is also used as a reserve area. On one side (to the right in the image) mass picking is carried out from pallets stored on sloping paths with rollers.

BAY WITH RESERVE IN AUTOMATED WAREHOUSE

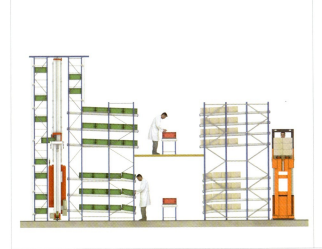

This example combines a high level live picking solution with a walkway, so as to make better use of the vertical space available in the preparation area. One racking unit (to the left of the aisle in the image) is automatically supplied using a stacker crane and the other structure (to the right of the aisle) is restocked with a combi type trilateral turret truck, which raises the pallets so that the operator handling the forklift places the boxes of goods manually on the different live levels.

Example of the pick to light system in a pharmaceutical laboratory.
Source: Mecalux.

Chapter 4 - Storage systems

Live picking racking units with the "pick to light" system

Live picking racking units minimise the journeys operators must make to prepare orders. A single aisle can be used to contain the same number of SKUs as four aisles of light or medium-duty classic racking units.

Reducing movement is one good way of improving operator efficiency, but not the only one. To go further and do away with the need for dispatch notes, pick to light (PTL) devices can be used.

In front of each channel in the live racking unit is a numerical sensor with buttons. These devices are controlled by the warehouse management system (WMS). This software turns on the light sensor (to indicate to the operator that goods have to be removed from this channel) and shows on-screen how many units of the SKU in question have to be picked.

When the operator finishes removing the corresponding units, he/she presses a key to confirm that the operation has been completed. This is relayed through to the WMS, which turns off the light.

When a new order is to be prepared, the lights in the positions from which the products have to be removed are automatically switched on. There are pick to light systems that enable several orders to be prepared at the same time.

The two major advantages of this type of picking are the speed they provide and the considerable reduction in errors that are possible in the preparation of orders.

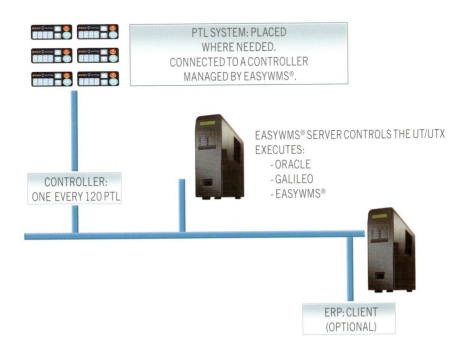

Chapter 4 - Storage systems

Car component warehouse. Source: Mecalux.

4.2.2 Goods-to-man solutions

Storing small and medium-sized loads using a goods-to-man strategy saves both time and effort, thus increasing efficiency. The operator does not have to move around; rather, he or she simply selects the units from each box or container brought over by an automated system at their workstation. The different solutions used to store and supply product units are described below.

Miniload

As mentioned earlier when discussing handling equipment in Chapter 3, a miniload is a storage system based on racking units for boxes or small containers, automatically supplied by stacker cranes. The robot transports the product to be prepared to the picking position, which is generally located at one end of the entire system that has been described.

On the miniload side, a conveyor system provides the basis for the circulation and recirculation of boxes, allowing them to enter and exit the picking position. Usually, the boxes used measure 600mm x 400mm and 800mm x 600mm. To expedite the picking process, as a rule they contain loose products.

Although the basic configuration consists of two racking units supplied by a single stacker crane, it is possible to install two or more aisles, each with its own robot, which together can supply one or more picking positions.

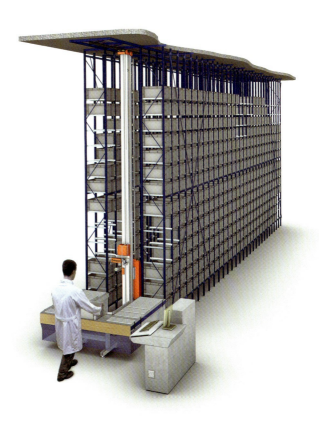

This type of system can also serve as a buffer (or reserve) for general or temporary storage and, instead of having picking positions, can use roller, belt or band conveyors to take complete boxes to distant work positions or loading docks.

The great advantage of miniloads, as opposed to other goods-to-man solutions, is the full use made of height, as warehouses of over 15m high can be built.

It is not only vertical space that is used well; full use is also made of horizontal space. Because it uses a stacker crane, the aisle can be narrower than one employed in traditional racking unit solutions, optimising the surface area. In this way, a machine that operates in an aisle 80cm wide can handle double-deep racking units for 600mm x 400mm boxes on both sides.

For all of these reasons, miniload storage is an excellent solution when a rapid picking system that takes full advantage of a building's height is required. To give an example, in an aisle 30m long and 10m high the double-deep version of the system can store 7000 boxes measuring 600mm x 400mm x 240mm and each box can contain one to eight different SKUs (in other words, an average of 28,000 SKUs). All of these SKUs can be accessed by the operator without moving from his or her position.

As well as making the most of available space, miniloads also save time. There are medium, high and very high performance solutions, and the choice of one or another will depend on the number of cycles required in the facility. The different machine models available can handle from 120 boxes per hour (60 coming in and 60 going out) to 540 boxes per hour (270 coming in and 270 going out) in combined cycles or, in other words, movements in which 1, 2, or 4 boxes (depending on the stacker crane) are placed in the racking units and the same number of units are removed, all in a single journey.

Source: Mecalux.

Chapter 4 - Storage systems

Warehouse for the manufacture of paper bags.
Source: Mecalux.

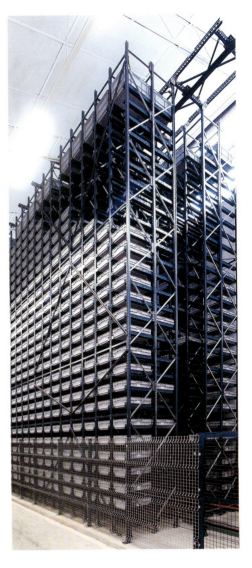

Automated warehouse for boxes for a company specialising in manufacturing textile machinery.
Source: Mecalux.

Vertical lift module (Clasimat)

The main virtue of vertical lift systems, such as Clasimat, is the maximum use made of the available height, minimising the surface area required.

A vertical lift module is made up of a closed structure, similar to an enormous cupboard, with internal positions in the front and rear with special trays for storing goods.

A vertical shuttle moves between the two columns of positions. The system can be up to 15m high and there are two models for the trays, one 600mm deep and another 800mm deep, which can be between 2000mm and 4200mm long (approximately). Each tray can contain anything from one SKU to more than 100, depending on the size and configuration used.

The trays can be open, and can have specific drawers or small flexible compartments.

When an operator selects the SKU required from a screen, the shuttle moves vertically to the level where the product is located, removes the tray and moves it vertically again to an opening in the structure at the level of the picking position. At this point, the operator must remove the required units from the appropriate tray.

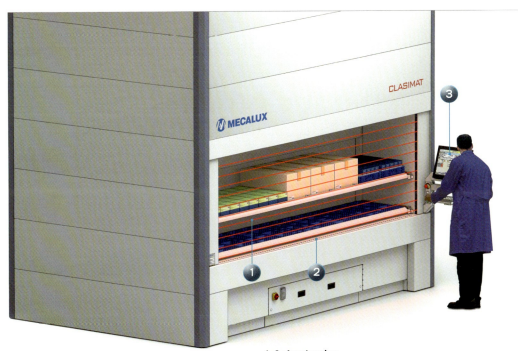

1. Safety barrier
2. Product position indicator (optional)
3. Screen

In a building with several floors, the vertical lift module can be integrated along the full height of all of these floors so that a picking position is created on each floor (or those that require one).

The following example illustrates the capacity of vertical lift modules compared with that of traditional manual load systems: A hypothetical vertical lift system that covers a surface area of 3220mm x 2400mm and a height of 10m could contain 57 trays of 3000mm x 600mm with products with a height of not more than 200mm.

To store these products using traditional systems, at least ten times the surface area required by the vertical lift module would be required.

Two or more vertical lift modules can be used at the same time in a single facility and can operate either separately or jointly, connected to each other to form a single working unit. The management system controls and coordinates the machines, and these can be connected to the company's ERP.

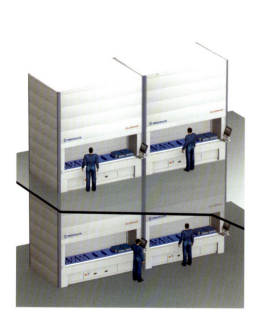

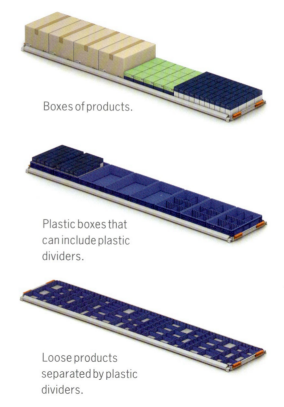

Boxes of products.

Plastic boxes that can include plastic dividers.

Loose products separated by plastic dividers.

In addition to the above, the basic configuration can be improved to expedite its operation. Based on the movements required, there can be two levels of trays in the same picking position, which enables the shuttle to take advantage of the time the operator requires to remove the product from one of the trays to go and collect the other, significantly increasing the cycles with Clasimat.

Likewise, to help operators with order preparations, lights can be included to indicate the position of the product in the tray from which units must be removed. Another option is to use multi-order tables with put to light devices that indicate the order associated with the product removed and where it must be placed in order to prepare the orders.

Vertical carousels

The family of vertical storage systems also includes carousels. The Clasimat Basic, for example, is a very simple vertical carousel for very varied products, as can be seen in the images below.

It consists of a structure containing a series of shelves, hangers, etc. where goods are stored and rotate vertically.

Vertical carousel for rolls.

Vertical carousel for cylinders and sections.

Vertical carousel for tyres.

Vertical carousel for clothing.

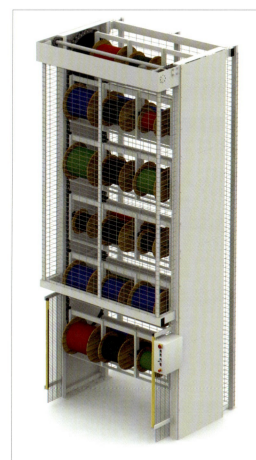
Vertical carousel for reels.

Vertical carousel for varied products.

Horizontal carousels (Spinblock)

Just as there are vertical carousels available, there are also horizontal carousels such as the Spinblock. These solutions use a mechanical system to transport goods to the operator, who then removes them without having to move from his or her workstation.

The system is based on a machine with guides from which compact modules, which have been joined together, are suspended. The guides form an oval so the modules move horizontally.

The horizontal carousel is a high performance picking machine. To facilitate its operation, different support elements such as pick to light and put to light devices, auxiliary screens, conformation buttons, multi-order tables, and barcode readers can be used.

Chapter 4 - Storage systems

1. Carousel system
2. Automatic door
3. Safety barrier
4. Control panel
5. Pick to light devices
6. Order management table
7. Management software system
8. Put to light devices
9. Complementary elements (labeller, for example)
10. Roller conveyor
11. Scanner
12. Confirmation button
13. Power and control cabinet

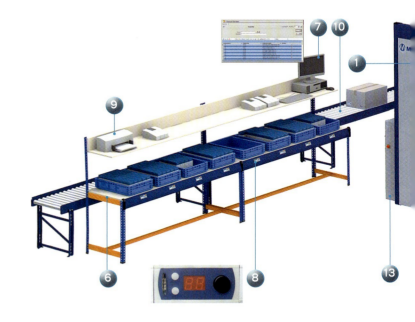

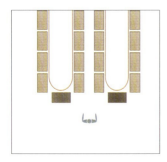

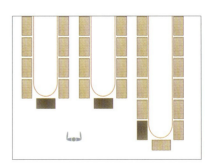

The usual procedure is to create working units of two, three or four carousels, each operated by one person. The layout of machinery in the warehouse installation is illustrated below:

Chapter 4 - Storage systems

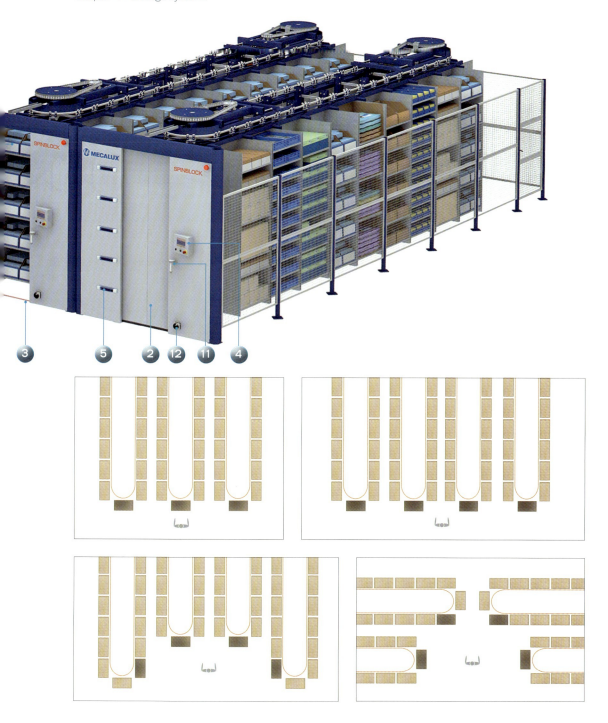

Horizontal carousels can be used for either specific or general storage, for example when supplying products to be sold in a store. In this case, the Spinblock can store SKUs that fit into the modules, as shown in the image below:

In any other case, carousels tend to form part of a larger warehouse and only products that will be picked are used.

Given that the greatest drawback to horizontal carousels is the difficulty in replacing the goods stored on them, with restocking being possible only when orders are not being prepared, they are generally reserved for medium rotation products (B) and, in some cases, for low rotation products (C). In any event, this depends on the size of the goods and their consumption.

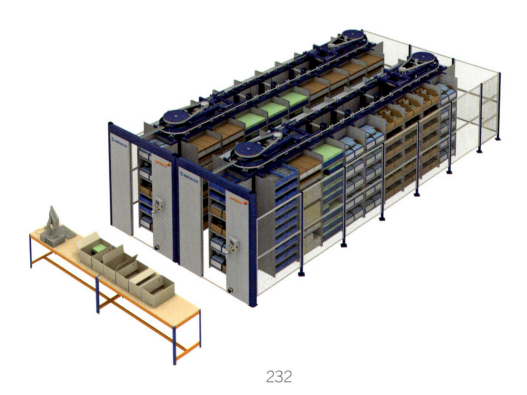

Although these solutions are not usually used to store high rotation products (A), there is a configuration for this. It consists of placing live picking racking units at the front of the carousel, so that order preparation operations do not have to be interrupted to replace the items. In these cases, the live racking unit can be considered an integral part of the carousel and the same management software system coordinates the operation of both elements.

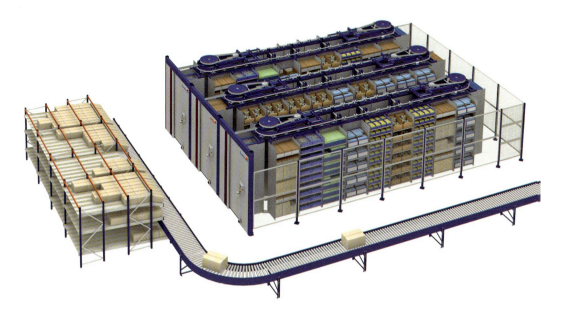

One final important issue affecting the use of horizontal carousels is ergonomics, a vital factor in obtaining the best possible performance from the machine. Among the rules that must be followed are, for example, the fact that the top level must not be more than 2m high and that the products in greatest demand must be positioned on the middle levels, at an average height. The operator's confirmation button (to inform the management system that the corresponding product has been removed and that it can move on to the next order) must be operated by foot. Likewise, whenever possible it is recommended that working units be arranged in an "L" or a "U" shape. If a scanner has to be used, then this must be of the fixed type (not handheld). These and other considerations improve the efficiency of the system and the safety of operations.

4.3 MIXED SYSTEMS

Although storage systems are rarely mixed in small warehouses, the larger the warehouse and the more varied the products being handled the more common it is to combine different options.

Section 4.1.3, which analyses the different capacities of each system, includes examples of combinations of conventional and drive-in racking units and an explanation of the criteria to be used when deciding which configuration to use. However, combinations in medium and large warehouses are not limited to drive-in and conventional racking units. Rather, it is common to mix these with options specifically for picking operations and to use a range of picking options.

Indeed, the combination of storage systems for boxes or loose products, using both man-to-goods and goods-to-man systems, will be increasingly prevalent in future. Each system is ideal for different specific circumstances. The secret is to combine them in the appropriate manner.

In seeking out the best possible solution, the aim is to treat every product individually, then group them together with others on the basis of rotation (ABC) and the families to which they belong, how orders are prepared, and the size of the products. All of these data can be extracted through an analysis of what is called the article master. With this, one can determine, for example, the advisability or otherwise of establishing separate areas or operations (or both), and therefore whether or not it will be necessary to create an order consolidation area.

The following are examples of combined systems, which give an idea of the (virtually unlimited) possible varieties and configurations.

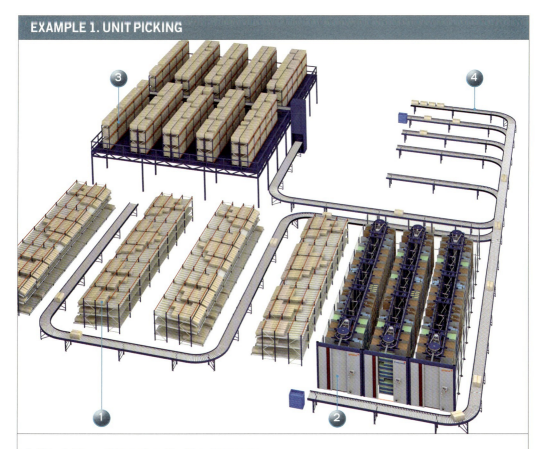

EXAMPLE 1. UNIT PICKING

1. Live picking racking units with pick to light systems
2. Horizontal carousels
3. Classic racking units positioned on a mezzanine
4. Consolidation area: Where orders prepared in other areas are sent

This case is also applied to unit picking, but it is simpler than the previous one.
There are four defined areas and operations are managed through a WMS. High consumption products are stored in live picking racking units with pick to light systems (number 1 in the above image). Medium consumption products are positioned on three horizontal carousels (number 2), while low consumption products are stored in classic racking units positioned on a mezzanine (number 3). The fourth area (number 4) is dedicated to consolidation, and is the area to which orders prepared in other areas are sent.

The different preparation areas are connected to the consolidation area through a system of automated box conveyors. Thanks to this configuration, the area below the mezzanine (which has a conveyor to connect it to the automated conveyor system) is available for depositing the goods ready for dispatch.

Chapter 4 - Storage systems

EXAMPLE 2. HIGHLY AUTOMATED UNIT PICKING

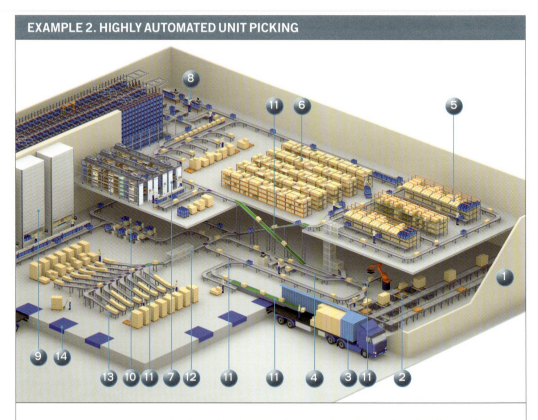

1. Entry of pallets, from the general warehouse, through roller and chain conveyors
2. Manual and automated destacking area with box conveyors
3. Unloading of maritime containers which transport cardboard boxes without pallets
4. Verification and quality control
5. Preparation of orders for high rotation products (A) in live picking racking units, with pick to light systems
6. Preparation of orders for low rotation goods (C), irregularly-shaped products, and unitary boxes
   These are classic picking racking units
7. Horizontal Spinblock carousel for high value A rotation products or B rotation products
8. Miniload for B and C rotation products, with picking positions in the P&D station

> 9. Vertical Clasimat lift modules, combined with multi-order picking tables, for storing small components or products
> 10. Consolidation of orders or assembly of components
> 11. Roller, belt and band conveyors that connect the different areas and transport the boxes in a totally automated way
>   The system includes various ramps and a lift
> 12. Sealing and identification area
> 13. Classification by destinations or routes area
> 14. Dispatch area and loading docks
>
> This type of facility is becoming increasingly common, as it can reduce operating costs.
>
> This is a fully integrated solution. Each area uses the most appropriate storage, picking and handling system for each product and, as a result, the various operations within the warehouse are as efficient as possible. A fully automated internal conveyor system has been installed that connects the different areas, meaning there is no need for personnel and handling equipment to be involved in this task. Thanks to this conveyor system, orders are automatically classified according to route and destination.
>
> In facilities of such complexity, a suitable warehouse management system (WMS) to control the entire operation is vital.

EXAMPLE 3. PALLET WAREHOUSE AND MINILOAD

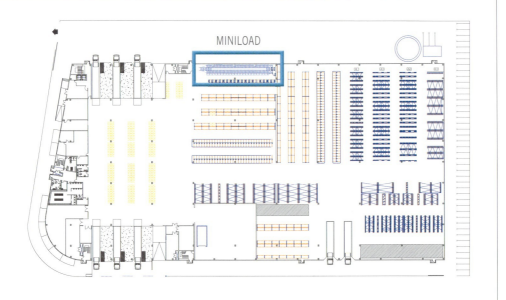

In this example, the miniload is located within a pallet warehouse for medium-sized and large products with many different consumption accessories.

Four areas with different processes have been created for picking. The first is a live pallet racking unit, with the pick to light system, for high consumption accessories in complete boxes.

The second area has a live picking racking unit with a pick to light device, which is used for medium consumption products (whole boxes or loose units).

The third operation takes place on a live picking racking unit with the pick to light system, supplied by a miniload, and is used for high and medium consumption loose accessories.

Finally, there is a conveyor system served by the same miniload, which used to complete orders with low consumption SKUs.

The entire system works in unison as a single working unit. When orders are launched, grouped into waves, the first task of operators is to prepare full boxes and place them on the conveyors to be taken to the consolidation area. Once this phase has been completed, personnel prepare the loose high and medium consumption accessories and place them in containers. The orders completed in this phase are moved on conveyors to the consolidation area. Those that have not been completed are sent to an area where the operator can add the missing products to the container. Once the order has been closed, the container will be transported to the consolidation area.

The rest of the warehouse operates as independent areas and the prepared product is consolidated in the loading docks themselves. In addition, the management system can separate and manage all orders and all areas.

Source: Mecalux.

Source: Mecalux.

EXAMPLE 4. SOLUTION FOR A FREEZING CHAMBER

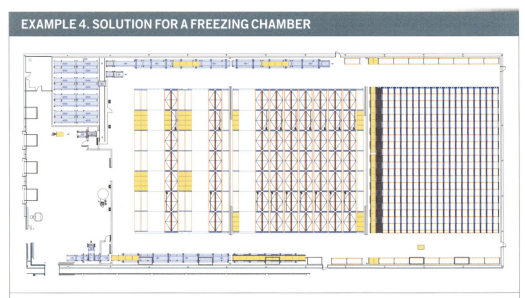

This hypothetical warehouse consists of live pallet racking units for high-consumption and high rotation products. There are also conventional racking units on mobile bases used for B and C rotation products (with the lower level used for picking individual boxes). Other conventional racking units are also used for rotation B and C products but, unlike the previous ones, these are static, since they have been added to make the most of the irregular spaces in the facilities. All of these areas are supported by automated conveyors which, in addition to moving the goods to and from the racking units, act as a buffer for prepared orders, so a group of these has been installed close to the docks.

Orders are prepared using radiofrequency equipment or through a voice picking system. The latter is the most appropriate for a freezing chamber, as it leaves operators' hands free.

Warehouse for a company producing and distributing pre-baked bread, frozen pastries, and baked products. Source: Mecalux.

Warehouse for a company in the food sector. Source: Mecalux.

Source: Mecalux.

EXAMPLE 5. PALLETISATION AND PICKING

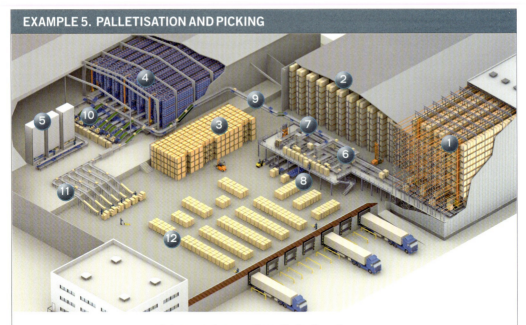

1. Automated storage for palletised goods
2. Conventional storage for palletised goods
3. Drive-in storage for palletised goods
4. Picking storage with miniload
5. Vertical Clasimat lift module
6. Area for picking from the automated pallet storage
7. Area for restocking the miniload storage with reserve product
8. Area for restocking the miniload storage from reception area and communication with the mezzanine
9. Overhead circuit consisting of roller and band conveyors
10. Order picking positions from the miniload warehouse
11. Sorter for sorting orders by routes
12. Consolidation area and dispatch docks

Automated pallet storage, with four stacker cranes, is used mainly for the reserves of medium consumption and large goods. In the outer area there is a mezzanine with conveyors and stations for preparing orders directly on the pallets themselves. The operator has support tools, above all computer resources and barcode readers, which, in addition to facilitating picking operations, allow goods destined for the miniload box storage to be replenished.

The conventional storage warehouse for palletised products is used to store low-consumption products of a medium size or irregular dimensions. It uses VNA trucks and high level picker machines to pick goods directly from the racking units.

High consumption products are stored in the drive-in racking units, which are generally sent on full pallets. Reach trucks are used to handle these.

The automated box storage warehouse, with nine miniloads, stores small and medium-sized products in boxes. Three levels of conveyors are used for picking positions: the lower level transfers boxes from the front of each aisle to the various picking positions and to the conveyor which leads to the restocking area; the intermediate level is used for the return and entries of boxes into the warehouse; and the upper level sends the boxes with picked orders to the classification sorter. The use of the three levels avoids interference and helps with the flow of boxes. The picking positions are ergonomically designed to facilitate the picking of the orders and avoid downtime.

Vertical storage is used for delicate or valuable small components.

Lifts are used to connect the conveyors on the lower part of the mezzanine to those on the upper part, both those for pallets and those for boxes, and can:

- Send pallets from the conventional pallet storage area to the automated storage and the picking and restocking area.

- Send complete pallets from the automated warehouse to the dispatch area.

- Restock boxes being sent to the miniload storage with goods from outside and that do not need a reserve.

The circuit of overhead roller and band conveyors on two levels connects the two automated storage areas and transports prepared orders to the classification sorter. The prepared orders coming from the sorter are consolidated, by routes, with those from conventional storage and the full pallets from automated storage, directly in the lanes positioned in front of the dispatch docks.

Electric and manual stacker cranes are used to transport pallets in the reception and dispatch area.

4.4 SPECIFIC SYSTEMS

In the previous sections, we examined storage systems commonly used to manage more standard goods, such as pallets, boxes, containers, and product items. However, in the logistics sector there is also work with many other types of goods that require specific storage conditions. This need for specific storage conditions can be due to their volume, weight, or shape, or to the specific requirements of the space available or different methods of operation.

The following is an explanation of the storage solutions available for less standard goods than those seen up to now.

4.4.1 Cantilever racking units

Long or variable length unit loads have a series of features that make their handling and storage in conventional racking units more complicated. Cantilever structures are specifically designed for goods of this type, such as metal sections, tubes, mouldings, wooden boards, metal or plastic sheets, etc.

These racking units are constructed with a row of vertical sections, each of which is connected to one or two horizontal sections (one on each side), to form a stable and strong structure. The vertical sections are fitted with cantilevered arms which support the load. The racking units can be configured for different heights and goods.

Warehouse for a company specialising in the manufacture of children's furniture. Source: Mecalux.

Warehouse for a company specialising in aluminium carpentry. Source: Mecalux.

Examples of the application of this system are illustrated on these pages. The top left image shows a warehouse for wooden products, in which the boards rest on cantilever racking units of a far greater depth than required for storing the aluminium sections in the image on the right.

Goods stored in this way can be handled by hand when they are light and the racking units are not very high. In all other cases, conventional forklifts are used to handle full packets or to handle goods higher up.

Warehouse for a company manufacturing accessories for the furniture sector. Source: Mecalux.

Chapter 4 - Storage systems

Side-loading reach truck Source: Mecalux.

Reach truck. Source: Mecalux.

Handling machines used with cantilever racking units can be counterbalanced and reach trucks (top right image) or side-loading reach trucks (top left image).

The use of side-loading forklifts reduces the width of working aisle and, therefore, increases the capacity of the warehouse. However, this requires an aisle with guides on both sides, as shown in the images below.

Warehouse for a company selling metal. Source: Mecalux.

Chapter 4 - Storage systems

The photograph below shows the cantilever racking units on mobile bases, which ensures the best possible use of space. It is important to bear in mind the explanations provided later on in section 4.4.4 as regards special and large goods.

Warehouse for a company specialising in the manufacture and sale of industrial fabrics. Source: Mecalux.

4.4.2 Racking units for reels and cylinders

In warehouses where it is required, there are two possible options for storing reels: using a shaft, or resting on a support. In some cases, the first option allows direct access to the product rolled onto the reel without the need to move it from its position. This is helpful in facilities where the product is supplied by the metre in quantities that are less than an entire reel.

Reels on shafts

With this option the product does not rest on anything, preventing possible deformation and, in some cases, enabling the reel to turn.

Two similar examples are shown in the photographs below.

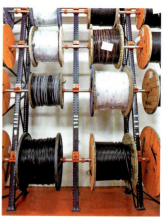

Warehouse for a company distributing electrical material. Source: Mecalux.

Supported reels

The bottom right-hand image shows how reels are stored by resting them on supports. The main structure used is a conventional pallet racking unit, with some frames added (as shown in the bottom left-hand image) on which the reels rest without any risk of them rolling.

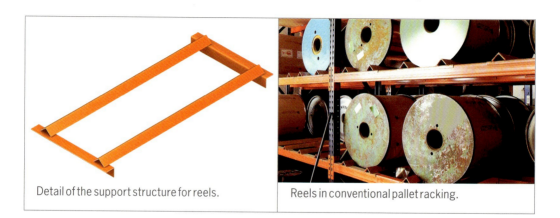

| Detail of the support structure for reels. | Reels in conventional pallet racking. |

Storing cylinders

When cylindrical goods, such as drums, have to be stored, conventional racking units fitted with the same supports used for reels can again be used. Beams fitted with stops to form a cradle, such as those shown on the right, can also be used. Both options remove the risk of the load rolling, hitting other items, or falling through a hole between beams.

Detail of the support structure for cylinders.

4.4.3 Mezzanines

As a complement to the racking units explained up to this point, mezzanines can double (with one floor) or treble (with two floors) a certain surface area. The following is an illustration of a basic configuration of this element, as well as its component parts.

Warehouse for a company specialising in the manufacture and distribution of bathroom furniture and accessories. Source: Mecalux.

Chapter 4 - Storage systems

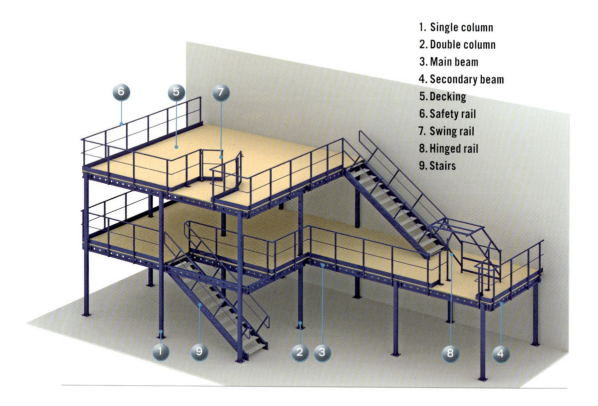

1. Single column
2. Double column
3. Main beam
4. Secondary beam
5. Decking
6. Safety rail
7. Swing rail
8. Hinged rail
9. Stairs

Although it is not a rapid storage system it is widely used, mostly for irregularly or variably-shaped products.

Loads are lifted to the floors using manual handling machines, for which hinged handrails are fitted, or using lifts and goods lifts. Where the weight and size of the goods in question so allow, they can also be taken up by hand using the stairs.

The following are different uses of mezzanine storage, which give an idea of the possible variations for these helpful elements.

Warehouse for a company specialising in the production and sale of paper products for access control, points of sale, and offices. Source: Mecalux.

250

EXAMPLE 1. TWO RAISED FLOORS

The facility consists of two raised floors. The lower floor has been fitted with racking units for storing small and medium-sized goods and those with most picking operations. The top floor is used to store lower consumption large products.

Source: Mecalux.

EXAMPLE 2. MEZZANINE OVER A WAREHOUSE

Here, the mezzanine is used as an area for receiving goods and preparing orders. It is placed above a picking warehouse with walkways. The floors are connected via a lift platform used to raise and lower the goods.

Logistics warehouse. Source: Mecalux.

EXAMPLE 3. MEZZANINE OF VARIOUS LEVELS FOR CLOTHING ON HANGERS

The mezzanine, in this case with several levels, is used as a classification and storage area for clothing on hangers. The structure itself also supports the elements required for the movement of trolleys with the clothing.

Warehouse for the textile sector. Source: Mecalux.

EXAMPLE 4. MEZZANINE FOR A SORTING AREA

This warehouse has a separate area for sorting documentation using a raised mezzanine over the loading docks. The conveyor belts hang from the mezzanine structure.

Logistics warehouse. Source: Mecalux.

EXAMPLE 5. MEZZANINE TO CREATE AN ASSEMBLY AREA

Here, the bottom part is used as an electrical panel assembly area and the top part as a storage area.

Warehouse for a company assembling electricity cabinets. Source: Mecalux.

EXAMPLE 6. MEZZANINE FOR SMALL AND MEDIUM SIZED GOODS

This example shows a mezzanine in which racking units are used for storing small and medium-sized goods. Large volume products are stored below it.

Warehouse for electrical supplies. Source: Mecalux.

4.4.4 Warehouses for special and large products

Special products and large products can cause serious difficulties when it comes to storage and handling, so it is best to be aware of their characteristics when planning a warehouse.

When assessing the storage options for these goods, which can be classified as atypical, we need to group them into three categories: sheet, tubular, and cylindrical. This classification is the most basic, given that shape has a direct impact on how most goods are handled and stored.

Nonetheless, the shape of the load is not the only variable to be taken into account: other factors also need to be assessed when classifying these goods, such as fragility, safety, hazard level and, above all, volume and weight. The following is an analysis of each of the three main groups and their characteristics.

<u>Sheet type goods</u>
This type of load has subdivisions moving from less fragile to more fragile: metal sheets, plastic sheets, and wooden boards and sheets.

To determine the best ways to handle and, in particular, store these different types of goods, it is important to take into account not only their shape and fragility but also the other factors mentioned above.

To determine the most appropriate handling method for **metal sheets**, one must above all take into account a fundamental characteristic of this type of goods, which is its degree of flexibility. This is determined based on the size and thickness of the sheet. The larger and thinner the sheet, the more flexible it will be.

For metal sheets cut into small pieces, the best approach is to place and strap them onto a wooden platform or pallet, creating a solid unit load that it is practically impossible to deform. This unit can be handled and even stored using the traditional systems for handling and storing materials described in previous chapters.

If the sheets being handled are large but thin in relation to their size, the problem is completely different. In that case, the damage that handling could cause to the material must be assessed. This damage can be of two types. First, the sheet could be permanently bent (becoming warped, for example). Second, inappropriate handling could lead to the material becoming marked, reducing the quality of the goods, with the resulting financial losses.

To minimise the possible effects of bending, the distance between the supports of the lifting and storing elements and the cantilevers of the loads away from these must be reduced. There are three ways to do this: using more forks, adding more supports than usual and, as already mentioned, handling the sheets on a platform.

In addition to this bending, it is crucial to consider a second factor: weight. These products have a density far greater than that of goods usually handled, and, as a result, machines and racking units must be of an appropriate design. One must take into account that a cubic metre of iron weighs around 8000kg.

A. Plastic sheets

The handling of plastic sheets presents a single significant problem, which is the bending of the material. There are many types of hard plastics handled in the form of sheets, so the amount of bending will vary. However, the behaviour of hard plastics is always very similar. The problem only arises in large sheets, which in fact have relatively little bend.

Small and medium-sized sheets are usually handled and stacked in exactly the same way as any other load of a similar size. Their storage does not create additional problems.

If, however, the sheets handled and stored are large, a procedure similar to that described for metal sheets is used: the standard approach is to store them on wooden trays and even pick them up directly, for which there are supports between the sheets to create a space sufficiently large for the forks of the forklift truck to enter. In contrast to metal sheets, plastic sheets do not create any additional problems due to excessive weight or the possibility of damaging the goods.

B. Wooden sheets and boards

If the wood is in the form of sheets, the factor to be considered is bending. This is the same issue as discussed above for plastic sheets, and therefore their handling and storing is the same as for plastic sheets.

The rigidity of wooden boards depends on the thickness of the wood. Usually their shape is similar to that of metal sheets. However, when it comes to weight, this material is not as dense as metal and one cubic metre of wood weighs between 650kg and 800kg.

Medium-sized boards can be stored on conventional racking units with special cross ties or in cantilever racking units (as explained in section 4.4.1.).

Tube-shaped goods

When planning the storage of this type of load, it is important to carry out an initial assessment of one of the characteristics which most affects their handling: their ability to retain their shape. Specifically, one must distinguish between rigid tubes (of steel or concrete, for example) and semi-rigid tubes (such as plastic tubes). The two types of tube are handled and stored in a completely different manner, and the system used to create their unit loads completely different.

In terms of the handling and storage of rigid tubes, this information applies to medium to large tubes, since small tubes fall under the category of large loads, already discussed in this chapter.

Very similar problems are encountered in the handling of metal and concrete rigid tubes. This type of large object is normally stored outside the facilities. They form pyramids, with the tubes strapped together into groups of three and stacked on top of each other. Some are stored with others inside vertical structures.

When stored on racking units (generally cantilever), the tubes must be prevented from rolling toward the edge. To this end, stops are fitted to the arms supporting the tubes where required. Where possible, they are stored in pyramid-shaped packs of three tubes strapped together, as this provides greater stability.

Chapter 4 - Storage systems

Handling and storage of semi-rigid tubes
Hard plastic tubes, which fall under the category of semi-rigid tubes, must be handled using unit loads. These consist of cages made from welded metal sections or wood (of the appropriate strength), with the tubes stored inside them. Given that the material is relatively light, the most important factor to take into account is the large volume of these cages.

These tubes are fairly simple to handle: they can be handled using side-loading or front-loading forklifts, with the difference between using one or the other of these being the space required. However, when using front-loading forklifts there is an additional problem in the transverse stability of the load, since its large volume and light weight can prove very dangerous, in particular during the storage process. Apart from this factor, the load is usually positioned using the cages themselves, which act as support for others, and therefore it is easy to stack them to considerable heights.

Generally speaking, semi-rigid tubes are stored outside. When positioned on racking units (cantilever as a rule), additional problems do not normally occur, provided that rigid cages are used. However, if the tubes are stored loose in racking units they must be prevented from rolling, as is the case with rigid tubes. Furthermore, however one must consider the potential bending of the material and more supports must be added if necessary.

Cylindrical type goods
Now that loads in the form of sheets have been analysed, we can move on to cylindrical loads. Cylindrical goods are those that are rolled up for handling, using either a mandrel or a structure (metal or wooden) or directly in the form of a reel. The three reel types analysed below are paper and cardboard reels, sheet metal rolls, and cable reels. Each type of reel is handled and stored in a completely different manner.

The handling of paper reels requires forklift trucks fitted with special clamps for gripping and turning. The size of machine required depends on the reel size. The machines lose some of their capacity once clamps are fitted, so their capacity must be from 1.5 to 2 times the original capacity needed to handling the weight of the reel. This margin will vary according to the diameter of the loads and how many will be stacked.

These paper and cardboard units are stored inside the warehouse. Given the high resistance of paper when wound tightly on a reel, they are stored directly on top of each other. In other words, units can be stacked on top of each other almost without limit.

Reels are manufactured horizontally but are stacked vertically (thus preventing them from rolling). They are turned from one position to another using the clamps on the handling equipment, which have this function.

There are two possible solutions for storing these goods on racking units: vertically on pallets, or horizontally on support cradles, handling them using specific forks or equipment. In any event, the size, weight, and protection applied to the goods will determine the best way of storing them.

A. Sheet metal rolls
These can be handled directly or on pallets. The main issue arising with these goods is their weight. Large sheet metal rolls can weigh between 20 and 30 tonnes.

When these reels are handled directly, lifting machines fitted with a shaft or spur are used, with this fitting into the space in the centre of the reel. Alternatively, an overhead crane is used. When stored on pallets, forklift trucks of sufficient capacity are used and fitted with conventional load forks.

Large heavy reels are usually stored outside the facilities, on the ground and in a pyramid shape. Lighter units can also be stored in this way, or inside the warehouse on special racking units created specifically for this purpose and with the appropriate sections. This unit forms a structure similar to a honeycomb, on which the reels rest (one for each cell created). In general, these warehouses are constructed for special materials, such as reels of stainless steel or other similar materials, which are more widely used in the processing industry than in primary industry.

B. Cable reels

In this section we address the handling and storage of reels of steel cables and multipolar electric and telecommunications cables, insulated for carrying high voltages or for transoceanic t sheet reels ransmissions. These two types of cables represent two different but typical handling problems, each with its own solution.

Steel cables are rolled to form a cylinder, creating a reel as a unit load. They are relatively simple to handle and can be handled by cranes, using the hook that these machines have installed in their boom. Another option for handling them is forklifts, for which forks are used as a shaft, entering the space in the centre of the reel. Alternatively, a shaft can be fitted instead of conventional forks. The handling method is the same in both these cases: the shaft enters the space in the centre of the reel.

In general, cable reels are stored outside and on the ground with no additional problems, although one must remember that it is difficult to place one load on top of another. One solution for storing them might be to construct conventional racking units, since these reels are not too heavy. For heavier reels, racking units similar to those for metal reels must be used.

The solution used for handling and storing multipolar electric and telecommunications cables is quite different, since they tend to be rolled onto large wooden or metal reels (metal ones are currently most commonly used), thereby constructing a unit load which at times is very large and can be difficult to handle.

First, the metal reels onto which these long cables are wrapped do not come with a central hole of the right size to be used to help lift it (by entering a shaft, for example), which means that they have to be grasped on the outside. This poses another problem, in that the reel is completely cylindrical in shape and cannot be easily handled with the conventional forks of a forklift truck.

The only practical way of gripping this type of reel is by using cranes or adaptors fitted to the forklift trucks instead of conventional forks.

Reels that are large or heavy (or both) are stored on the ground and, in some cases, stacked to form pyramids. Smaller ones can be lodged on racking units by fitting a shaft of the appropriate size and strength through the hole that this type of reel normally has, as explained previously in this chapter.

4.5 WHERE TO FIND MORE INFORMATION ABOUT STORAGE SOLUTIONS

Although this chapter has extensively analysed all the different types of storage structures and systems, the ongoing development in the sector means that it is helpful to consult the specific reference information on each of these to ensure that you are up-to-date with recent developments. This reference information is to be found for the most part in the specific catalogues and manuals for each product.

Catalogues are designed to provide clear, visual, and concise information about the different systems available, setting out their advantages and uses, but without going into detail on certain construction issues or some features.

Product manuals are used to examine solutions in greater detail and provide practical information about the technical characteristics and assembly of the structures. These documents tend to be used internally by specialist companies, and are not usually available to the general public.

Whenever possible, these two documentary tools should be used to complement this *Technical Warehouse Manual* and as sources of information for the training initiatives being run.

Source: Mecalux

CHAPTER 5
THE IDEAL STORAGE SOLUTION

5.1 WHAT IS THE IDEAL STORAGE SOLUTION?

This is undoubtedly the most difficult question to answer. Despite the extensive experience in storage solutions at our disposal, there are still no fixed rules for determining the most appropriate solution, since this depends on various factors.

In general, the ideal solution is that which responds to the needs and conditioning factors of each specific case, taking into account everything set out in the earlier chapters in this manual. However in practice this simple principle can be difficult to apply.

The first chapter discussed the different factors involved in and influencing a warehouse, such as the product, available space, personnel, the company's management and policy, scope for investment, available and required storage equipment, flows, rotation, and other aspects.

Bearing this in mind, what are the possible scenarios? One is that the planner establishes the need for a warehouse with specific features, but the customer is unable to create this facility because it does not have the required financial resources. Another is that, given the nature of the product, a certain storage system is required but the available space does not allow it.

Yet another is that by classifying products into A, B and C, it becomes clear how helpful it would be to combine different types of storage system. However, this requires a number of processes that make the warehouse difficult for the customer to manage.

These examples illustrate that **the ideal solution is that which, taking all factors into account, is best suited to the customer and has been created jointly with that customer.**

The customer has information that is difficult for it to transmit, while the storage company understands the technical aspects of designing storage facilitates. If they can work closely together, hand in hand, they can achieve the best possible understanding and outcome, where each and every one of the factors comes together, even if this solution is not ideal from a technical point of view.

Bearing this idea in mind, when visiting a firm that has requested the services of a warehouse solutions firm, one commonly encounters one of two situations. The first is that the customer knows it wants a certain type of racking unit or storage equipment, with specific measurements and levels, and has allocated a certain space for this. In other words, the customer knows, or at least thinks they know, what it needs. The second common situation is that the customer simply describes the product it needs to store and the space it has available for this, and asks for technical advice.

For any sales technician, the first situation is very practical and does not pose complications. The discussion is limited to offering the requested solution, and it is just a case of waiting for the customer to agree to this. In other words, the salesperson simply processes an order.

Yet if a sales technician working for a competitor shows more interest in the problem or in the customer's needs and, as a result, offers a better solution, this company will win the contract (unless a counter-offer is received that improves on the original price and proposal). It is important to remember, then, **that the customer values the supplier who can advise them.**

The second situation, where the technical supplier is asked for their opinion, can be simple or complex to resolve depending on the specific case. It is the skill of the technical salesperson and the support teams that determine how difficult it is to identify the best solution. It is here where the company must differentiate itself from its competitors.

In short, there is a maxim that must be observed when marketing these solutions: in the personnel of a company, the customer must find experts in applied storage and logistics. The company that lives by this maxim need never worry about the competition.

5.2 BASIC CRITERIA FOR SELECTING THE MOST APPROPRIATE STORAGE SYSTEM

The first stage is simply to examine some basic issues, addressing the more complex issues once these simpler ones have been understood.

Finding the best storage solution depends on the correct decisions being made on these issues. These decisions this must be made jointly with the customer.

There are four basic issues: the capacity to be obtained; the speed to be reached; the variety and type of products to be stored; and the general cost of the solution. The following is an explanation of how each of these will condition the planning of the facility.

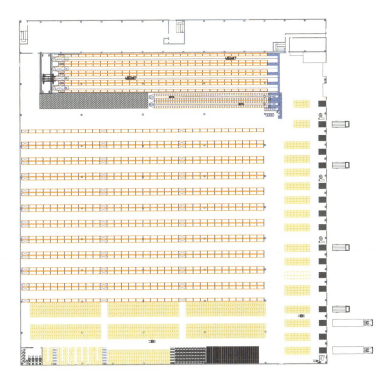

5.2.1 Capacity to be obtained

Section 4.1 of the previous chapter, which discussed storing pallets on racking units, highlighted the potential capacity to be achieved with each of the possible systems. There, we saw that compact systems offer greater storage capacity or, in other words, that the same available surface area can house a larger number of goods.

At this point it is important to remember the issue discussed in chapter 4.1.3 concerning physical and effective capacities, since with compact systems there can be significant differences between the two, owing to the large number of empty spaces that can exist in a normal work flow.

Conventional racking units, in contrast, offer lower physical capacity than their compact counterparts. Yet as long as the right management system is used this physical capacity is very similar to effective capacity, since there are almost no empty spaces in the standard work flow.

Maximum effective capacity in a pallet warehouse is obtained by using a system that combines the best features of these two options, namely conventional racking units on mobile bases. With this system, as long as a competent management system is employed then high physical capacity is achieved, similar to that reached with compact solutions, plus effective capacity that is very close to physical capacity.

Warehouse for a company selling floor and wall tiles. Source: Mecalux.

In addition to making the most of the warehouse's available surface area, the solution must also take into account the available vertical space. To this end, as long as the regulations so allow, it is helpful to use systems that make use of the full height of the facility or to build tall automated warehouses (as illustrated in the image above).

5.2.2 Desired speed

Often, it is essential to minimise the time spent performing operations in the warehouse, particularly if the facility is medium or large in size. The number of operators required is directly related to this factor and, as a result, so is the added cost for each operation performed.

To measure the time taken to perform each task, one must calculate the time spent covering the distance between the initial point and the point where the goods are stored and add this to the time taken to return to the starting point. The exception is a combined movement (taking advantage of the journey to collect some goods to leave other goods, or vice versa); in which case, these times are measured separately.

When analysing the different operations, we can see that for goods on pallets the slowest and least dynamic system is the drive-in racking units system, followed by push-back racking units. The fastest option is gravity-flow live racking units, followed by a system based on conventional racking units. Between these two extremes are the mobile base and radio-shuttle solutions, but the results of these depends on the number of consecutive operations carried out in each lane.

Automated warehouses, for their part, are quick if tasks are properly programmed.

5.2.3 Product variety and type

With this factor, the suitability of the chosen solution depends on the range of SKUs, the number of pallets or boxes per product, and the time the goods will spend in the warehouse.

If the goods are on pallets, there is a wide range of SKUs, and there are few pallets of each of these, the ideal system is static conventional racking units. However, another very good option is to install these on mobile bases.

In the opposite situation, where there are few SKUs and lots of pallets of each of these, any compact system is optimal. If, in addition, the goods are going to spend a great deal of time without being moved, drive-in racking units are also ideal.

When the goods to be stored are handled in boxes or loose in specific positions, individual storage and loose product solutions can be used, except when the products are of an irregular shape.

In addition to these considerations, another factor that determines the system to be used is rotation. Thus, any storage system can be used for rotation A products (high consumption) on pallets, but compact systems are particularly appropriate. It is common to use these systems with such products; however, one must not forget the greater time required to perform manoeuvres.

In terms of B products (medium consumption), the ideal options are those that use conventional, push-back, and shallow live racking units.

5.2.4 General cost

The fourth factor to be considered when choosing a storage option is its set-up and operating costs. Its ultimate purpose is to help generate company business. For the company to be competitive, operational costs must be as low as possible.

It is also important to estimate the period required to generate a return on investment (ROI), which must also be as short as possible. Some companies have a policy of not undertaking investments which have a ROI of more than three years.

As a result, in most cases the solution chosen will be that which offers the most competitive price and the shortest period required to obtain a return on the investment. In addition, the customer must be capable of financing the chosen solution.

While the choice of the appropriate storage system, adequate flows, operating method, warehouse location, etc. all have significant repercussions on the financial performance of the warehouse, the factor will have the biggest impact on this performance is the solution chosen for the picking or preparation of orders (the operating methods of which are explained below).

Chapter 5 - The ideal storage solution

STORAGE SYSTEMS COMPARISON TABLE
DIRECT ACCESS STORAGE SYSTEMS

	Conventional pallet racking	Conventional pallet racking on mobile bases	Double-deep conventional pallet racking	Narrow aisle conventional pallet racking	Automated conventional pallet racking	Automated double-deep conventional pallet racking
Use of surface area	2	5	3	3	3	4
Use of volume	2	4	3	3	3	3
Access to any pallet	5	5	2	5	5	4 (A)
Speed of access/agility (movements per hour)	4	3	2 (B)	3	5 (C)	4 (A)
Stock rotation	4 (D)	4 (D)	2 (B)	4 (D)	5	4 (A)
	FIFO	FIFO	relative FIFO	FIFO	FIFO	relative FIFO
Height of the top level (m)	2	2	1	3	5	4
	< 10	< 10	< 8	< 14	< 45	< 40
Width of aisles (m)	3	2	3	4	5	5
	2.20/3.50 (E)	3.00/3.50 (E)	3.00 (E)	1.55/1.80 (F)	1.55	1.55
Initial investment	4 (low)	3 (medium)	4 (low)	3 (medium)	2 (high)	2 (high)
Handling equipment (forklift)	· Stacker · Reach · Counterbalanced	· Reach · Counterbalanced	· Specific reach	· Turret trilateral · Turret trilateral	· Stacker crane	· Stacker crane
Advantages (average score)*	3.25	3.50	2.50	3.50	4.12	3.75

(A) With WMS and relocation bay
(B) With WMS and A-B-C management can be greater
(C) Programmed operation
(D) With suitable WMS
(E) Depends on the forklift
(F) Depends on whether it is bilateral or trilateral
(G) It is vital to ensure that the pallets are of good quality
(H) Depends on the forklift and simultaneity in an aisle

SCORE: 1 (low) to 6 (very high). For "initial investment" the values are reversed.
*Average obtained from the eight numerical variables.

COMPACT STORAGE SYSTEMS							
Drive-in pallet racking	Push-back with trolleys	Push-back with rollers	Radio-shuttle	Live with rollers	Automated radio-shuttle	Automated live with rollers
5	4	4	5	5	5	5
5	4	4	4	4	4	4
1	2	2	1	2	2	2
2	3	3	3	4	4	5
1	2	2	2	5	2	5
LIFO	LIFO	LIFO	LIFO	FIFO	LIFO	FIFO
2	1	1	2	3	3	4
<10	<7.5	<7.5	<10 (E)	<14 (E)	<40	<40 (G)
2	2	2	2	3	4	4
3.00/3.50 (H)	3.00/3.50 (H)	3.00/3.50 (H)	3.00/3.50 (H)	1.80/3.50 (H)	1.55	1.55
4 (low)	3 (medium)	3 (medium)	3 (medium)	2 (high)	2 (high)	1 (very high)
· Reach · Counterbalanced	· Reach · Counterbalanced	· Reach · Counterbalanced	· Reach · Counterbalanced · VNA	· Reach · Counterbalanced · VNA	· Stacker crane	· Stacker crane
2.75	2.62	2.62	2.75	3.50	3.40	3.75

This table shows a comparison of the different pallet racking solutions, although it only includes the factors with the greatest influence. The final score is merely intended as a measure of the scale of the advantages and disadvantages of the different systems; it does not imply that the system with the highest score is always the best. In each case, one system will be better suited than another. In formulating this comparison, no consideration has been given to picking operations, only an assessment of the storage of pallets, accessibility, and capacity.

Chapter 5 - The ideal storage solution

Warehouse for car parts. Source: Mecalux.

5.2.5 Combination of factors

It is common to find facilities in which a number of the factors described above have been taken into account. It is also normal to use several storage systems, each for a specific type of product. We have already seen some examples, such as that in section 4.3, in which conventional racking units are combined with racking units on mobile bases, drive-in pallet racking units, live systems and, in addition, roller conveyors to reduce manoeuvre times.

The combination of factors and storage solutions allows unique facilities to be created that are best adapted to the specific needs of the companies that operate them.

5.2.6 Optimisation of the factors in automated warehouses

The tables on the previous pages show that automated storage systems combine the optimisation of basic criteria. The only problem here is their higher initial cost. However, they provide significant advantages, such as their large storage capacity, greater construction height, perfect control and management, high performance at points of entry and exit (these are totally automated), a minimal requirement for personnel, greater accessibility to products, easier rotation, etc.

Warehouse for a cosmetics distribution company. Source: Mecalux.

Automated systems can be used just to position goods, for internal transportation, or both. The latter is most common, since it considerably increases the number of movements that can be carried out and, in addition, operators only have to load and unload the lorries or containers.

Fully automated solutions have suitable conveyors installed in the dock areas. In general, these conveyors are configured to operate with stacker cranes. This system is used in both exit and entry areas, but for entry areas gauge and pallet control elements must be fitted to guarantee the smooth running of the automated machines and devices.

Entry to the control position of the automated warehouse.

Automated warehouse. Source: Mecalux.

5.3 ORDER PREPARATION (PICKING)

Order preparation (also called "picking") consists of picking and combining non-unitary loads to put together an order for a customer. This can be done in almost any type of warehouse, and always takes place when there is a need to combine packages, parts, products, or materials and, once combined, to transfer them.

The picking and handling of unit loads are connected to the restocking cycle and to the dispatch of orders prepared.

This activity can be carried out in many ways, from the simplest method (in which the operator moves around the facility collecting the units) to the most sophisticated (such as that based on a fully automated system with mechanised picking). Each of these methods is ideal for certain circumstances, but also has its own limitations.

Example of a conventional pallet racking unit and picking. Source: Mecalux.

5.3.1 Impact of picking on investment

The significant impact of picking operations on operating costs was referred to in the section on flows in Chapter 3.

To understand the financial impact of this activity on a warehouse, one need only say that in a badly-planned facility, picking costs can account for more than 60% of operating costs. Reducing the impact of picking to the minimum tolerable level can mean the difference between a competitive company and an uncompetitive one, between staying in the market and going out of business.

This section (order preparation) is where the greatest planning effort needs to be focused. It is also the activity that is experiencing the most advances in applied technology and it is expected that in the future, new products will become available to reduce the added cost of order picking.

Picking can be done in many different ways and, while all of them are valid, some have greater financial impact than others and a different level of initial investment.

The example of an order prepared directly from a pallet located on the lower levels of a racking unit with storing reserve pallets in the upper part is a valid solution when there is not much picking to be done or the warehouse is small. With the right equipment, picking can also be carried out using the full height of the racking unit. This is a good solution for low rotation products.

These two options use the man-to-goods strategy, which requires the operator to move around the warehouse. In most cases, this leads to high costs.

So should other alternatives be considered? That depends. The use of an alternative picking solution will only be profitable if the reduction in the added cost is sufficiently large and if it provides the best ROI, an issue that can be addressed by studying each available option and the tools and strategies applied. This is explained in the following sections.

Chapter 5 - The ideal storage solution

5.3.2 General strategies to improve picking

All picking operations are measured by the number of preparation lines. There are several options for storage systems based on the man-to-goods principle to increase these lines.

The first is to install a warehouse management system (WMS) which, among other things, minimises the journeys made by the operators in terms of both number and distance. The right layout of the warehouse and the goods will also help with product picking operations.

Similarly, personnel can work more quickly when the use of paper is avoided. To do this, staff can be provided with radio frequency or voice picking terminals and equipment.

Operations can be improved by preparing orders in waves (several at the same time) or by grouping them together.

Of course, infrastructure can also speed up operations. One example is live racking units with the Pick to light system, where lights are placed in front of each station. These lights indicate from which positions the product has to be removed, and in what quantity.

Put to light systems, where light devices indicate where the units have to be placed for each order and in what quantity, can also speed up operations when fitted in picker trolleys or machines.

Beyond these measures, further increases in the capacity to form order preparation lines can only be achieved by using goods-to-man strategies, in which the operator does not have to move from his station and the goods come to him.

The following is an analysis of the different ways of preparing orders. They are divided into the two strategies mentioned above: man-to-goods and goods-to-man.

5.3.3 Order preparation methods using the man-to-goods principle

When studying the preparation of orders there are four initial approaches to consider, each based on the height level at which the process takes place: on the ground, low-level, mid-level, and high-level.

There are different methods, advantages, equipment used, etc., associated with preparing orders at each height. Therefore, each level must be examined individually.

<u>Order preparation at ground level</u>
This refers to preparing orders by positioning full loads (pallets, for example) on the ground, and taking units from these to create final orders.

Warehouse installed for a company in the distribution sector. Source: Mecalux.

A. Possible systems

The most appropriate system for preparing orders at this level consists of grouping full loads in a suitable area, in order to make order preparation as fast as possible. To do this, loads can be arranged in a single file, in two or more parallel lines, or in a "U" shape.

Loads can be arranged in a single file when the number of components in the average order (the most common of the warehouse operations) is not too high and, therefore, a row of the appropriate size can be established. The person preparing the order can do their work in an acceptable time, without becoming excessively tired. This arrangement can also be used when the space available for picking so demands, either because the picking area is elongated or because there is no other alternative.

Full loads can be arranged in two or more parallel rows and is appropriate when there is an option to duplicate or multiply the picking area. An aisle must be left between rows so that the people preparing the orders can move around.

The third configuration that can be adopted is a "U" shape. This can be useful when there are both few or many full loads. It offers the significant advantage of very quick picking, although it has the disadvantage that it requires more space.

The objective for each of these three layouts is the same: To enable more than one person to work in the picking area at any given time, speeding up the work in the process.

B. Reasons for preparing orders at ground level
This strategy involves lower investment costs and, while this could be a reason in itself to choose it, it is not the only one.

Picking speeds are faster with this system, given that positioning unit loads on the ground reduces the time involved in searching for the pieces or parts for the order.

Since the units are located on the ground, access to them is also easier than when they are positioned on racking units at different levels.

There is less chance of making mistakes, since the operator can be physically close to the part or pieces to be picked, thereby helping them identify these parts or pieces and providing more accurate control. This significantly reduces the likelihood of mistakes, both in picking and in immediate control.

The main disadvantage of this option for positioning loads is that if there is not much space available, it can only be used for a small number of SKUs.

Warehouse installed for a company in the distribution sector. Source: Mecalux.

Chapter 5 - The ideal storage solution

Source: Mecalux.

C. The most appropriate equipment for preparing orders at ground level

The most appropriate equipment for picking at ground level is pallet trucks, both manual and the self-propelled variety with the driver mounted or on foot.

In general, all versions of pallet trucks, or even a simple manual trolley, can be used as handling equipment for picking at ground level. However, the ideal vehicle, which is designed to prepare several orders at the same time, is a low-level selector or picker (discussed in Chapter 3).

Order preparation at low levels

Order preparation at low levels is performed above ground level. To fall under this category, the units must be positioned at a height that enables them to be accessed by an operator on foot or, at most, riding on the highest part of the body of a self-propelled pallet truck.

A. Systems for low-level picking

Orders can be picked at low level by taking individual pieces or packages stored as unit loads, or stored in the spaces in racking units enabled for this (through shelves, for example).

Chapter 5 - The ideal storage solution

Source: Mecalux.

As we have already seen, picking at ground level invariably involves taking parts of a unit load. At low level, this does not necessarily have to be the case. Rather, orders can be prepared by taking loose pieces or parts that have first been separated and placed in the spaces on a racking unit configured for manual picking.

B. When to use low-level picking

The choice of the most appropriate system is directly related to the number of orders that have to be prepared each day. Therefore, the factors that influence this decision are the time and space available.

In terms of space, when the number of SKUs to be included in the average order exceeds the capacity of the space allocated for order preparation, orders cannot be prepared at ground level. To solve this problem a system of racking units can be installed with two or more load levels in this preparation area.

The choice of the number of load levels and their size will be determined by the volume of the unit loads or individual parts to be handled.

As regards time, if an excessively large number of orders has to be prepared each day, the classic preparation sequence (in which a unit load is taken and placed in the order) may prove too slow. In this case, it would be helpful to use a low-level manual picking racking unit system.

When using this type of structure, there is a radical change in the way of working and orders are prepared in two phases. In the first phase, racking units are loaded with units, loose pieces, or parts, which are supplied either from the reserve area or from another preparations area at ground level. The second phase is to prepare the orders, taking pieces from the spaces in these racking units.

For this system to operate smoothly, different shifts should be set up for each phase so that the working day is divided into two, four, or more parts. Depending on the number of orders to be prepared and the size of the racking units, the duration of each shift can be as long as a full working day.

C. Equipment for low-level picking

The appropriate equipment for picking at low levels is low-level pickers, as discussed in Chapter 3.

D. Position on manual picking racking units

When picking products stored on racking units, the quickest man-to-goods system is that which is carried out in the most manual way possible.

This circumstance arises when the operator, either on foot or mounted on a pallet truck or self-propelled trolley, can pick pieces or parts for orders without needing a machine to reach higher levels and without having to climb down from a machine to do so.

However, when there is a large number of SKUs stored in a facility, picking at height must be used and, therefore, machines are required to access the goods.

Source: Mecalux.

When planning the position of racks for the preparation of orders on low levels, there are two options. The first is to prepare the orders on the general storage racking units. The second is to install racking units exclusively for manual picking, i.e. without the worker having to be lifted on a machine or climb down from it

When the designer chooses the second option, it is important to remember that these racking units must have specific characteristics.

These units must be capable of being loaded manually, with the height of the top load level no higher than the average shoulder height of the employee preparing the order. The maximum weight of packages positioned there must not exceed 25kg.

These characteristics lead to a very specific racking unit design. Given that it will have to be loaded manually, the compartments or spaces do not have to be large and only need to be able to contain the average number of pieces to be picked in each picking shift (plus a percentage stipulated as the margin to ensure that there is no shortage of stock).

Given that the height of the racking units is limited, if the number of SKUs is very large and the available surface area is relatively small, orders must be prepared on two or more levels, for which mezzanines are used, connected using staircases.

Since packages must weigh no more than 25kg, the racking units used are light or medium-duty. It is also advisable to store the heaviest pieces or packages on the intermediate levels and the lighter ones on the rest. The distribution of the units according to weight is illustrated in the image below. This will result in more efficient order preparation.

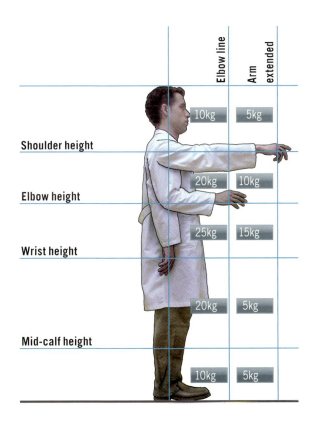

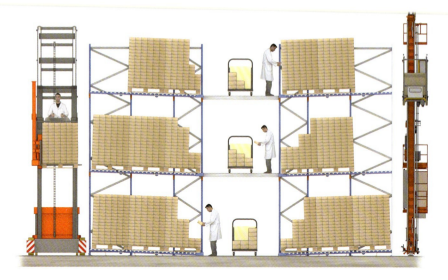

Order preparation at mid-level

Mid-level order preparation is always carried out on racking units, both those for general storage and those exclusively for picking. Mid-levels are located at heights no more than 3.5 to 4m.

This order preparation system is a midpoint between low-level picking and high-level picking (the system on which it is based).

Preparing orders is always much faster when less time is lost going up and down between racking units. As a result, although the higher levels provide an advantage through making better use of the available volume, it is always useful to create a picking area at the mid-level or, in other words, place products with heavy rotation in the low to mid-levels of the racking unit and pick orders for these products only from that area.

A. Use of mid-level order preparation

There are two circumstances in which this strategy is recommended. The first is in warehouses or areas used exclusively for picking a high number of orders per working day.

The second circumstance is in a distribution warehouse with a large number of orders concentrated into a limited number of SKUs. When designing a warehouse (or a storage area exclusively for picking) with a very large number of orders, the installation of this type of system provides the necessary speed of preparation.

Ideally, the area or warehouse with mid-level order preparation should be designed with manual picking racking units. Unloading and restocking occur in alternate shifts. Where so required

Warehouse for an electronic components company. Source: Mecalux.

by the speed of preparation, the system can be complemented with multiple low-level picking machines that will produce the best performance as long as they leave the aisle as little as possible.

When the speed required is very high, one machine can be used per picking aisle in the warehouse, ensuring unbeatable picking performance. In this case, a horizontal transport system must be placed in the aisle at the front of the racking units, using either conveyors or automated vehicles. With these conveyors or vehicles, individuals preparing orders only need to unload the completed orders onto these conveyors or vehicles, preventing any time from being lost.

In distribution warehouses with a large number of orders concentrated into a certain number of SKUs, these SKUs must be stored in the intermediate area of the facility. As a result, products can be picked using a mid-level picker, averting the significant loss of time that would occur if these orders were to be picked using high-level pickers. Furthermore, given that the cost of mid-level pickers is substantially lower than that of high-level pickers, the investment required is significantly lower.

B. Mechanical equipment for mid-level picking

The most suitable machines for picking at these levels are mid-level pickers. These have already been described, in Chapter 3.

Order preparation at high levels

This type of preparation consists of picking from the full available height of the racking units, taking complete advantage of this height. There is a single SKU in each compartment of the racking unit.

Different high-level picking methods can be used: using a single space for each SKU, using various spaces for the same SKU in the same aisle or over several aisles, allocating a single aisle to the full preparation, or using different areas with the SKUs grouped into batches in various aisles.

Each of these options is explained below.

A. How to perform high-level order preparation

In the first method mentioned, **each SKU has a single space** (no more than one space) in the warehouse. This helps set a routine which improves preparation to such an extent that if the entire warehouse is unified in such a way that the SKU-space relationship remains constant over an indefinite period, orders can be prepared in a fully automated procedure.

Although the above cannot be achieved in full, the memorisation of the SKU location-space by the preparer helps reduce preparation times. On reading the SKU to be picked, the person simply moves, almost mechanically, to the location for that SKU without having to check where the space is located.

The second system involves **several spaces in the same aisle for a single SKU**. This method also helps reduce preparation times, in particular when the aisle contains a large number of spaces due to its height or length. Placing the same SKU in different locations along a single aisle helps reduce movements along that aisle.

However, this method can only be applied if there is a system for real-time communication between the operator and the management software. The final decision as to whether to remove the specific SKU to be picked for an order from one space or another is made by the operator preparing the order. The order must therefore be immediately communicated to the system, so that the system can program the restocking of this SKU in the position from which it has been removed, and not in another position.

The third method mentioned, **with several spaces for the same SKU in several aisles,** makes it easier to conduct operations. It is only suitable when there are several preparing orders at the same time. With this system, operators avoid long and complicated movements along the length and height of the various aisles. In this case, the use of a system for real-time communication between operators and the central computer is highly recommended (even more so than with the previous method).

The fourth working system, **that which a single aisle to complete the entire line,** is useful when the ratio of orders to the number of SKUs is very high and the operation must be extremely fast. To achieve this, the quantities of each SKU stored can be distributed across different aisles, so that they are all available in each aisle and, therefore, the complete order can be prepared. This does away with the need for operators to move between the aisles, enabling them to prepare orders at high levels in very little time.

The fifth operating system is a variant on the previous method and consists of **grouping the SKUs into different areas,** so that an order can be consolidated in each area, independently of the other areas. Using this system, operators work in a specific area, although they do need to change aisles frequently. This system is slower than the previous one but, since it does not require such a continuous change in personnel, its effectiveness is fairly similar. Furthermore, it is more cost-efficient due to the fact that fewer operators are required.

B. Equipment for high-level order preparation

Orders can be prepared on higher levels using three different types of equipment. High-level pickers are specifically designed for this task and are very similar to mid-level pickers in their construction, from which they are derived. These machines can operate to a height of up to 10m to 11m.

It is also possible to use combi VNA trucks, in which the driver is lifted along with the load, providing direct access to loose units or pieces stored higher up.

The third option is to use medium-height stacker cranes (between 10m and 12m), which include an element which allows a man to ride on board, removing units from the racking units. This type of machine is practically no longer in use, since automated picking stacker cranes (explained later), which adopt a goods-to-man strategy, or picking robots, can now be used.

Source: Mecalux.

Warehouse for an electronic components manufacturer.

5.3.4 Devices to improve picking from pallets or boxes

All of the manual picking options and strategies discussed in the previous sections can be made more efficient with the addition of four technologies: radio frequency terminals, pick to light, put to light, and voice picking systems. All of these can be used to pick from both pallets and boxes.

Section 1.9.5 of Chapter 1 in this manual explains how the radio frequency system works and the importance of these very useful devices for improving warehouse management. It is important to choose the type of terminal (hand-held, wrist-mounted or truck-mounted) best suited to the work being performed, and to have a powerful and intuitive management programme.

Handheld terminal

Truck terminal

Pick to light systems use devices with lights and numbers to indicate to the operator the position from which the product has to be picked, and in what quantity. They are connected to the WMS of the warehouse.

The previous chapter, Chapter 4, describes how this works in live picking racking units for boxes, although it can also be used in racking units for pallets. In terms of the issues raised in this chapter, it should be noted that Pick to light devices can incorporate lights of different colours, which allows several orders to be prepared at the same time, assigning a different colour to each order.

Warehouse built for a company in the pharmaceuticals sector. Source: Mecalux.

The third type of system that can improve picking efficiency is put to light. Put to light works in exactly the opposite way to pick to light, with the device, which is of similar characteristics, used to indicate to the operator position the goods must be left in and what amount or number. Often these systems are combined. The put to light system can be used in fixed positions for pallets, or in mobile equipment in which more than one order is prepared.

Chapter 5 - The ideal storage solution

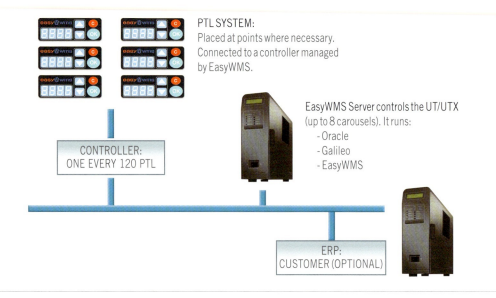

The final technology to be discussed in this section is voice picking.

Voice picking is based on computer terminals fitted with voice synthesisers and voice recognition systems, whereby instructions can be given and confirmations received through oral communication with the operators preparing an order.

Each operator carries a terminal that includes a headset and a microphone, allowing personnel to keep their hands free. This leads to a considerable increase in the number of operations that can be performed. Furthermore, it is a very good solution for working in cold chambers, since the use of gloves makes it difficult to manage any other type of terminal (think, for example, how difficult it would be to use the buttons).

Image of the voice picking system which is currently used in an automated logistics centre for the storage and distribution of frozen products.
Source: Mecalux.

284

5.3.5 Picking systems in automated warehouses with products on pallets

The need to reduce order preparation costs means that the use of solutions based on automated systems is now increasingly common. This is due to the significant advantages of this option, such as the reduction in personnel required, perfect stock control and management, the possibility of constructing warehouses of great height, the absence of handling equipment for picking, etc. The goods normally stored in this type of system are, generally, of medium consumption and complement full pallet orders.

There are four basic configurations used for automated picking from pallets: creating picking posts at the front of the automated warehouse, doing the same but on one side of the automated warehouse, establishing picking positions in annexed areas, and using special picking robots. Each of these is discussed below.

<u>Picking positions at the front of the automated warehouse</u>
This is the most commonly used solution for small or medium-sized warehouses in which picking is not the main operation. There are different solutions that can be adopted depending on the number of orders to be picked, and each of these has different applications and performance. Therefore, each individual case must be analysed to determine which configuration of elements is the most appropriate. An example of a picking area at the front of the warehouse is shown in the photograph below.

Source: Mecalux.

Source: Mecalux.

Picking positions on one side of the automated warehouse

The configuration of this alterative is based on using live racking units at the lowest level (ground level) on one side of the automated warehouse, facing outwards so that the end forms an aisle. This layout can be seen in the above photograph. These live positions, which can allow for two or three pallets per channel, are used for pallets containing the most consumed goods (see example in photograph above).

Full reserve pallets are stored in other conventional positions, mainly those above the live ones, so that the stacker crane can restock these as they are emptied.

The operator moves along the whole side of the automated racking unit with the help of a pallet truck or picker.

Other products, which are stored in other aisles and consumed in smaller volumes, are picked in the picking positions located at the front of the warehouse.

This system of picking on one side is compatible with the use of pick to light devices, which help the operation and expedite the preparation of orders.

Picking in annexed areas

For high-consumption products, and to reduce preparation time, a good solution is to create an area for live picking from pallets on both sides of a working aisle. Products are handled by shuttles that supply the live channels.

Reserve pallets are stored in an automated warehouse with a stacker crane. Communication between this warehouse and picking shuttles is via the use of roller or trolley conveyors, electrified monorail systems, or automatic guided and laser guided vehicles (AGV/LGV).

The handling equipment recommended for use by operators is the self-propelled pallet truck or ground-level picker.

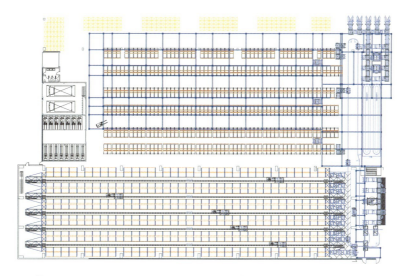

Source: Mecalux.

Image of an anthropomorphic robot. Source: Mecalux.

Chapter 5 - The ideal storage solution

Automated picking with robots

Picking robots can be used for large-scale picking and as a complement to automated warehouses. These robots can automatically handle individual boxes or complete levels of boxes (called layers).

There are three types of robot: anthropomorphic, two-axis gantry, and three-axis gantry. The choice of robot used is largely based on the number of cycles per hour sought and the combination of orders.

Anthropomorphic robots, which can rotate 360°, have an articulated arm that combines different movements. This allows them to access boxes or layers anywhere within their radius of action. Their operation is similar to that shown in the image below, which illustrates an automated picking system with a depalletizer robot:

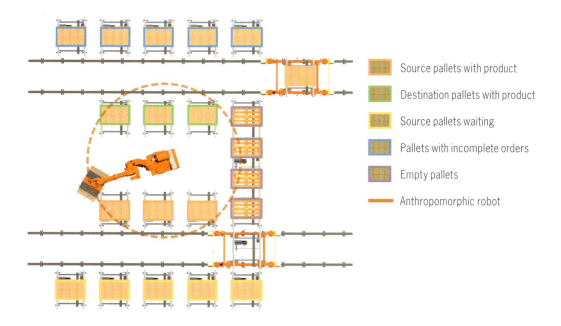

Two-axis gable robots have a rigid handling arm which can only move vertically. The body to which this arm is fixed moves horizontally along the gable, allowing the robot to access any point on this line. It can access several pallets, generally located in four or five positions (two source positions and the remainder destination positions).

Chapter 5 - The ideal storage solution

The operating system is illustrated in the following image:

■ Source pallets
■ Destination pallets
■ Finalised pallets
■ Source pallets waiting
■ Destination pallets waiting (empty)
— Two-axis gantry robot

Image of a two-axis gantry robot. Source: Mecalux.

Chapter 5 - The ideal storage solution

Image of a three-axis gantry robot. Source: Mecalux.

Three-axis gantry robots work in a similar way to the two-axis variety, but the entire gantry moves along a third axis on a side structure. This enables the machine to access two different lines of pallets, each being assigned as source or destination positions. As a result, there can be greater diversification in the orders and more orders can be prepared.

The operating system is illustrated below:

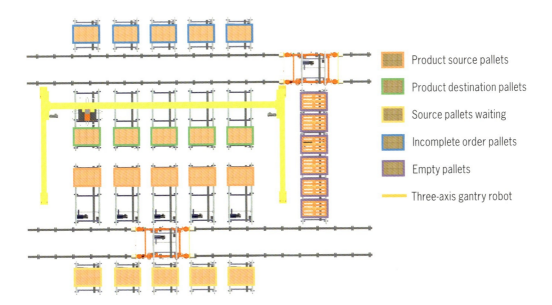

5.4 STORAGE OF SMALL PIECES

Having analysed storage systems for pallet picking, we can now examine another type of facility, namely that used for small pieces.

There are two main problems that can occur with the storage of small or lightweight units. First, there can be a large number of SKUs, i.e., a wide range of units to sort. Second, a high rotation ratio is required. Bearing this in mind, the following are the preliminary considerations to be assessed before examining the options available on the market, an issue that will be addressed later.

5.4.1 Preliminary considerations in the design of a warehouse for small pieces

This section will establish the factors that must be taken into account when creating an almost perfect warehouse for small pieces. Such a warehouse will provide sufficient capacity, both now and in the short- and long-term, and the highest possible rotation ratio.

This is achieved most efficiently and rationally through automation. However, when designing a warehouse, above all if this is robotised, it must never be forgotten that the cost of the facility must be proportional to the total cost of the operation. In other words, there must be a balance between cost and utility. To achieve these objectives it is essential to analyse each of the parameters that can be involved, and these are set out in the following sections.

The importance of warehouse storage to the production chain

A warehouse is not a passive element within the production chain of an industry; rather, it is one of the most active and strategic elements. It can be just as or more productive than the assembly or distribution line, since if the warehouse does not operate correctly any such line could be brought to a halt due to a lack of supplies. These supplies can only be properly controlled when the warehouse runs smoothly.

Owing to the above, it is vital that companies that need a warehouse to perform their operations first consider issues such as whether the pieces with the most movement need to be positioned for easier access, whether the most delicate items have been deposited in clean locations, and the degree of safety required, at least for certain products.

Obtaining sufficient capacity for current and future needs

The warehouse is an element of the production chain which must be viewed as a living organism, since any change in demand directly affects it.

When the economy is experiencing rapid growth, for example, the warehouse must become faster, expand its capacity, increase the number of SKUs handled and, as a result, adapt to a reduction in the number of pieces that must be stored initially, and which will rapidly tend to rise.

These ups and downs must be considered from the moment the earliest stages of the warehouse design process. However, there will be unforeseeable circumstances that may force the designer to use other systems. For this reason, it is vital to know how to adapt to sudden growth once the warehouse is operational. This is the subject of the following section.

Warehouse installed in a hardware component and assembly company. Source: Mecalux.

How to increase capacity in an existing warehouse

Increasing capacity for the storage of goods can be relatively simple or very complicated, depending on the facility. There are two basic strategies for achieving this. One is to redesign the warehouse using more modern techniques. The other is to construct new facilities with larger capacity.

The first option can be more or less complicated, since not all warehouses can be extended. If they cannot, the only solution is to choose the second option.

There are several alternatives on the market to increase the capacity of an existing warehouse or a new warehouse. First, one could use ultra-compact storage, which focuses on height and very narrow aisles and uses conventional, semi-automated, or fully automated handling equipment.

A second option is horizontal carousels, which can even be combined to offer the capacity required and extended in the future. Vertical lift modules, which can also be combined and extended in the future, are another option.

Another alternative is to modify part of the existing facility and construct a self-supporting warehouse.

These four solutions should help the planner design the most appropriate warehouse, given the type of product handled in the facility. It is possible that the ideal solution in a specific case is none of these on their own, but rather a combination to offer the almost perfect storage defined at the start of this section. However, in making the right choice between these it is vital to bear in mind the second of the factors discussed above. This is analysed below.

How to obtain the highest possible rotation ratio

The rotation ratio measures the frequency with which stored goods leave the facility. To calculate this ratio, the volume of a good consumed is divided by the average stock of that good in the warehouse. For example, if over the year 100 units of a product have been consumed and the average stock of this product during the year was 25 units, the rotation ratio is 4. This is the number of times that this product has been restocked.

The rotation ratio of a warehouse can vary significantly. Whether or not a rotation ratio is acceptable depends on whether or not it applies to all goods.

Warehouse for a car company. Source: Mecalux.

It is not enough to reach an optimal overall rotation ratio, which in some cases can be 12, in others 20, and in others just 3. If there is a single product with a rotation ratio of, for example, 0.01, this signifies that the facility has a serious error, or at least that something is going on with this SKU, since the company will be storing a large quantity of a product which is not leaving the warehouse, wasting space and reducing efficiency.

It would also be unacceptable to have a situation in which there are high rotation ratios for all low-priced products, but not for more expensive products.

Therefore, having a balanced warehouse is almost more important than a high average rotation ratio.

The effect of streamlining on the storage of small pieces
Any increase in streamlining has a highly positive effect on the total cost of storing small pieces.

This factor is improved by using the appropriate equipment for handing and storing materials, as this eliminates downtime and, above all, unnecessary movements.

Streamlining can also be increased through the use of faster and safer channels for the flow of materials. This avoids the use of unsuitable, complicated and tortuous routes that increase the time taken for cycles, with the associated increase in handling costs.

Another issue that influences this factor is the correct planning of the layout of the storage elements within the facility, as this optimises the supply and exit routes.

An efficient system to control and administer each and every resource also helps improve efficiency and improves the smoothness of operations at the facility.

A final element that should be considered in this section is the creation of workstations inside the warehouse that have a pleasant environment and effective task planning, which makes the facility more efficient.

5.4.2 Key principles when creating storage for small pieces

Once these initial considerations – which are required as a starting point for the analysis of both general and specific objectives and circumstances – have been taken into account,

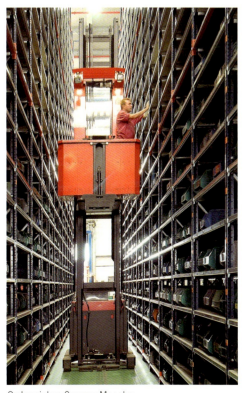

Order picker. Source: Mecalux.

the next step is to analyse the various options available when creating the best possible design for the storage of small pieces.

There are two basic key strategies when planning a facility of this type. One or the other can be used, or both. As already mentioned in other sections of this chapter, these are the man-to-goods strategy (in which the operator moves) and the goods-to-man strategy (where the load moves to the operator's position).

There is no single standard or perfect solution when choosing between these two options. It is even possible for there to be no single best solution, or for the most appropriate solution to be a combination of both. There are many questions related to this issue which are difficult to answer, since these strategies must adapt to each specific product and industry.

The aim and contribution of this manual is simply to provide information which is fairly disperse and which changes as new solutions and elements are developed.

In this way, even if they do not have much training in the latest storage systems, the reader can have an overview of the options available. With the essential involvement of specialists, he or she can look at more decision factors when analysing options for its facilities and any improvements that could be made there. Starting this premise, the following is a discussion of the options offered by the specialist industry.

Man-to-goods strategy

The man-to-goods strategy is the most conventional and classic of current strategies. It has the disadvantage of high handling costs and the fundamental advantage of its low investment costs.

With this option, products are stored on racking units positioned in various ways depending on the system chosen. These elements are handled manually, with the product positioned piece by piece, or mechanised, whereby complete unit loads, generally boxes or containers, are handled.

Units are usually picked manually, with the operator moving on foot or riding on board a machine to where the SKU required for the order is located.

The systems used for this approach are racking units on one floor, racking units on several floors (through the use of walkways or mezzanines), mobile racking units, narrow-aisle storage, and live picking racking units.

The degree of automation in these systems is very low, and depends on the characteristics of each application. Only the live picking system with pick to light devices and the use of trolleys with put to light involve a significant degree of automation.

Not all man-to-goods systems are exactly the same. The various options can be classified using a scale of 0 to 10 for four criteria.

These four criteria are: the total cost of the investment, the cost of handling in terms of labour (handling cost per item, which is independent of the investment), handling capacity in terms of the number of movements per unit of time and, lastly, the area usage index in terms of its effective use.

Facility for the chain of self-service stores. Source: Mecalux.

The following section goes through these solutions one by one and scores them on the basis of these four criteria.

A. Racking units on a single floor

These racking units, which are generally low-duty, are distributed throughout the warehouse, leaving a small aisle for the operator and the picking trolley.

There are very sophisticated systems with drawers of different sizes and layouts that are suited to all possible product sizes and industrial activities. Usually, heavier products are stored on the lower levels.

Although these racking units are not usually very high, this feature will depend on the requirements of each industry and each warehouse.

Chapter 5 - The ideal storage solution

Publishing warehouse. Source: Mecalux.

It should be remembered that in very tall structures, it can be difficult to rapidly access products stored in the highest positions. At times it may be necessary to use ladders or ladder-trolleys (which are almost always manual), but this slows down the process of picking and dropping off units.

Other mechanised equipment can also be used in warehouses with these systems, such as manual or self-propelled stacker cranes and low and mid-level pickers, as explained in Chapter 3.

Scores for this system:

CRITERION	SCORE	COMMENTS
Total investment cost	1	Low
Handling cost	8	High. In general, handling is completely manual.
Handling capacity	4	Average
Use of the surface area	3	Fairly good, as a result of the narrow aisles. Inefficient use of volume.

B. Racking units on several floors

This storage system follows the same principles as the previous one: in practice, it involves two or more one-floor storage areas, installed one on top of another to increase storage capacity or create high racking units with walkways (which has the same effect as having several floors).

With this system there is no need for manual ladders or ladder-trolleys. As a result, the time required to pick and deposit each item is shorter.

In warehouses with this system mechanical devices cannot be used, except on the lower floor or on heavy-duty mezzanines (which are more expensive to install). However, forklift trucks and other devices, such as lifts or goods lifts, can be used to supply the upper floors with full pallets.

Scores for this system:

CRITERION	SCORE	COMMENTS
Total investment cost	1.5	Slightly above that of single-floor warehouses.
Handling cost	9	Higher than with single-floor warehouses. Mechanical devices cannot be used in positioning and picking on upper floors (their use would require major investment).
Handling capacity	3	Lower than obtained with single-floor warehouses, since it slows down the operation in upper floors as mechanical devices are not used there.
Use of the surface area	5	The use of the surface area is similar to that of a one-storey warehouse, but it doubles or triples the volume offered by such a warehouse.

C. Mobile racking units

The mobile racking unit system saves a great deal of space by reducing the number of aisles, generally to a single aisle. Nonetheless, when racking units are used very frequently or there are a very large number of racking units, these can be designed with more than one aisle, with racking units grouped into several blocks.

Products are placed and picked exclusively by manual means and, given that the distances to be covered are much shorter than when using fixed racking units, the time required to open up the aisle (or aisles) is more than made up for.

With these systems, in which the racking units are hermetically sealed to form blocks, products are stored free of dust. In addition, when the movement is electrically controlled, these blocks of racking units come with a safety system which automatically halts the manoeuvre if an obstacle is encountered, preventing potential accidents such as a member of personnel being crushed.

Mobile racking units can be controlled by computer, so that the opening and closing of the aisles is programmed. This system speeds up operations.

Scores for this system:

CRITERION	SCORE	COMMENTS
Total investment cost	3.5	The smaller the facility, the more expensive the investment (in proportion to its capacity). Mobile racking units can be positioned on several levels.
Handling cost	8	The ease of opening and closing the aisle in automated systems reduces the operating time, with the resulting increase in productivity and lower labour costs per item picked or deposited.
Handling capacity	4	The reduction in operating time means an increase in the number of items deposited and picked per time unit.
Use of the surface area	7	The much-reduced number of aisles required by these facilities considerably increases the area usage index. This can be even greater if the system is installed on several levels, although this also means a considerable increase in investment that is not offset by a positive impact on handling costs and capacity.

D. Warehouses with narrow aisles

As part of the category of man-to-goods systems, storage structures with narrow aisles score highest in terms of use of the surface area, handling capacity, and handling cost. However, the investment cost for this option is higher than for the others, although it is still at acceptable levels.

The surface area occupied is very limited with the layout of very narrow aisles that, depending on the type of load, can be as narrow as 1000mm between loads. Nonetheless, the most common option is to create aisles from 1500mm to 1700mm wide, in order to be able to use full loads. These systems allow the full height of the warehouse, up to the roof, to be used.

Chapter 5 - The ideal storage solution

The handling devices used are exclusively mechanical. These devices include turret-type trucks, VNA trucks, high-level pickers, and manual stacker cranes, all of which were explained in Chapter 3.

With these systems, a high level of streamlining is crucial in order to maximise capacity. The use of roller conveyors, pallet trucks, forklift trucks, and even auto-guided and laser-guided vehicles (AGV and LGV), which connect the various picking phases in the warehouse, is crucial to achieving this objective.

The correct working position whilst picking and depositing goods on the shelves is also vital. The operator must be able to move vertically and horizontally between the racking units and perform operations that are ergonomically correct and, therefore, safe and efficient.

There are other essential allies in achieving high productivity levels. These include the incorporation of a good warehouse management system (WMS) and the use of radio frequency terminals, which help the operation take place in the proper sequence and, among other things, enable each operator to manage several orders simultaneously.

The system can be more efficient if computer terminals, printers and other data communication systems are installed on the trucks. With this, the operator must instantly notify the central computer of the changes to the stock. The result is an improvement in management, which increases the efficiency ratios of the warehouse.

Productivity can also be increased by installing height and position pre-selectors in the aisle, so that the operator does not have to be concerned about the situation on the racking unit and only has to automatically direct the machine toward the correct position.

These storage systems must be designed for the equipment that is going to be used and the loads that are going to be handled. Therefore, an exhaustive initial analysis of the goods entering and leaving the warehouse, their dimensions, and the proportion of one type or another of exit for the goods is essential. The greatest efficiency is achieved when a high proportion of exits involve uniform goods or, in other words, complete unit loads.

Source: Mecalux.

Scores for this system:

CRITERION	SCORE	COMMENTS
Total investment cost	3	The investment required is fairly high, but can be worthwhile given the improvement in the other criteria.
Handling cost	2	The labour costs for handling are lower because the entire operation is carried out using mechanical equipment.
Handling capacity	5	The speed of movements obtained with the system means this factor grows spectacularly.
Use of the surface area	6	This ratio is very high, thanks to the use of very narrow aisles and the entire height of the warehouse.

E. Live picking racking units

In terms of man-to-goods strategies, the picking system for small pieces providing the best performance is that based on the use of live racking units.

Each box along the picking aisle is for one SKU, with those behind them reserve boxes. The number of aisles required in a warehouse is reduced considerably, as is the distance that the operator has to cover.

Thanks to this minimum space used for aisles, this system makes much better use of the surface area than other types of system.

Warehouse for an airport retail company.
Source: Mecalux.

Warehouse for a CD distribution company.
Source: Mecalux.

Orders can be prepared in three ways. The simplest is to use a trolley (or a picker) with which the operator moves around the racking units and prepares the order.

The second possibility is to install conveyors on one side of the aisle, adjacent to one of the racking units.

The third option again uses conveyors, but in the centre of the aisle. Here, the emphasis is on the operability of the warehouse at the expense of its capacity.

The image on the right-hand side of the previous page illustrates this third option.

The different structural solutions available allow live picking racking units to be adapted to meet different needs. For example, the higher levels can be used to store pallets with reserve goods, and can even combine live picking from boxes and from pallets. The different options are discussed in more detail in Chapter 4.

These systems can be improved, considerably increasing the number of operations, with the installation of a pick to light system, which indicates from where and in what volume each SKU must be removed. The management system is responsible for managing and controlling these devices.

Live picking racking units are essential when preparing lots of orders with lots of SKUs. If pick to light devices are also used, these systems come very close to what is considered automated or goods-to-man picking. In fact, it is common to install these systems along with a miniload or horizontal carousels when handling mass consumption products. In these cases, live picking is managed as part of these automated systems.

Scores for this system:

CRITERION	SCORE	COMMENTS
Total investment cost	8	The cost of the investment is average (even though it is an 8, this is offset by the advantages and efficiency it provides).
Handling cost	2	The handling cost is very low, given that the efficiency of the personnel is greater with this system.
Handling capacity	8	Very high in environments with a large number of operations, particularly if pick to light is used.
Use of the surface area	8	Very high, due to fewer aisles. Inefficient use of height, except when the space above the live picking racking units is used for reserve pallets.

The goods-to-man strategy

This principle, the complete opposite of the man-to-goods principle, involves bringing the units to the operator so that the movement of the operator is reduced to a minimum. This system eliminates the downtime produced when moving from one position to another to deposit or pick goods.

Unlike the systems seen previously, the process for depositing of the product in position and its picking are practically manual, although the movement of the units is almost totally automated.

The storage systems that use this strategy are vertical storage (Clasimat), horizontal carousels (Spinblock), and miniload stacker cranes.

Source: Mecalux.

Chapter 5 - The ideal storage solution

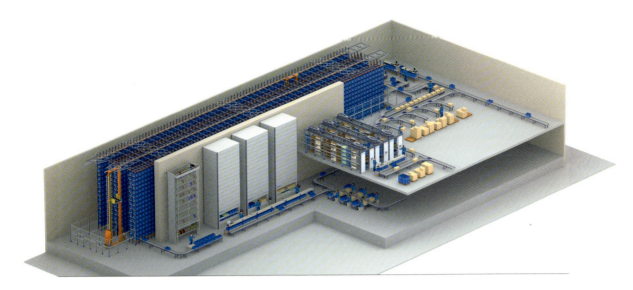

Although some of these systems have already been described in Chapter 4.2.2, they are examined again below from the perspective of the four productivity and efficiency measures used in this section.

A. Vertical lift modules (Clasimat)

Clasimat is an ultra-compact storage system specifically designed for small pieces. These pieces are stored on trays that are moved vertically and horizontally to store them in the positions created inside a large cupboard.

The products stored are completely dust-free and boast a very high degree of safety, since the vertical warehouse is always hermetically sealed and is only opened when the correct code is entered into the computer.

The trays inside the cupboards are moved around using an automated shuttle, resulting in a silent and vibration-free manoeuvre.

The use of space is optimal, since the Clasimat uses a very small surface area in relation to its storage capacity. There are versions different heights that can exceed 15m, but above 5m they start to become very efficient.

The goods-to-man strategy allows for the design of ergonomically suitable work stations and even allows other functions, such as packaging and labelling, to be performed in the same position.

One way to improve how the capacity of the equipment and the operators is used is to create working groups using several Clasimat units, and to mechanise the flow between various groups of these. It is very common to find these systems connected to the warehouse's central computer, which, through the appropriate program, can control and handle various groups of these.

Chapter 5 - The ideal storage solution

While in principle these machines are designed for the storage of small pieces, this is not their only use and there are models with dimensions that are suitable for the storage of larger units.

The use of these vertical storage systems can result in highly sophisticated levels of control, depending on requirements. The device has a keyboard so that the operator can select the position or product desired at any time, while the computer controls in detail the positions of goods and the stocks of SKUs, allowing for the complete management of the system.

Scores for this system:

CRITERION	SCORE	COMMENTS
Total investment cost	7	Average cost.
Handling cost	2	This cost is dramatically lower than the systems seen in the previous section; this is true for all the goods-to-man systems. The fact that the operator does not need to move leads to an improvement in efficiency.
Handling capacity	8	Very high.
Use of the surface area	9	This score shoots up because there is no need for aisles and space is used to full advantage. When reaching heights of above 5 metres, the storage area obtained is 10 to 20 times greater than the surface area used.

B. Horizontal carousels (Spinblock)

Horizontal carousels consist of a series of suspended mobile racking unit modules, which are propelled by electric motors to the point where the load is added or removed. The system is controlled by a person or an automated system. The carousel is generally loaded manually.

Carousels act almost as compact storage, since loading and unloading occurs at one end, without the need to operate on the sides.

Furthermore, several of these systems can be used at the same time, combined and coordinated to act as a single picking station. Indeed, the standard procedure is to have a single operator controlling two, three, or even four Spinblock systems. Each carousel (including when only one is used) has a control computer and is connected to a warehouse management system (WMS).

Certain issues should be taken into account when planning the use of a carousel or group of carousels in a facility. For example, with pick to light and put to light devices, each work unit consisting of more than two machines can pick more than 400 picking lines per hour. As a result, their low cost when compared to other systems and the performance that can be achieved makes this one of the most interesting picking options.

This is a very good option when storing small items with medium or low rotation (B or C). It should be remembered that goods cannot be restocked while orders are being prepared, so the use of carousels is not recommended for storing high rotation (A) products, unless using live picking racking units placed in the front of the point of entry and exit of the carousel. In this configuration (managed by the WMS as a single combined system), type A SKUs are stored in the live racking units, so that the product can be restocked as orders are prepared.

Horizontal carousels are also a good solution as general storage or for retail operations, due to the speed of response to any request.

Scores for this system:

CRITERION	SCORE	COMMENTS
Total investment cost	8	Average. Depending on the type of industry and the degree of use required, the cost can be very justifiable, particularly when taking the other criteria into account.
Handling cost	2	Extraordinarily low. The carousel eliminates the time spent by the operator on the move. In addition, in configurations of more than one carousel, while one is being handled the others can be automatically moving to reach the following position, saving even more time.
Handling capacity	7	Handling capacity reaches exceptionally high levels. Four carousels can be installed around a single picking position, and up to three high.
Use of the surface area	8	Very high, similar to that achieved with compact storage. However, unless several floors are used it leads to a loss of capacity (due to its height).

C. Box stacker cranes (miniload)

In essence, the miniload is a compact storage system supplied by a fully automated stacker crane. The units handled by these systems are boxes or containers, which normally measure 600mm x 400mm or 800mm x 600mm and are adapted to the size of the pieces they contain.

This system can also handle trays, instead of boxes, which can be used to house many different very small products at once, forming a mini unit load. In fact, this is where it gets its name: miniload.

This storage option requires very little space and, given that it follows the goods-to-man principle, allows for the creation of ergonomic and very efficient working positions. Miniloads can also be combined so that a single work position can work with several devices at the same time.

This system can handle loads of up to 100kg per unit (box, container, or tray) and reach lifting speeds of up to 90m/min. It can also reach good horizontal movement speeds (up to 250m/min.).

One of the most important advantages of these systems is stock control. Normally, items are identified using barcodes read by scanners. The IT system that incorporates the miniload both controls and manages the goods, and operations that need to be carried out.

When it comes to miniloads, one must remember that there are different configurations for this type of automated storage, with different capacities and speeds. As a result, the solution can be adapted to the needs of each company or industry. Specifically, miniloads are classified as medium, high, or very high performance.

Medium performance miniloads are those that can move up to 150 boxes per hour (75 in, 75 out) in a combined cycle (the movement to add one unit is combined with the removal of another unit, or vice versa). As with the pallet stacker cranes, one side of the racking units that houses the load can incorporate inclined live racking levels for picking rotation A products using a parallel aisle, while B and C rotation SKUs are served through the P&D station of the miniload. They can also be fitted with pick to light and put to light devices to speed up the operation even further.

High performance miniloads can move 150 to 180 boxes per hour in and out in combined cycles. As with medium performance systems, they can include levels of live racking units on one side. They are also suitable for installing various P&D stations in the header if this is considered worthwhile. With these systems, it is essential to use pick to light and put to light devices.

Lastly, very high performance miniloads can handle more than 250 boxes per hour coming in and 250 going out in combined cycles. Generally, with these models the boxes are only supplied through the front of racks and picking positions can be established in an annexed area. In these warehouses, ergonomic resources, very intuitive support systems, and advanced management and control software are essential.

Chapter 5 - The ideal storage solution

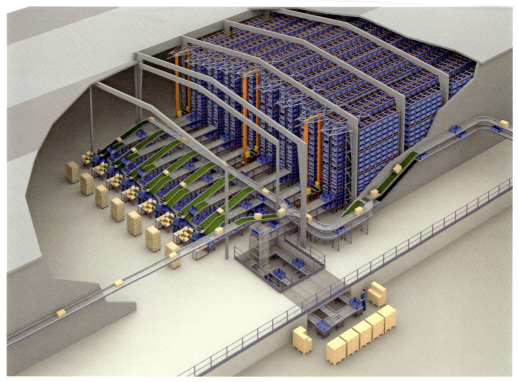

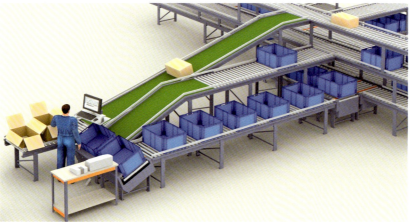

Owing to their characteristics, very high-performance miniloads are a good choice when picking large numbers of boxes in extremely short periods of time. As a result, they can be ideal as temporary storage for picked orders (buffer), storage for supplying assembly and handling positions, or as a sequencer for very quick delivery of sorted boxes.

Scores for this system:

CRITERION	SCORE	COMMENTS
Total investment cost	7	Medium to high.
Handling cost	1	Because it is an almost completely automated system, the influence of the cost of the labour for handling is almost zero.
Handling capacity	6	The handling capacity score is medium-to-high/very high, depending on the model.
Use of the surface area	8	Storage capacity is very high, given the surface area used. It can occupy the full height of the warehouse.

Although these three systems (vertical lift modules, carousels, and miniloads) are the most widely used, other solutions are constantly appearing on the market. Therefore, it is useful to be aware of the options available at any time and suppliers of storage facilities must keep up to date with any new developments, so that they can offer their clients the best service and the most suitable options.

5.5 RETURN ON INVESTMENT CALCULATIONS

The last – but by no means least important – criterion to be analysed when deciding on the ideal storage system for a company is the return on investment.

Analysing the cost of an installation and the return on investment is an exercise that can, and must, be included in any project. In most cases it is very simple, and warehouse operators or owners can do it themselves. In other cases, the supplier of storage solutions will need to help its clients with this calculation.

The calculation of ROI consists of deducing the approximate time it will take to recover the initial investment. This calculation must always be performed by comparing at least two scenarios: the current situation compared with the new project (for companies with a warehouse they want to replace), or a comparison of two different solutions (for companies starting from scratch).

When completing the detailed calculation it is vital to consider all investment costs, plus operating costs (direct savings) and estimates of gains to be made in terms of corporate image, service, control, etc. (also called indirect savings). While all these factors are taken into account in real-life cases, to make the calculation easier to understand the analysis in this manual has been simplified and only the largest figures are included, namely civil works (the warehouse building and its annexes), the storage system (racking unit), handling equipment and its performance, and personnel.

To compare two options it is essential to have comparable starting data. In this example, these data are as follows.

Chapter 5 - The ideal storage solution

A warehouse with a capacity of 8000 pallets measuring 800mm x 1200mm x 1450mm is required. It must be possible to move 700 pallets in and another 700 pallets out each day. There is no picking. Furthermore, in the first phase the working day will be 8 hours. The space available for construction is 100m long and 60m wide, within a larger enclosed area.

Here, two options to meet these needs and limitations are proposed. ROI will be calculated to compare these options. The costs shown are for orientation purposes only, and may vary given the time and circumstances; they are provided here merely to illustrate the calculation.

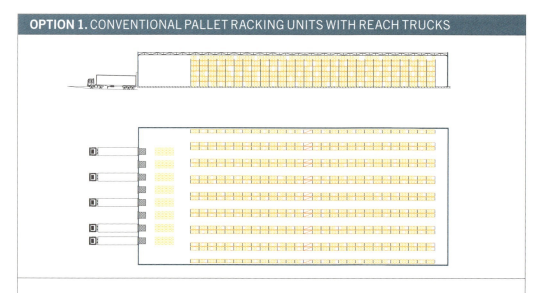

OPTION 1. CONVENTIONAL PALLET RACKING UNITS WITH REACH TRUCKS

This first option involves a warehouse 84m long by 49m wide, with an internal height of 11m. The occupied surface area is 4,851m², and the scope for expanding the occupied surface area of the warehouse is 19% of the total surface area of the plot. It is a conventional industrial building, with 8 loading docks and a reception and dispatch area of 735m².

As requested, the facility has a capacity of 8,000 pallets. The number of movements that can be performed with one forklift are 11 pallets in and 11 out each hour (22 in total), so nine forklifts will be required. With these resources, it will take 7.4 working hours per day to reach the 1,400 movements required (700 in and 700 out). If the warehouse becomes a 24-hour operation, its capacity for growth is 224%.

COSTS OF THIS OPTION		
Item	Quantities	Total cost (in euros)
Forklift operators	9	216,000
Forklifts	9	315,000
Racking units	8,000 positions	312,000
Civil works (warehouse + dispatch)	4,851m²	1,454,400

Chapter 5 - The ideal storage solution

OPTION 2. CONVENTIONAL PALLET RACKING SERVED BY DOUBLE-DEEP STACKER CRANES

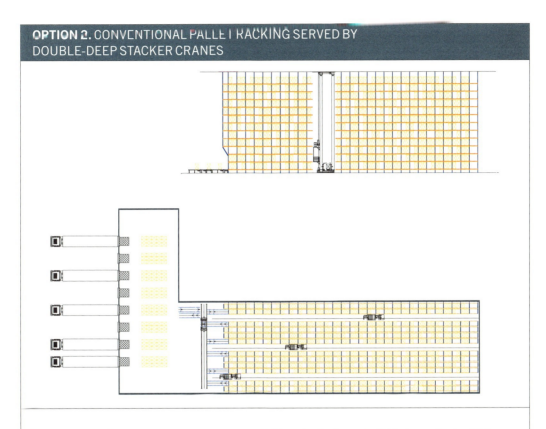

This second option uses the same space as the first, but only part of this is used to build the warehouse, leaving the rest available for future expansion. The height of the warehouse is 24m under the roof truss, inside an industrial building, as in the previous option. The total built area is 2,953m^2, of which 2,218m^2 is the warehouse and 735m^2 used for reception and dispatch. The capacity obtained is 8,000 pallets, as requested.

A stacker crane can perform 29 double cycles per hour (29 pallets in and 29 pallets out), so in this case three stacker cranes will be required. With these resources, it will require 8 working hours per day to carry out the number of movements per day required. Operating 24 hours a day, this facility could grow by 200%. The margin for expansion of the warehouse is 51%.

COSTS OF THIS OPTION

Item	Quantities	Total cost (in euros)
Forklift operators	2	48,000
Forklifts	3	855,000
Racking units	8,000 positions	760,000
Civil works (warehouse + dispatch)	2,953m^2	1,099,926

ROI CALCULATION

The simple return on investment table is formulated based on the total money spent on the facility each year. With this information, as with the workload, one can determine which facility is best from a financial point of view.

The calculation uses annual spending, taking into account that the cost of the facility is only included once (in the first year) and recurring costs, such as personnel, are included each year.

CONVENTIONAL RACKING UNITS WITH FORKLIFT TRUCKS

	Year 1	Year 2	Year 3	Year 4	Year 5	Year 6	Year 7
Figure for previous year		2,297,400	2,513,400	2,729,400	2,945,400	3,476,400	3,692,400
Forklift operators	216,000	216,000	216,000	216,000	216,000	216,000	216,000
Forklifts	315,000	-			315,000		
Racking units	312,000	-					
Civil work (warehouse + dispatch)	1,454,400						
Cumulative total	2,297,400	2,513,400	2,729,400	2,945,400	3,476,400	3,692,400	3,908,400

Figures in euros

AUTOMATED WAREHOUSE WITH SINGLE-DEEP STACKER CRANES

	Year 1	Year 2	Year 3	Year 4	Year 5	Year 6	Year 7
Figure for previous year	-	2,672,926	2,720,926	2,768,926	2,816,926	2,864,926	2,912,926
Forklift operators	48,000	48,000	48,000	48,000	48,000	48,000	48,000
Stacker cranes	855,000	-					
Racking units	760,000	-					
Civil work (warehouse + dispatch)	1,099,926						
Cumulative total	2,672,926	2,720,926	2,768,926	2,816,926	2,864,926	2,912,926	2,960,926

Figures in euros

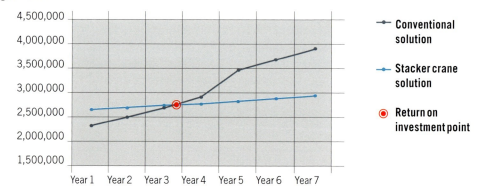

As can be seen, the conventional facility requires less investment when the warehouse first becomes operational, but personnel costs are so high that after two years and eight months the automated option, with its lower annual fixed costs, has absorbed the difference between the two options. From this point on, for the entire lifetime of the warehouse, the second option provides savings. This is a clear example of the importance of planning projects with a view to the medium- and long-term.

How would the calculation vary if this facility, rather than being new, were an existing warehouse no more than three years old? In this case, the only savings would be in relation to personnel, i.e., €168,000 per year, and the forklifts would be replaced every five years (with the first option, they would have to be replaced in year two).

With the change of warehouse, the value of the building (€1,454,000) and some of the equipment (€150,000 in ranking units and machines) would be recovered from its sale. This would have to be subtracted from the initial investment in the new warehouse, leaving a differential of €1,068,926. The return on investment point would be in year five and, from this point on, for the rest of the useful life of the new warehouse, its use would be beneficial. Again, thinking about the impact over the medium- and long-term helps the company.

5.6 CONCLUSION

This chapter poses the question, *What is the ideal storage system?* The answer is complicated, since all the options and variations examined are ideal in some circumstances but not in others because of the investment required, for example. Success in finding the most appropriate configuration is the result of a number of factors, such as information, knowledge, the desire to find the perfect solution, customer involvement, and having the most appropriate product given the specific circumstances and needs.

Trying to summarise the issues explained in the various chapters of this manual is not an easy task, particularly for complex solutions. It is highly probable that in certain cases, the best option will require a combination of various systems.

To find the optimal solution, it is vital to bear in mind everything discussed previously. However, the size of the warehouse, the number of SKUs, and the operation to be performed will mean that only part of the discussion in this chapter and in the rest of the manual is relevant.

The intention of this manual is not to turn the reader into an expert, as it is only a guide. Professionals and companies, with their extensive experience, are the ones that must to solve, plan, and develop the different storage options, particularly the more complex ones.

In Chapter 6, we will look at the principles involved in constructing the buildings and the warehouse environment. You will find that this issue is very closely related to the choice of solution.

CHAPTER 6
THE DESIGN AND CONSTRUCTION OF THE WAREHOUSE

Once the alternatives available for addressing the specific needs of a company requiring a warehouse, along with the flows, loads, operations, investments required, etc., have been analysed, it is time to take action and build the new warehouse, or alter the existing one. This is the focus of this chapter, which looks not only at the techniques used but also at the various issues, limitations, and conditioning factors involved, and the decisions that must be taken in relation to these issues.

6.1 THE IMPORTANCE OF LOCATION

One of the primary issues when building a warehouse is where to build it. This has a bearing on its construction and, even more importantly, on the strategy of the company. Therefore, it can be crucial to the success or failure of the business.

The process of deciding on the location of a warehouse will be longer and more complicated the larger the company and, therefore, the larger its distribution system. In any event, this process must always consider four basic factors: production, demand, costs, and competition.

For each of these elements two different aspects must be considered – financial and commercial – to create as realistic an analysis as possible. Bearing this in mind, the analysis must include a range of variables.

First, as regards the product, an assessment must be carried out on the type and total quantity of the product to be stored.

In terms of costs, these relate to infrastructure (land, buildings, and equipment), direct and indirect labour, transport and handling costs, and parallel costs of the activity, as well as services and insurance policies that must be bought.

In terms of demand, one must estimate the quantity and location of consumers, the number and size of orders, the demand curve, the relative importance of proximity, and speed of delivery.

Chapter 6 - The design and construction of the warehouse

Lastly, with regards to competition, one must examine the location of their warehouses, and the efficiency and service provided by these.

Some of the aforementioned variables have already been explained in previous chapters. Others are beyond the scope and purpose of this manual, and must be assessed by the owner of the warehouse.

The analysis to determine where to locate the facilities must be carried out by examining these variables and the four parameters discussed in the following sections, such as the characteristics of the product, the manufacturing capacity of the industry, and the specific features of the distribution network required.

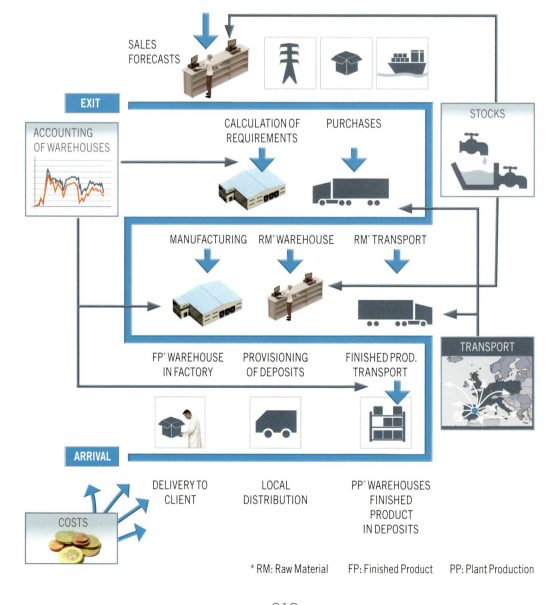

* RM: Raw Material   FP: Finished Product   PP: Plant Production

6.1.1 Product characteristics

Three factors must be taken into account when analysing the characteristics of the product that may influence the location of the warehouse: durability, intrinsic stability, and manageability.

<u>Durability</u>
This characteristic determines how close distribution warehouses should be to points of consumption.

Thus, products with low durability, such as fresh fruit and vegetables, require facilities that are very close to final purchase points, since the time between their production or picking and their consumption must be very short. Therefore, transit warehouses cannot be used with these items because even the short period of time that the product spends there could prove disastrous in terms of its conservation.

For very long-lasting products, such as almost all industrial items, however, there is no need for warehouses to be very close to points of consumption, at least from the perspective of how time impacts on quality, since time has little or no impact on their condition. Therefore, this type of item can be stored in any of the different types of warehouses (central, regional, or transit).

Detail of a pallet. Source: Mecalux.

<u>Intrinsic stability</u>
Intrinsic stability refers to the stability of the product itself, which can affect its transport and safety. If the product is intrinsically very unstable it will need special warehousing facilities, since its storage could affect the physical safety of the location and even the health of nearby residents. A typical example would be chemical products, whose intrinsic instability means it advisable for warehouses that handle them to be located in one of only two locations: the point of production or the point of consumption, with no intermediate warehouses.

The size of the warehouse will be very different for each of these two options, since at the point of production it is possible to have a large storage facility (an actual warehouse), while at the point of consumption there will only be room for a storage area of a size which reflects demand and the average transport time between the two locations.

This is not a determining factor when storing goods of great intrinsic stability, for which any of the options discussed earlier in this manual can be used.

Manageability

The options for handling a product and the ease with which it may be handled can be restrictive characteristics in terms of the number of movements that may be carried out with the item.

Very hard-to-handle products, such as liquids and loose aggregates, must be stored in as few locations as possible, since their characteristics mean that costs increase exponentially as transfers and movements take place. In addition, in most cases such movement can also lead to a reduction in quality and a loss of volume. The perfect solution is to have just two types of warehouse: a central warehouse, located at the production plant, and a warehouse for raw material, which must be located at the product packaging plant.

Once packaged, these items are reclassified as very manageable. At this point, where they are stored is totally independent of their manageability.

6.1.2 Manufacturing capacity

The manufacturing capacity of the industry served by the warehouse determines the quantity of goods that need to be stored. This is a relative factor, which must also be assessed on the basis of the demand for the product in question.

Its influence on the location of the different types of warehouse depends on the degree of processing that takes place in the industry.

Degree of product processing

Not all industries have the same degree of product processing, as this depends on their specialisation, their preparation, and, above all, on their capacity. To study possible locations for warehouses, this factor can be split into three levels: low, medium, and high.

The low level of processing is present in those industries which, due either to the nature of the product or their capacity, are limited merely to sorting and packaging raw material. This is the case, say, of food companies in the primary sector. In this sector, only a central warehouse, located at the production plant itself, it required. The facility must have two sections: one for raw materials, and another for the packaged product. In any event, its location does not depend on the quantity of goods that must be stored.

A medium level of processing is that in which raw materials are received, sorted, and transformed into various different products. In this type of industry, the quantity of goods that must be stored starts to be a factor in the location of the warehouses. As a general rule, given that it is normally a question of mass production, whether for a single product or for several in parallel, these industries need three independent warehouses: one for raw materials, one for products used in processing, and one for finished units.

If the quantity of items stored is small, the three warehouses can probably be located in the same place as the manufacturing plant. When production volumes are very large, local or regional warehouses must be installed, and even intermediate warehouses at times for semi-finished products, or transit warehouses for the finished products.

Finally, industries with a high degree of processing are also highly influenced by the quantity of product obtained. Thus, their case is almost the same as for the medium level, the difference being that it will almost certainly be necessary to use intermediate warehouses to control the various stages of production.

The necessary distribution network

The composition and availability of the network required to sell an item will influence the location, number, and type of warehouses needed.

This point involves the analysis of two separate factors: the composition of the network, and how the products are distributed. Both are explained below.

A. Influence of composition

The distribution network can be composed of independent concession holders (such as independent companies) or the company's own agencies. In the case of the former, the amount of product that must be stored will be determined exclusively by demand and the number of orders received from this network. Under no circumstances should a staple warehouse be created, because the network itself takes care of this.

For own agencies, in addition to having the classic central, regional, and transit warehouses, there must be a centre for staple items in each distribution point. These must be as close to the areas of demand as possible.

B. Influence of the distribution of the sales network

The geographic spread of the distribution network influences the location, number, and type of warehouses required. As with the previous factor, there are two possibilities: a network of independent concession holders, or own agencies.

Chapter 6 - The design and construction of the warehouse

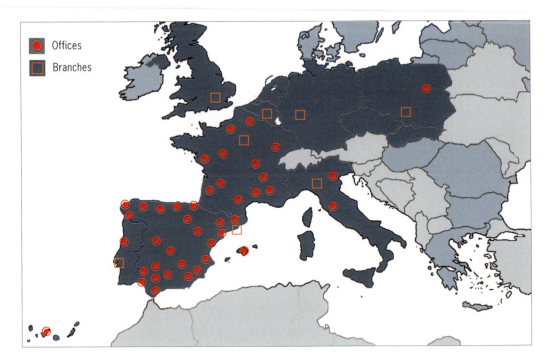

In the case of the former, which involves an external sales network, its positioning in the territory and its area of influence may or may not reflect actual demand for the product.

If agents are positioned in the correct locations, they should be considered as if each were a storage area. A distribution centre is placed in each of the strategic positions and, if demand in a specific area so requires, the corresponding transit facility is created. The purpose of this strategy is to minimise the time required to supply the agents, who must be considered points of consumption.

When concession holders are located in positions that are not the most appropriate for the sale of the product in question, the first step is to rectify this aspect. Once this limitation has been resolved, proceed as set out in the previous paragraph. An incorrectly positioned sales network within a territory will inevitably lead to an increase in the use of transit warehouses and can even lead to delays in supplying points of consumption, two factors that increase the cost of distributing the product and, therefore, result in a loss of market competitiveness.

If the sales network consists of own agents, it is also necessary to ensure that they are correctly positioned within the territory to avoid, as far as possible, the need to create more transit warehouses than is strictly essential, and to ensure that the time required to supply points of consumption perfectly reflects demand.

In any event, for both physical and commercial distribution it is possible to operate without intermediate or regional centres, working with just a central warehouse, if you have a good transport and distribution service.

Services can also be outsourced to a logistics operator, who will manage the transport and distribution, and even the storage and picking of the orders if so required.

6.2. THE DESIGN AND LAYOUT OF WAREHOUSES

Once the location of the warehouse has been determined, along with its requirements and purpose and available space, the first step in designing the facility is to decide on the layout. While this is apparently a simple issue, in practice it is difficult to resolve.

Generally speaking, warehouse designers have to work with a space in which certain factors limit the surface area available. This is why the layout has to be carefully planned.

When deciding on the internal and external layout of a warehouse, there are three possible scenarios that could necessitate a different assignment of space. These are the installation of new warehouses, the extension of existing facilities, and the reorganisation of currently operating facilities.

The last of these three options does not involve any need to take extremely important decisions that will affect the development of the business over the medium- to long-term.

Nonetheless, regardless of the specific circumstances, the general layout of a facility must be in keeping with a good storage system Such a storage system makes the best use of space, reduces the handling of goods to a minimum, provides ease of access to the stored product, has the highest rotation ratio possible, and offers maximum flexibility in the positioning of products and the ability to control the amounts stored.

To achieve these objectives, the first step is to create the layout, where the design of the warehouse is represented in the form of a plan.

First and foremost, the layout created must respect the basic rules of good storage mentioned above and avoid areas and points of congestion, facilitate maintenance tasks, and establish the resources required to obtain the greatest possible movement speed, with the associated reduction in working times.

The following areas must be perfectly defined when designing the layout:

A. Loading and unloading areas
B. Reception area
C. Storage area
D. Picking area
E. Dispatch area

An example of a layout which includes all of these areas is shown below:

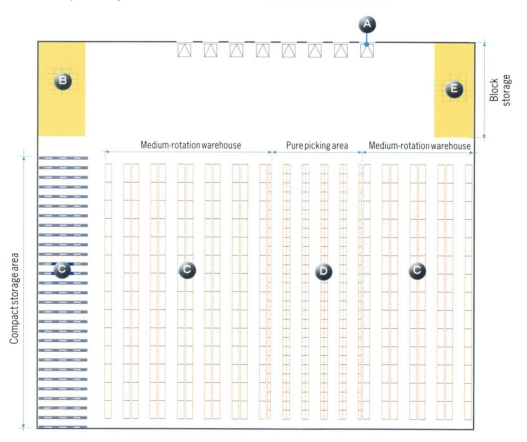

6.2.1. Loading and unloading areas (A)

Loading and unloading areas, which are normally located outside the warehouse or incorporated into it, are those to which lorries and vehicles transporting and distributing goods have direct access.

In a well-organised warehouse, it is useful to separate these activities from the rest of the facility, allowing sufficient space for loading and unloading. This area can be integrated into the warehouse or be independent.

Dock with platform attached to a warehouse.
Source: Mecalux.

Dock with intermediate platform in cold chamber.
Source: Mecalux.

Loading and unloading areas integrated into the warehouse

If loading and unloading areas are built directly into the sides of the warehouse so that goods are deposited and collected without the need for any detours, it is said that they are integrated into the facility. The main advantage of this is the greater handling speed for the load, which means it is preferable to non-integrated options if there is sufficient space for it.

Lorries are connected to the warehouse via docks, which can be separated from the building by a platform or built into the building with an access door (flush).

Docks separated by an intermediate platform are appropriate when this is separation is advisable as determined by the nature of the goods or the need to maintain the internal warehouse environment, or when there are safety issues relating to the material stored.

A typical example of the use of this type of separate dock is for cold chambers, where the loss of cold that could occur if using a flush dock with access door must be avoided at all costs. Yet there are many other circumstances in which this design is preferable, particularly when the safety of the warehouse could be compromised.

Flush docks allow lorries to back right up to the warehouse wall. To avoid affecting the internal environment of the facility, access doors must have, as a minimum, a hermetically sealed system. This seal can be metal or created through using a dock shelter.

Docks with direct access to the inside of the warehouse. Source: Mecalux.

Access points with metal seals have a manual or automated system that operates a flat barrier that can be fixed, folding, or rolling (as shown below). It opens when the lorry backs up to the building, and closes when the vehicle has finished the operation. The internal environment can be more effectively preserved if the closing system is automated.

In addition to a metal seal, doors with inflatable shelters have a tunnel that encircles the lorry when it is connected to the entrance, so that the internal environment is less compromised by conditions outside.

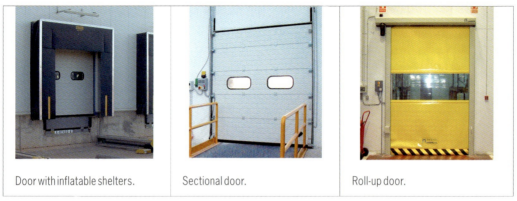

| Door with inflatable shelters. | Sectional door. | Roll-up door. |

Images provided by Vinca Lagenför.

When this type of loading area is created, it is advisable for the warehouse floor to be above the level of the ground on which the lorries drive.

Loading and unloading areas can also be designed where lorries are driven into a pit. However, movement and operations are faster if the warehouse is at a higher level instead.

The necessary height difference can be achieved in several ways; therefore, it is not vital for the warehouse floor to be above ground level. Instead of this, for example, the area in which the lorries drive can be at a lower level, creating a gradual descent that avoids the steep ramps which, ultimately, make manoeuvres more difficult and slow down movement.

Two different scenarios need to be considered when determining how to achieve this height difference. The first is when lorries accessing the loading and unloading areas are owned by the company. The second is when the lorries used are owned by third parties.

If only the company's own lorries are going to use the loading and unloading areas, and

View of a dock in a pit. Source: Mecalux.

the height of the trailer is exactly the same in each case, the difference in level can be established precisely and no further considerations are required.

However, if the lorries that are going to access these areas are owned by third parties and come from different sources, they will have different trailer heights so a system must be created that allows the difference in height to be adjusted.

In general, an adjustable leveller system is essential because even when the company uses its own fleet (which in theory means there is no variation in the height difference between the vehicles and the dock), in practice this difference is always present.

Image provided by Toyota.

One of the reasons for this is that the springs in the lorries give way over time, either because different loads cause the height of the lorry to vary or, more commonly, because over time the company is obliged to purchase or lease other types of transport. Ultimately, a difference in trailer heights is practically inevitable.

Mechanical or hydraulic devices can be used to deal with these height differences. Mechanical devices are based on the use of (usually metal) bridges or walkways fitted manually between the dock and the lorry, as shown in the following images.

Manual walkway.

Image provided by TM Pedane.

Manual foldable walkway.

Images provided by Waku.

These elements are used so that forklift trucks, stacker cranes, and any other mechanical devices used to load and unload lorries can enter and exit the vehicle.

Another option is to use the second system mentioned above, which consists of a metal platform with one or more hydraulic cylinders. This platform facilitates access by acting as a ramp,

Chapter 6 - The design and construction of the warehouse

Images provided by Hörmann.

when integrated into the dock itself, or by raising and lowering the lorry. The image to the left illustrates the second option, with the platform integrated into the dock.

Independent loading and unloading areas

Located away from the warehouse, but within the surrounding area, they operate completely independently of the warehouse itself. They normally consist of a large flat area to which the lorries have direct access, with the lorries positioned so that they can be loaded or unloaded using forklift trucks.

This option is best used in warehouses where only one of the two functions is carried out, i.e. where goods are loaded or unloaded. This option can achieve the necessary handling speed, as there is no need for the lorries to back up to the building, so the time spent positioning them is reduced. In addition, with this option the process of loading and unloading goods is totally independent of the work cycle of the warehouse.

In these areas, goods in the lorries can be handled through the side or the rear of the vehicle. If using the side of the vehicle, forklift trucks are used to handle the goods, as shown in the image to the left.

Forklift handling the goods from the side.
Image provided by Toyota.

Access by ramp.
Images provided by Vinca Lägerfort.

If, however, the operation is carried out using the rear of the lorry, there are two different options.

The first is to access the lorry using forklift trucks and ramps, which are normally made from metal and connected to the lorry either manually or mechanically. While there is a wide choice of such products available on the market, at the moment two are most commonly used: modular ramps and those connected to the unloading docks.

Modular ramps are metal structures with a non-slip surface which can either be fixed (when the lorries used are all of the same height) or mobile (when using vehicles of different heights).

Ramps connected to the unloading docks are made with a brick or concrete structure, which can also be fixed or variable in height. If variable, their construction is similar to that of the integrated loading and unloading docks described previously.

The second option for the loading or unloading lorries by the rear is to use roller conveyors.

Automated loading using sliding elements. Source: Mecalux.

With this system there is no need for the forklift to enter the trailer to carry out the operations. Instead, rails are installed which allow goods to slide along the inside of the lorry. Movement is generated by pushing some loads against others.

The loading process starts by placing one or more units at the entrance to the vehicle, which are then pushed in by a second group that takes the place previously occupied by the first group. In this way the loads accumulate, one after another, until the trailer of the lorry has been filled.

6.2.2. Reception area (B)

The reception area must be located as independently as possible from the rest of the warehouse, so that it can be used not just for receiving goods, but also for quality control and sorting.

Chapter 6 - The design and construction of the warehouse

Source: Mecalux.

Once it has been ensured that the characteristics and quality of the delivery received matches those of the products ordered, the next stage is to determine where to position the load within the warehouse.

Depending on the type of warehouse, it may or may not be necessary to transform the units received. If this is necessary, a suitable area must be established for this function. For example, it may be necessary to break up the pallets that have arrived into smaller units, remove parts that are strapped together, etc.

Given the impact that accurate checking and, above all, correct positioning, can have on the future performance of the warehouse, this area must be as large and independent as possible.

Currently, almost all products handled in a warehouse come with barcodes that can be read using a scanner. Therefore, once the warehouse's central computer has identified the units, it can in turn immediately generate the position label for the goods. This label can subsequently be read by a forklift truck operator or by the scanners of the warehouse's automated system so that, in both of these cases, they can be positioned in the correct location.

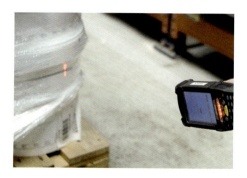

Source: Mecalux.

6.2.3 Storage area (C)

A storage area is, strictly speaking, an area used only to store goods.

Goods can be stored in a number of different ways: directly on the ground; directly on the ground but stacked or in blocks; or on racking units. The choice of one or the other will depend above all on the type of product to be stored, whether it can be stacked, and on the storage quantity and time.

Storage in stacks involves placing unit loads on top of each other without anything in between them, other than the pallets that support them. This method has the advantage of making better use of space, given that it does not generate unused positions. However, not all materials can be stored like this and it must be remembered that even goods that can be stacked have their limits in terms of strength and, therefore, have a maximum stacking height. The main disadvantage of this system is that it does not allow for access to the loads, and a load can only be accessed by first removing all the loads on top of it.

The use of stacking is mainly limited to two types of load: those with great internal strength, and those in rigid packaging.

Goods with great internal strength, such as ceramic bricks, concrete blocks, etc., can be stored directly, at times even without the need for pallets or other support systems. Other goods, such as feed, cements, and aggregates in general, which are stored in sacks, can also be stored in this way thanks to their resistance to compression, although pallets or other support systems are required for their proper handling.

Rigid packaging, such as cardboard, wooden or plastic boxes, can be stacked in this way without problems, although the rigidity and resistance of these packages will determine the number of units that can be stacked, and therefore the height of the stack.

Racking units must be used when unit loads are not strong enough to be stacked to the required height, or when there is a greater need to access the product.

Goods are stored on racking units by placing them on metal structures, which are basically made up of suitable braced frames and beams. These elements create a multi-cellular structure that generates spaces into which unit loads can be placed.

As we saw in Chapter 4, the configuration and layout of these spaces (or compartments) can vary to suit different operations and different needs in terms of the accessibility and accumulation of the load.

Chapter 6 - The design and construction of the warehouse

Warehouse for a distribution company. Source: Mecalux.

6.2.4 Order picking areas (D)

These areas are not required in all warehouses, only when the goods that must have a configuration or composition when leaving the warehouse that is different to the one with which they entered, or when they require any other modification.

Areas for preparing orders can be integrated into storage areas, as is the case when picking from racking units. They can also be separate from storage areas, creating specific picking areas, generally with automated or semi-automated systems.

The various order preparation systems are described in Chapter 5.

The image shows the picking area in a warehouse for tapware and bathroom accessories. Source: Mecalux.

6.2.5 Dispatch areas (E)

These areas are used for packing orders prepared in the areas described in the previous section. Even if this packing operation is unnecessary, this area also can be used for goods that have to be dispatched and loaded into the delivery or distribution vehicles.

To ensure the correct speed of movement within the warehouse, these spaces must be designed in a specific location and differentiated from the rest of the facility.

If separate reception and dispatch areas have been created, these must also have separate loading and unloading areas. If, however, the reception and dispatch are close to each other, a single loading and unloading space can be created. However, this option makes it more difficult to control the flow of goods and the movement of vehicles.

Warehouse for a distribution company. Source: Mecalux.

6.2.6 Service areas (F)

Part of the warehouse must be assigned to support activities at the facility, such as general and control offices, changing rooms, toilets, and the area for recharging the batteries of handling devices.

The ideal solution is for the control office to be located in the reception and dispatch area and, if possible, between these two areas. This provides greater operability and efficiency in the work of the personnel in this department.

Changing rooms, toilets, and general offices can be located anywhere in the warehouse, although it is more logical to locate these close to the control offices. A good solution for bringing together these resources is to construct a mezzanine over the reception and dispatch area, and to locate these functions there.

Lastly, the space for recharging the batteries used by handling devices must be isolated and well ventilated, to improve health and safety and avoid any incidents involving operations taking place in this area.

6.3 THE CENTRAL WAREHOUSE: FUNCTIONS AND DESIGN

In addition to storing the finished products obtained from one or more industrial processes (which, therefore, can come from one or more sources), a central warehouse also acts as a distribution centre for these products.

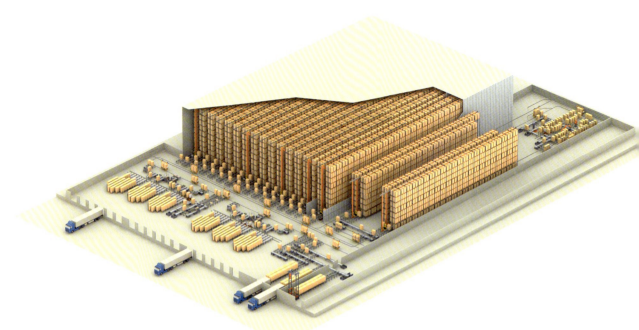

Unlike other types of distribution centres, the central warehouse dispatches the products stored there almost exclusively to supply other regional or local warehouses, and it is these other warehouses that are responsible for the final distribution to the consumer. As a result, the central warehouse acts as a reserve.

It is not always necessary to follow this strategy; the best option will depend on the product and delivery speed. If the company has, or has access to, a good delivery service at a competitive price operated from a central warehouse of the appropriate scale, this warehouse can supply items directly to all of the customers.

In view of the above, the central warehouse is a crucial part of a distribution network. Therefore, it is useful to go into greater detail about the strategic, operational, and functional issues related to such a facility. These are discussed in the following sections.

6.3.1 Factors when choosing the location of a central warehouse

One of the most important issues when building a facility of this type is where to locate it. This must be based on a balance between the location of sources of supply for the materials and products and the geographical location of the distribution and customer centres to which the goods must be delivered.

6.3.2 Influence of the location of the sources of supply

A central warehouse can have a single source of supply (for example, a facility that dispatches dairy products produced in an adjacent factory) or several sources (such as a central warehouse for a chain of clothing stores that receives items from different manufacturers).

Where should the central warehouse be located in these two scenarios? When there is a single source of supply, the facility is the central warehouse for a factory and the logical solution is for this to be integrated into, or at least be very close to, that factory. If, however, there are several sources of supply, it would be better to locate the facility at a strategic point determined as a function of the location of these sources.

6.3.3 Influence of the location of the points to be supplied

The location of the points of distribution to which the goods managed by a central warehouse are to be sent has less influence on its positioning than the location of the sources of supply.

In general, one of the missions of a central warehouse is to prepare the product for the next stage of the distribution chain. As a result, the transfer to another distribution centre is always less traumatic for the product than the transfer from the point of production. This is why the positioning of the secondary centres is less important than that of the main warehouse.

Thus, the only aspect to be considered is the choice of a point with good links to the rest of the region and which provides access to the transport options used.

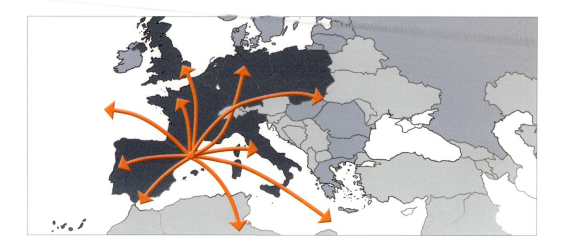

6.3.4 Functions of a central warehouse

A well-designed central warehouse must be capable of performing the functions explained in the following sections. These functions are summarised as follows:

- Reception of all products involved in the industrial activity of the company that owns the warehouse.
- Instant quality control.
- Control and inventory of the products stored.
- Correct storage of the goods.
- Preparation of orders to be sent to regional warehouses, clients, or both.
- Rapid dispatch of orders.

Receipt of all products

To correctly receive all the products that comprise the industrial activity of the company that has built the central warehouse, a series of initial tasks must be carried out to determine the mechanical, human, and computing resources required.

The first step is an exhaustive analysis of the products to be received at the facility. This analysis must take into account the size and weight of the unit loads, the consistency of any packaging used, the arrival frequency of each material, and the quantity of goods received in each delivery.

A. Weight and size of products to be received

The analysis of these two factors determines requirements to be met in terms of the goods received, the type of machines used, and their load capacities, which will not necessarily be the same as those used later for storage. It must be ensured that the machines used in the storage area are suitable to receive the goods in question and, if possible, for dispatch as well.

The goods received can be of different shapes, sizes, and weights. Indeed, this is almost always the case: the more varied the sources of supply, the more common this is.

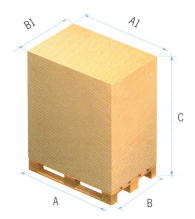

Measurements to take into account for goods on pallets.

Once of two situations normally arise: either all of the units are of the right size and shape to be stored directly, or many do not and need to be modified prior to being stored.

In both cases, the central warehouse must be ready to receive, prepare, and store any type of goods. Therefore, it must have one or more docks, handling devices for unloading the lorries, a reception area and, when necessary, a preparation area.

B. Mechanical means used for loading and unloading

The mechanical devices or means that can be used (and are often used) to load and unload goods are pallet trucks, stackers, and counterbalanced trucks.

All of these elements are discussed in Chapter 3 of this manual. Refer to this section if further information on their characteristics and use is required.

Baked goods, confectionery, and bread manufacturer. Source: Mecalux.

Instant quality control

Quality control in a central warehouse must be limited to checking that the contents of the container in which the product is received match the actual container.

To facilitate this operation, unit loads must be accompanied by a delivery note that sets out the characteristics of the product received, its trade name (where applicable), and the number of units contained in each container or package (for example, in each pallet, container, or box).

With this delivery note, personnel who receive the goods must carry out selective sampling, opening a random package if necessary and checking its contents. This is done to check both the quantity and quality of the delivery.

A second aspect of quality control is checking that the container is strong enough to withstand the anticipated storage time and conditions. This is the point when the packaging is modified to adapt it to the characteristics of the warehouse, where required. This is required, above all, when a central warehouse receives goods from various sources or suppliers.

Control and inventory of the products stored

As soon as quality control has been completed, the products are counted. Once this has been done (and never before), the data are entered into the central computer. The reception department must have one or more terminals, so that if any discrepancy is detected between the goods delivered and the accompanying delivery note, immediate notification can be sent to the manufacturing centre or relevant supplier.

Once receipt of the load has been recorded in the computer, the computer must provide the precise position assigned to each unit, in accordance with the pre-established warehouse program.

When dispatching the goods this operation in conducted in reverse, with the central computer providing notification of the removal or exit of the corresponding units. The management system can then record the space as empty and assign it to a new load.

This departure of goods must be recorded once the operation to remove the goods has actually taken place. Although the computer generates a delivery note, the position is still occupied from the time this document is issued until the load is actually moved from its position. Therefore, if the goods are considered to have left when the delivery note is produced, the system could record this position as being free and assign it to a new load. However, since the load has yet to be picked, the operator could find that the space is still occupied, a situation which could occur if goods enter and leave at different speeds. To avoid this, the computer does not record the position as empty until the operator has picked the unit and this has been communicated to the system. The use of a suitable WMS guarantees all the processes involved in this point, and avoids this type of potential error in the management of the positions.

Correct storage of goods

Central warehouses must have the necessary mechanical devices in sufficient quantity to store goods correctly. If goods are received on pallets, the company must have one or more of the handling

Source: Mecalux.

resources or devices described in Chapter 3 so that it can handle these goods comfortably and safely, and take them to the storage area.

If, however, goods are received in bulk, not only is it necessary to have the resources required to move them, but also at times to have the tools or machines to package them. This can involve the use of hoppers, buckets, or other suitable mechanical elements, such as skid steer loaders or even front loaders, if the volume and characteristics of the goods so require.

In general, it is impossible to correctly store goods and achieve a good financial return and efficiency if a facility does not have the appropriate physical, human, and material resources.

Preparation of orders for regional warehouses

As noted at the start of this chapter, one of the main functions of a central warehouse is to act as a reserve for regional or local centres. As such, one of its primary tasks is to prepare orders requested by these centres. This can be done daily, weekly, monthly, or bi-monthly (or even less often) depending on the required frequency, the products being handled, and their size of the orders.

The following section discusses the different systems and methods available for preparing orders. All of these are designed for specific circumstances, so their use is based on adapting to the specific needs of each company.

It should be noted at this point that for a central warehouse to be efficient in preparing orders, it is essential to have areas set aside for this activity on racking units or on the ground. For this, it is vital to have appropriate storage.

Chapter 6 - The design and construction of the warehouse

Normally, orders must be prepared in a central warehouse on the ground or through automated or semi-automated systems, or at least it must be planned this way. This offers greater storage capacity and better ease and speed in the operation.

The reason for these two advantages is that, first, it offers the option to completely fill the spaces in the racking units, which obviously offers more storage capacity than preparing orders on racking units, since the space or spaces set aside for this purpose are mostly half-empty.

Second, the ground is the ideal level for operators to perform these tasks, so there is an improvement in their performance. This brings with it the ease (fewer errors) and speed mentioned earlier.

In addition, preparing orders using automated or semi-automated systems reduces the time required. However, to achieve the best possible performance orders need to be properly programmed; therefore, it is very important for these to involve complete unit loads whenever possible. Another factor that influences speed and efficiency is the ability of the central warehouse to be constantly aware of the requirements of the other points in the chain and to anticipate their requests as far in advance as possible.

How can this forecast be made? The only efficient way to do this is to have all the relevant information. The faster and more accurate it is, the better the results will be. Therefore, it is vital to establish real-time communication between all the links in the chain, from the most remote final point of consumption (for example, the business that sells the items) to the central computer of the production or picking point.

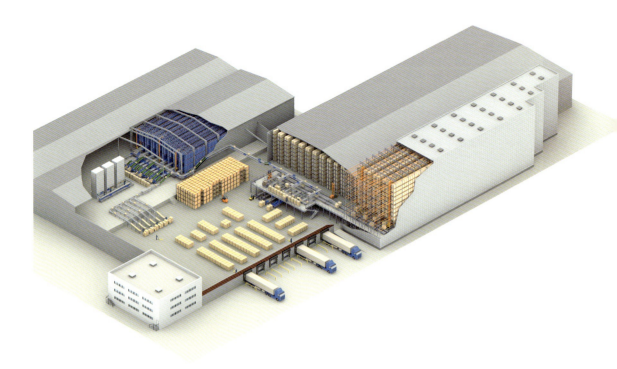

One model for linking these points that generate information is as follows: communication between the business and the controlling warehouse takes place via computers, using modems that send messages over the telephone line. The link between the controlling warehouse and the order picker takes place from operator to computer through a scanner that communicates using radio waves. Finally, communication between the controlling and central warehouses takes place computer to computer, again, through the use of modems connected via the telephone line.

There are several variations of this system. Other alternatives exist as well.

Companies that specialise in information technologies are best-suited to planning and designing the communications required.

In addition, to ensure that everything remains under control it is vital to have a good warehouse management system (WMS).

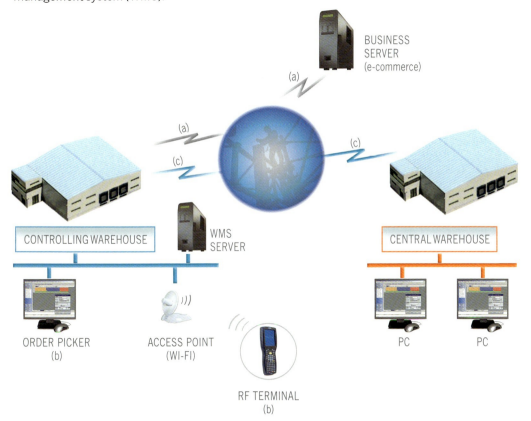

Rapid dispatch of orders
The time required to dispatch orders is vital to prevent delays and disruptions in distribution chains. As a result, one of the functions of a central warehouse is to perform this operation in a prompt manner.

Speed in dispatch operations is simply the product of the correct organisation of all of the aspects explained in the previous sections. If all of these tasks are performed as well as possible, the dispatch of orders is simplified and accelerated.

If not, if there are hold-ups and bottlenecks at any earlier point in the process, then the dispatch of orders becomes chaotic and slows down. For this reason, it is essential that operations in the warehouse be well-coordinated. This is the most important part of the warehouse manager's job.

6.3.5 Design of a central warehouse

Once the exact needs have been determined in terms of location, volume of goods to be stored, the mechanical devices that must be used, the tasks that need to be performed, and the role of the central warehouse in the distribution network, it is time to assign the spaces inside the warehouse and start to design the facility.

Bearing in mind everything seen previously in this chapter, the central warehouse must consist of six sections: reception, quality control, adaptation of unit loads, storage, order preparation, and dispatches. Usually, these six sections or departments can be grouped together into three areas: reception, storage, and dispatches. These are explained below.

Reception area

This area covers the receipt of goods, quality control and, where required due to the nature of the product or goods, the adaptation of unit loads.

The reception area must be adjacent to the unloading docks, and of an appropriate size to manage all goods that could arrive in the warehouse during a full normal working day. If possible, there should be an additional area large enough to be able to deal with any possible unscheduled increases in goods received.

If it is necessary to adapt unit loads received, the surface area must be increased and the resources required to carry out this task must be made available. This includes having the necessary personnel, suitable working benches and tools, reserving part of the storage space for empty packages, and having a system to remove the original packaging.

Warehouse for an urgent transport and distribution company. Source: Mecalux.

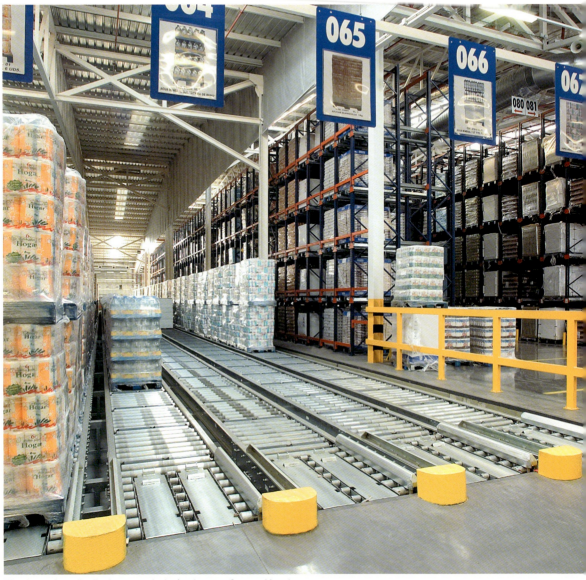

Warehouse for a distribution centre in the food sector. Source: Mecalux.

Storage area

The design of the storage area will depend on whether or not orders will be prepared in the facility, and whether this preparation will take place on the racking units.

In a central warehouse, this area can be made up of one or more sections. Since the objective of this manual is to provide the reader with as much information as possible about the different op-

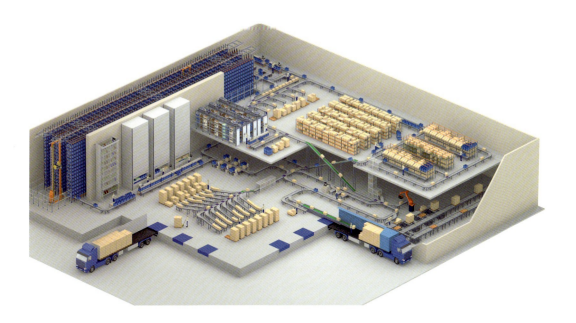

tions, we can consider, for example, a facility that receives various types of products, in different quantities, with a number of different rotation ratios and with complicated storage requirements.

To design a warehouse with these characteristics, the first step is to study the products' rotation ratios, sorting them into three categories: low-, medium-, and high-rotation.

The determination of these three categories is, of course, very subjective. Nonetheless, it can and must be determined by creating an average ratio as the point of reference. Products with a ratio close to this will be classified as medium-rotation. Those with much lower figures will be classified as low-rotation, while those with much higher figures will be classified as high-rotation.

Once the products, their volumes, and their corresponding rotations have been established, the next step is to position them inside the warehouse. In doing so, three factors must be taken into account. Firstly, low-rotation goods are generally those consumed in small quantities and, as a result, they normally need less storage space.

Secondly, medium-rotation SKUs are normally picked regularly and in moderate quantities (in other words, they are requested in average and regular batches). As a result, they need an exit speed which is neither very fast nor very slow, and must be easily accessible.

Finally, high-rotation goods are normally requested often and are in excessive demand (so the situation is normally one of medium-to-large batches requested very frequently). For high-rotation products, the most important thing is to ensure great accessibility and a high picking speed.

Thus, a central warehouse with these characteristics could include:

- **A block storage or compact storage area**, used for high-rotation products for which volume is more important than accessibility or picking speed. Based on the quantity of the product and capacity available, it is possible to use a configuration in blocks or any of the compact storage systems described in Chapter 4.

- **An area with racking units** which, based on the quantity of high-rotation products that exist, can be for pure storage (where the load is only positioned) or mixed, with picking racking units built in.

If the storage is pure, there are a number of options in terms of handling equipment to use, including conventional forklifts (which need aisles of 3500mm to 4000mm wide), reach trucks (aisles must be 2500mm to 3000mm wide), VNA trucks (aisles 1700mm to 2200mm wide), and stacker cranes (aisles of less than 1700mm). The choice of handling equipment is not determined simply on the basis of the space required between racking units, but also, fundamentally, on the relationship between the storage volume required and that available. It is also vital to take into account the different lifting height limits of each type of machine (see Chapter 3).

Another very important factor is the investment required if adopting one system or another, an aspect discussed in the previous chapter. The more sophisticated the handling equipment used, the greater the cost. Similarly, one must not forget the return on investment, since the most

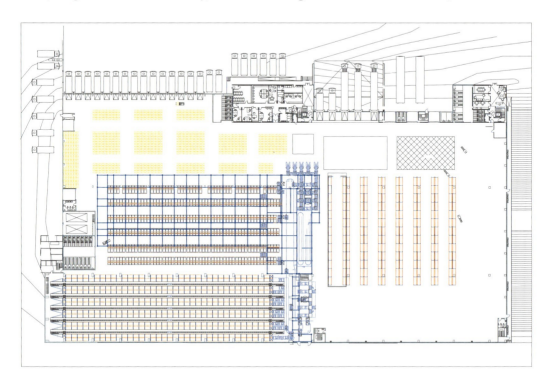

sophisticated systems, with a largest initial cost, can be the fastest to generate a positive return on investment (ROI).

On the other hand, if the number of products with a high rotation is very significant, a mixed storage area can be useful. Given that the fastest picking is normally carried out at the lowest possible height, while the most profitable storage is at the greatest possible height, it is useful to design a configuration of racking units with the preparation of small pieces at medium height (and storage in the rest), or to install automated systems.

Dispatch area

This area contains both the order preparation department (with orders prepared on the ground or on racking units) and the dispatch department.

This is the area that must be used for the preparation and, where necessary, the packaging of orders received from the rest of the warehouses in the chain. To this end, it must have the right resources and no expense must be spared on these resources under any circumstances, since this is the part of the warehouse that has the greatest bearing on the company's public image and reputation.

The preliminary preparation of order on racking units simplifies the work of this area significantly.

In any event, order preparation personnel must report to the dispatch department, since this will be responsible for regulating their activities in response to external demand.

Consolidation of orders in the dispatch area. Source: Mecalux.

Chapter 6 - The design and construction of the warehouse

Sorting of orders by customer or route.
Source: Mecalux.

Buffer for orders
picked in dispatches
with automated
sorting.
Source: Mecalux.

In terms of operation, if the warehouse has a management system and this has been programmed correctly, the task of preparing orders is limited to placing the products in batches in an area set aside for that purpose.

This space reserved for the load must be sufficient to store all items being dispatched on a normal working day. However, it is both useful and necessary to plan an expansion area that can absorb unscheduled peaks in demand.

This outbound dispatch area must be as close as possible to the loading docks.

When orders are prepared in a separate area (particularly for picking or individual boxes), an appropriate consolidation area is required. Sorting conveyors that distribute the picked units by order or route can be added nearby. An example of this configuration can be seen in the top right-hand image.

Other alternatives to conveyors for taking consolidated loads to the dispatch area are pallet trucks, forklifts, and auto-guided vehicles (AGV and LGV). The image on the right shows an example of the use of laser-guided vehicles. These LGVs leave the pallets on five tables with rollers, from where they are collected by a shuttle which, in turn, deposits the loads in one of the various disbursement lines fitted with accumulating conveyors.

6.4. STARTING CONSTRUCTION AND THE IMPORTANCE OF FLOORING

Up to this point, this chapter has addressed the way a warehouse must be organised and the factors that influence its initial design. It is now time to move on to issues relating to the construction which affect the smooth running of the warehouse. The first element to be built, and which has a huge impact on the facility, is the flooring, the foundation on which all work takes place and which sustains the storage structures and external shell of the building.

To obtain the best performance in any industrial activity, it is vital that all elements of the production chain be constructed or manufactured on the basis of certain standards for quality, dimensions, etc.

In a warehouse, flooring is another element of the production chain. Therefore, it is vital that it meet certain construction conditions and under a series of scrupulous quality controls.

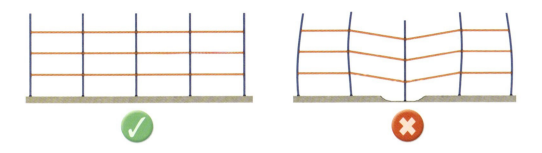

Each and every one of the elements that makes up a warehouse must be designed with a reasonable level of interdependence, and all must play their part in the overall handling operation. Both the designer and constructor of the facility must provide the proper conditions so that this work can be done as smoothly as possible.

When, as a general rule, the construction project for an industrial plant includes the creation of complex manufacturing plants and office blocks (in which aesthetic and decorative aspects are involved), there is a high risk of paying little attention to the installation of flooring that is suitable for supporting forklift trucks and storage elements.

It is surprising how often, for example, construction companies ignore the specifications for levelling the floor in high dock warehouses, arguing that such requirements are unrealistic and impossible to obtain when, in fact, they are not merely achievable, but essential.

As a result, there is a need to raise awareness among construction companies to ensure that the entire project is planned jointly and as a team with all the parties involved (including the providers of the storage solutions and the customer itself). This is a very important issue, and must be given sufficient attention.

In the sector, there are companies that create specialised flooring for high dock warehouses, and so it is possible to have highly effective floors that satisfy the levelling and resistance demands required by the devices working in these warehouses if they are to perform well.

6.4.1 Loads that flooring must withstand

The loads applied to the floor of a warehouse, which must be able to support the structure and all of its machinery, can be very considerable.

First, there is a series of static loads under the pillars of the racking units. Then there are some dynamic loads produced by the handling equipment itself.

Loads generated below the pillars of the racking units are point loads of great intensity, concentrated into a very small surface area and distributed evenly across the entire grating of the warehouse floor. These are disconcerting to most construction companies, causing them a great deal of alarm, since they are concentrated into a reduced surface area (that of the section of the pillar, just 80 to 100cm^2) and can reach 7 or 8 tonnes, or even more.

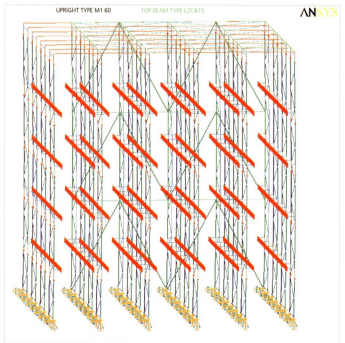

Source: Mecalux.

Dynamic loads, which are produced by handling devices moving along very narrow aisles, are also very large and vary according to the type of machine used. In the most extreme case, a stacker crane, this load can reach 18 tonnes and be concentrated into a small surface area, i.e. the footprint of the load wheel. Yet this effect can easily be minimised, since it is distributed across the entire guide rail along which the machine moves.

With other types of handling devices, the heaviest loads are produced when they are at rest. One very significant example is VNA trucks, whose greatest impact on the floor is when they are depositing or taking a weight at the maximum height and with the forks extended to the side. At that moment in time, the pressure on the load wheels is so high that the resistance limits of the floor can be exceeded, as can those of the wheels and their bearings. This force is transmitted directly to the sides of the aisles.

Other machines, such as counterbalanced forklifts, produce their maximum pressure on the floor when they are unloaded. This pressure is produced through the rear wheels, since this is the part where the counterbalance rests. When this forklift is loaded, there is a levelling of the load in the front (through the lever principle) and, although the total weight increases, this is distributed throughout the entire surface area of the machine. In this case, the load is also supported by a small surface area, that of the footprint of the tyres.

6.4.2 What do we mean by "suitable flooring"?

The purpose of flooring (and its foundations) is to withstand and transfer the loads just described from the surface of the floor downwards, until they reach the subsoil level. This applies both to dynamic loads (produced by devices in movement) and static loads (loads generated by the racking unit pillars). Therefore, suitable flooring is that which has the strength and stability required to meet these requirements.

The finish of the surface must be correctly level within the margins and tolerances required for a certain type of facility, with its specific devices and storage system. Achieving these objectives and qualities is the responsibility of the designers and construction companies.

6.4.3 The importance of the substrate

Before starting to install a good floor for the warehouse, it is essential to examine the substrate or firm layer on which the flooring must be firmly supported. The substrate is very variable and there can be enormous differences between two points, even if they are very close to each other and even within the same plot. For this reason, variations between points within a facility can be substantial.

The most important parameters that must be taken into account in relation to the substrate are its compressive strength, its tendency toward slippage, and its water-absorbing capacity. To determine the extent to which these factors are present in a specific location and to discover how these vary with depth, an analysis must be conducted on-site.

It is essential to ensure that the warehouse's substrate will behave appropriately given the load that will be borne by the flooring laid over that substrate. The exact location and area in which the facility will be built will be determined by the results of the necessary examinations.

The characteristics of this very important part of the floor are a decisive factor influencing the foundations. The foundations can be laid using anything from simple support pads or strips of varying width to, in extreme cases, a complete grating. At times, the characteristics of the substrate require a change in the position of the racking unit pillars, so that these coincide with the points that offer the necessary guarantees.

6.4.4 Composition of the flooring

The flooring is constructed on the substrate, which normally consists of a sub-base of agglomerated material, firmly compacted to withstand the load. This layer consists of any type of material, either natural or filler.

A concrete slab designed to support the pressure is placed onto the sub-base.

Image provided by Pavindus.

Image provided by Pavindus.

Concrete slabs have high compressive strength yet little tensile strength. During their curing process, the concrete contracts but the conglomerated sub-base does not. These contractions produce tensions in the slab, which can lead to accidental breakage and warping.

To minimise these problems, one must ensure that the surface of the substrate onto which the slab is placed is completely flat and smooth.

Once this point has been checked, a type of membrane or film is placed between the sub-base and the substrate to reduce the friction between the two. During the curing process, this film allows the slab to move independently and acts as a barrier against humidity, which is required to limit the loss of water in the concrete and achieve better curing.

Another measure to relieve the problem of potential breakage and very frequent warping consists of installing a light metal reinforcing mesh that remains close to the surface. This is a very common practice that allows for the construction of larger slabs with fewer expansion joints.

Image provided by Pavindus.

Reinforcement can also be provided using steel bars, which increase the resistance of the cured layer despite the inevitable contractions and slippage suffered by the concrete during the process.

Whether or not this reinforcement is included, it is inevitable that cracks will appear in the cured slabs, even if the greatest possible care has been taken in their construction. If these cracks are a casual and random, the impossibility of carrying out the appropriate filling due to their irregular shape invariably causes problems in terms of fluctuation in the loads.

Cracking is often induced so that these openings appear in specific places that can be observed and controlled. This is done by sawing the slab along a given strip, cut to a depth of between one-quarter and one-third of the thickness of the layer. In this way, the breakage takes place in these positions as opposed to others, and can easily be filled following a simple and clean process.

6.4.5 Joints in the flooring

Joints that can be found in the floors of the facility can be caused by various factors: they may be produced by individual strips in the flooring resulting from construction (produced by the end of one working day and the start of the next), created to avoid or surround columns or walls, or produced through cutting with saws. Irrespective of their origins they can be a source of problems, creating ruts caused by the continuous passing of forklift trucks.

Joints must be bonded or bolted to the structure of the sub-base to prevent transfers of movement beneath the adjacent slabs. In expansion joints, the bolts must be properly built in and in complete alignment. These bolts must have a free sliding end with a plastic sleeve embedded into one of the slabs.

On the other hand, the width of the expansion joints must be proportional to the thickness of the slab, although never more than 10mm. While they can be positioned at any point, it is always preferable to avoid places with very large point loads, i.e. far from the uprights of the racking units.

Warehouse for a consumer electronics company. Source: Mecalux.

6.4.6 The finishing layer

A third layer (the finishing layer) is applied to the sub-base and slab. It is monolithic, and constitutes the actual working surface.

Normally, the finishing layer consists of a granulite concrete mixture layer around 50mm thick.

The smoothness, hardness, and properties of this material are the most suitable to ensure that the flooring can withstand the conditions that exist when devices are in use in the warehouse.

At this point, a decision must be made in relation to a specific issue: should the finishing layer be done together with the slab and, thus, also be subject to its problems and treatments, especially with regard to the joints? Or should it be applied completely separately?

This layer can be applied independently and separately on a dry slab, but this requires the minimum thickness of the latter to be around 125mm. In this case, a new layer of concrete is laid, with the same fragility and warping problems as the main slab, since the surface of the finish will act and contract independently. To avoid this, a new separation film or membrane, which forms a very fine layer with no appreciable joints, must be added. Extremely fine concrete mixtures can be obtained by adding bitumen or a wide range of copolymers.

If using synthetic resins, a layer of only 3mm thick can be used, providing flooring with an excellent finish. If, however, a more comfortable surface is sought, one option is to use resins with greater resilience or, in other words, those with a greater elastic capacity to absorb deformation and return to its original shape when the pressure is removed.

One must bear in mind, however, that some layers created using special mixtures can be unstable or have insufficient complete granulite features, as occurs when using inappropriate resins to correct defects in the upper layer. These mixtures can end up being not only unstable, but also very expensive.

Warehouse floorings therefore need to be very carefully laid and require preventative maintenance while in use. In this way, imperfections and ruts that can be produced by the wheels of the forklifts when they move and cross the joints can be avoided and corrected. The use of such high specification finishing layers is not necessary in automated warehouses, since there is no movement over the floors

6.4.7 Laying the flooring

Once the basic concepts and the elements that make up the flooring have been explained, the next step is to analyse how it must be laid.

After preparing the foundation and levelling the sub-base, the next step is to decide what type of frame to use and the method for laying the flooring. This will vary depending on whether the flooring needs to be low- or high-tolerance.

The method for laying the floor is based on the use of a compaction rod, handled by two operators, which ensures that the concrete is perfectly embedded in the frame. Meanwhile, other operators, equipped with a road roller, move over the surface. This is a typical construction method, but although the road roller can help to smooth the surface it does not achieve the flattening required, as explained below.

To prevent heavy granulates and additives from falling to the bottom of the flooring or the layer, the concrete must not be manipulated to excess. To achieve good tolerances in the finished surface without the need for an extraordinary amount of work, the concrete must not be laid where there are significant height differences or holes in the sub-base.

Great care should be taken to ensure that the flooring is laid with a high degree of levelling; otherwise, it becomes progressively more difficult to obtain the required tolerances at each stage of construction. The frame used also has an influence here. For a relatively low-tolerance floor a wooden frame can be used, but if high tolerances are required at least the sides must be metal. The reason for this is that the accuracy of the linearity and levelling depends on the frame used. The more reliable this is, the better the results will be.

Success in creating the flooring depends not just on the use of the right frame, but also on another basic factor: the personnel who build it and their skills in using mechanical compacting and finishing devices.

Image provided by Pavindus.

Image provided by Pavindus.

A typical system for creating conventional flooring is to lay concrete strips that are finished as they are poured (this technique is illustrated in the top right-hand image).

This system can raise two problems when laying high-tolerance floorings. The first is disorganised access to the filling areas during the verification process. The second is the physical difficulty of laying broad strips. Therefore, long, narrow strips may be needed.

Strips 9m to 15m in length are currently achieved in premises with very high-tolerance floorings. This requires highly specialised personnel and the use of compaction rods specially designed for this purpose.

In any case, the most common method consists of creating wide or narrow alternative strips which are poured and finished. After a short period of curing, the rest is completed later.

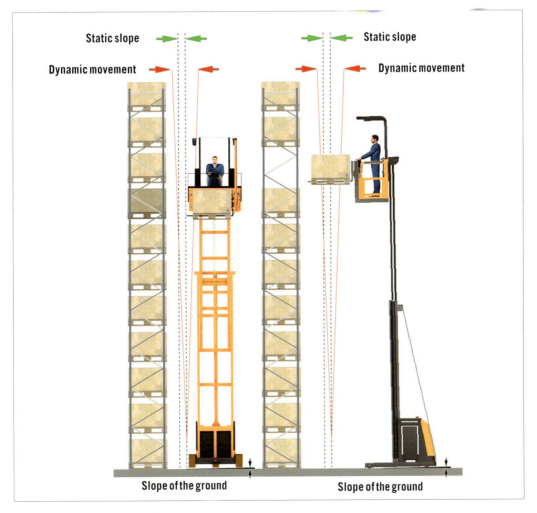

6.4.8 The importance of flatness

Apart from having to support point and dynamic loads, flooring must fulfil another function: it is the surface used for the movement of the handling equipment in the warehouse. Some of these demand a high degree of flatness in the flooring to avoid problems with the machines and, even more importantly, the facility itself.

The most serious problems are in systems with turret trucks (either trilateral or bilateral), due to their great lifting height and speed of operation. With these machines, the levelling of the flooring is an extremely critical factor, since they work with minute clearance in the aisles between the shelves. Any variation in the floor can lead to a tilting of the device which, no matter how small, poses a risk to the entire facility.

When a very narrow aisle forklift moves over an unlevelled surface it rocks. In the absence of a suspension system, this immediately transmits the motion to the mast and, given the considerable height of this device, a single millimetre of unevenness at the base can be converted, at great heights, into several centimetres of movement, as shown in the illustration on the previous page. This may lead to accidents with the loads or shelves being hit, with the danger that this entails.

Deviation will also decisively influence the height positioning of the forks in the head, creating the risk of blows when they are extended to collect or deposit a load.

Because of the above, and to avoid any danger or unfortunate incidents in the future, the flooring in a working environment with narrow aisle machines must be extremely level.

It is not enough for the construction company to assure that the surface is properly levelled. Experience shows that it is essential to have the relevant certification, and even the table of the sampling performed after completing the flooring.

Checking the levelling of the floor is hard work, requiring great care and the use of very accurate optical instruments.

Image provided by Pavindus.

The floor must comply with parameters that vary depending on the storage system used.

Levelling requirements differ depending on whether the facility is class 100, 200, 300, or 400. This class is determined by certain factors that are taken into account in the quality standard EN 15620. In terms of handling equipment used, storage systems are classified as follows:

CLASS	AISLE TYPE	SUITABLE FOR:
100	Very narrow	Pallet racking unit less than 18m high, with very narrow aisles and operated by automated stacker cranes.
200	Very narrow	Pallet racking unit with very narrow aisles, operated by automated stacker cranes and with an additional system for positioning unit loads.
300	Very narrow	Pallet racking unit with very narrow aisles, operated only by forklifts that do not need to turn in the aisle to load or unload units. The forklifts are guided along the aisle by mechanical or induction guides.
300 A		The operator continually moves up and down with the unit load and has manual height positioning. When the driver is at ground level, he or she has a closed circuit vision system or equivalent.
300 B		The operator remains at ground level at all times and does not have indirect vision devices.
400	Wide	Pallet racking unit with narrow aisles, wide enough to allow the forklifts to turn 90° for loading and unloading.
	Narrow	Pallet racking unit with aisles with less space, which can be used by more specialised forklifts.

Before analysing floor levelling requirements, it is necessary to explain the difference between floor levelling and flattening, for which the following illustration is used:

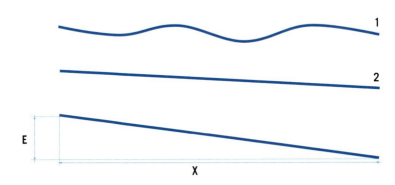

1: Profile of a levelled but not flat floor.
2: Profile of a flat but not levelled floor.
X: Distance between two fixed points on uneven ground (in this example, 3m).
E: Height difference between the two fixed points 3m apart.

The term "3m grid" when used in the following section refers to a set of points on the surface of the ground, 3m from each other in directions perpendicular to the building.

Requirements for a class 400 floor (for wide and narrow aisle).

All points in a 3m grid must be within ±15 mm of the horizontal reference. The table below contains the maximum values of E (the height difference between two points), according to the truck used and the height of the top level of the racking unit installed.

TYPE OF TRUCK	HEIGHT OF TOP LEVEL	MAXIMUM VALUE OF E
Without sideshift	Over 13m	2.25mm
Without sideshift	From 8m to 13m	3.25mm
Without sideshift	Up to 8m	4.00mm
With sideshift	Up to 13m	4.00mm

Requirements for a class 300 floor (very narrow aisle)

Facilities with trucks for class 300 (very narrow aisle) must meet very strict levelling requirements. One must bear in mind that a small slope of millimetres in the flooring can become centimetres of tilt for the mast of the truck, with the associated risk of accidents.

The requirements for proper levelling of the ground in 300 class facilities are specified in the standard EN 15620. The following table is provided as a summary to show the maximum values of parameter Z_{slope}, which indicates the cross-slope of the aisle between the centres of the front wheels of the truck and E, which represents the height difference between two adjacent points 3m apart.

HEIGHT OF TOP LEVEL	VALUE OF Z_{SLOPE}	MAXIMUM VALUE OF E
Over 13m	1.30mm	3.25mm
From 8m to 13m	2.00mm	3.25mm
Up to 8m	2.50mm	3.25mm

All points on the flooring must be within ±15 mm of the horizontal reference.

Requirements for class 100 and 200 floors (very narrow aisle)

For classes 100 and 200, despite being facilities with very narrow aisles, levelling requirements are not as strict as those for class 300 floors, given that the stacker crane does not move on the flooring, but rather on a lower guide rail.

In accordance with EN 15620, the flooring levelling requirements are as follows:

LENGTH OF THE AISLE	LEVELLING WITH RESPECT TO HORIZONTAL REF.
Up to 150m	±15mm
250m	±20mm

For intermediate aisle lengths (between 150m and 250m), the data can be interpolated linearly.

6.4.9 Racking unit clearances

As well as machinery, the levelling also affects the racking units. Racking units must have particular clearance once assembled and before being loaded. Again, it is EN 15620 that provides the acceptable parameters. These parameters must be observed in order to avoid the potential problem of machines colliding with the structures or hitting them when positioning loads into spaces.

Clearance values will depend on the type of facility and its class (100, 200, 300, or 400), with the data set out in the attached table referring to classes 300 and 400. The illustration accompanying the table indicates to which element each measure applies.

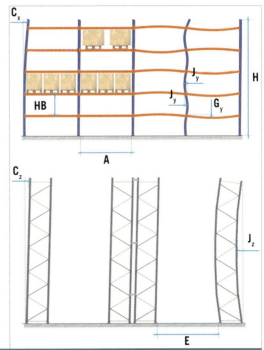

A: Clear width of the space.
E: Clear width of the aisle.
Cx: Lack of verticality.
Cz: Lack of verticality.
Jy: Straightness of the upright.
Jz: Straightness of the upright.
Gy: Straightness of the beam.
H: Height from the top of the base plate to the top of the upright.
HB: Height from the top of a beam to the top of the beam at the next level.

CLASS	CLEARANCES (mm)						
	A	E	C_x	C_z	J_x	J_z	G_y
300	±3	±5	±H/500	±H/500	±3 or ±HB/750	±H/500	±3 or ±A/500
400	±3	±15	±H/350	±H/350	±3 or ±HB/400	±H/500	±3 or ±A/500

In addition to the parameters set out above, the specific clearances contained in the standard EN 15620 must be adhered to.

6.4.10 Strength, porosity, bonding and durability of floorings

In addition to the construction characteristics mentioned earlier, warehouse floors must also have other features that make them particularly suitable for their intended use.

Thus, they must be resistant to abrasion, an issue addressed in UNE 41008, which establishes a scale known as MOHS that goes from 0 to 10.

They must also withstand compression, and be able to support over 500kg/cm^2 in general areas. Depending on the devices used, they may be required to support up to 800kg/cm^2 on the routes used for the movement of the devices. In terms of requirements for flexural resistance, these tend to be around 150 kg/cm^2 to 250kg/cm^2.

The floor must also be resistant to the effects of elements such as oil, grease, and hydrocarbons. While these materials are not stored in the facility, they are used for the forklifts and there will inevitably be stains on the floor. Allowable porosity must be very low (below 3%).

The flooring must form a monolith together with the support base to prevent slippage and downward movements that cause bumps on the surface.

Finally, the floor must be durable and resistant to wear and tear, although it is inevitable that over time ruts will form as a result of the constant movement of the wheels of devices along the same routes again and again and given their tremendous weight. These ruts can become very deep and cause misalignments in the facility, with the resulting implicit risks.

Using a company that specialises in flooring for narrow aisle forklifts is, undoubtedly, the best way to ensure a perfect and longest-lasting surface. Skimping in this respect can seriously compromise the entire facility. A very expensive project can be ruined due to savings in one area that appears less important, but which in practice is crucial.

6.5 WHEN SHOULD SELF-SUPPORTING WAREHOUSES BE USED?

The flooring discussed in the previous section is used as the base on which the warehouse and the structures used to store the goods must be built. There is one special case where these two aspects come together: self-supporting warehouses.

With self-supporting warehouses, the structure of the building consists exclusively of the racking units themselves, with the roof attached to these. Inside, goods are handled using completely automated and semi-automated elements.

Chapter 6 - The design and construction of the warehouse

Warehouse for the car industry. Source: Mecalux.

This type of structure has all the advantages of very high storage (over 40m) while at the same time being an affordable option, in that there is no need to construct a civil building. As a result, this type of facility is becoming increasingly popular.

To examine the elements that make up a facility of this type, it is important to first explain the two types of devices that can operate in this type of warehouse: fixed-route and free-moving. The clearances used in the racking units and aisles, as well as the characteristics of the devices, are vital in developing the internal structure of the building. As an aside, we also explain how other elements that form part of automated warehouses, such as conveyors, are integrated.

6.5.1 Fixed-route devices

Fixed-route devices are devices or machines (normally automated) used in a warehouse that always follow the same route on a pre-established circuit.

This category of devices includes conveyors, electrified monorail systems, automated guided vehicles (AGV and LGV), and, of course, stacker cranes.

Other vehicles commonly used in a warehouse, such as all types of forklifts, cannot be included in this group. Despite operating along routes inside the warehouse that are more or less pre-established, guided and wire-guided turret trucks do not belong to this group either, since they can move freely around the warehouse without restriction if so desired.

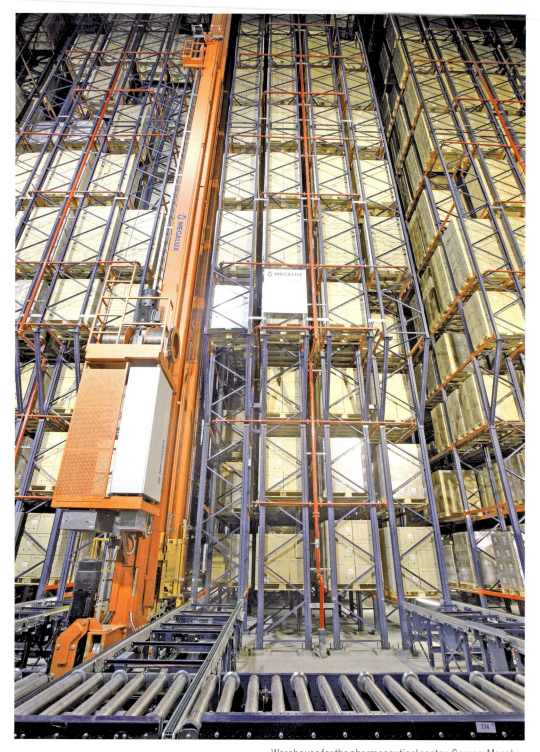
Warehouse for the pharmaceutical sector. Source: Mecalux.

Fixed-route devices are ideal for use within a self-supporting warehouse. However, it is useful to establish how to use them and in what way. This issue is addressed below.

Precision positioning

The different systems within this group have elements that guarantee that they are correctly positioned inside the facility or among the racking units at all times. Stacker cranes, for example, have laser rangefinders, electronic stopping systems, devices for dynamic detection for accurate positioning, etc.

These devices act as the eyes and ears of the automated systems, so that the devices used are perfectly positioned at all times and can handle loads without bumping into, or bumping the goods into, the racking units. They can also, for example, detect whether a space is already occupied or whether there are obstacles impeding their movement. These positioning systems are essential in the safe construction of very high self-supporting warehouses.

Warehouse for a publishing company. Source: Mecalux.

Chapter 6 - The design and construction of the warehouse

Supports for fixed-route elements

Supports for the fixed-route devices are designed on the basis of the specific characteristics of each. Roller conveyors are supported on stands attached to the floor. Stacker cranes are supported on two rails, with one attached to the floor and the other attached to the upper bracing of the racking units.

A. Supports for roller conveyors

As explained in Chapter 3, roller conveyors are adapted to the features of the working cycle and the fixed route that must be taken by the goods being moved. To this end, they consist mainly of straight stretches, which can be split into branches using various types of standardised switches. There is also the option to connect conveyors on different height levels by using lifts.

These devices are manufactured in standard sections varying in length between 1.5m and 3m. Depending on the characteristics of the floor and the weight of the section and load, at least one support stand is fitted to each end of a section. These stands are bolted into the ground using adjustable bearing plates.

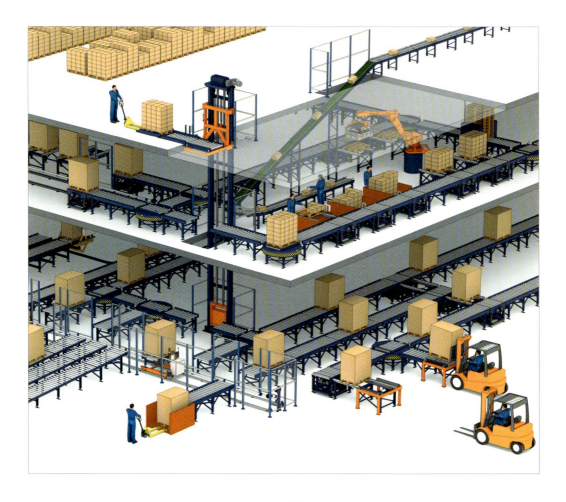

Chapter 6 - The design and construction of the warehouse

At times, conveyors are located at points where loads from different sources within the warehouse come together, so special fixing to the floor may be required depending on the total weight of the group of transport elements and loads.

B. Supports for stacker cranes

Due to their height, stacker cranes require more support than conveyors. They use two rails, with one fixed to the floor and another fixed to the upper bracing of the racking unit's aisles.

The lower rail must be extremely strong, given that a machine of this type can transmit loads in excess of 18 tonnes to each wheel.

The lower rails used are at least 150mm high and have welded footings of 250mm x 150mm installed along the rail every 450 mm. These footings are fixed to the ground using four screws (two fixed and another two for levelling), which come with a nut and locknut and have a pathway below ground level of around 150mm.

For large-scale stacker cranes, which are commonly used in self-supporting warehouses, on the other hand, the upper rail is fixed to the highest bracings of the racking units, since there is no other structure above these (even the roof is attached to the racking units).

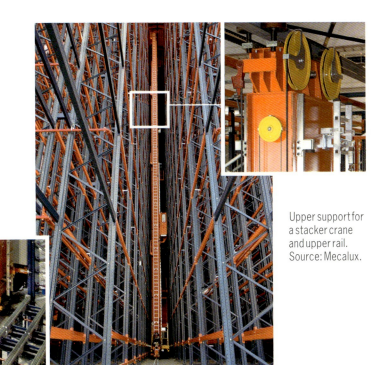

Detail of a lower support or frame for a stacker crane and of a rail. Source: Mecalux.

Upper support for a stacker crane and upper rail. Source: Mecalux.

Chapter 6 - The design and construction of the warehouse

Source: Mecalux.

Clearances for fixed-route devices

In self-supporting warehouses margins are very tight (practically only a few millimetres). Therefore, it is very important to specify the minimum clearances that must be observed by the designer.

For design purposes, the critical points that require maximum attention in terms of clearances are the working aisles, the load levels, and the longitudinal positioning of the loads.

Clearances in working aisles

The required width of a working aisle in a self-supporting warehouse is determined by the circulation space required by a stacker crane moving through the aisle and the width of the loads that will be transported.

Source: Mecalux.

Given that these machines are guided at both the top and the bottom, the chance of deviation from the route is almost zero. There is only a calculated risk of buckling, caused by the great height of these devices. In general, this buckling has been foreseen by the manufacturer, who will have implemented the necessary measures to prevent this.

Positioning of loads on racking units

The greatest problem in a warehouse is normally due to the potential for the loads to fall. Some goods may protrude from the racking units, and take up more space than planned.

This type of problem can be avoided by correctly establishing the characteristics of the units that will be stored in the facility, before it is designed, and strictly complying with the standards for safety and the use of devices once the facility is operational. Determining clearances for the positioning of loads is an issue of vital importance at this stage.

Clearances are the distances that must be left between unit loads and elements of the racking unit. They are expressed in relation to the total size of the units, including any overhang that may exist.

Depending on the weight of the goods and the height of the warehouse planned, two or three units may be placed lengthwise in each compartment.

Chapter 6 - The design and construction of the warehouse

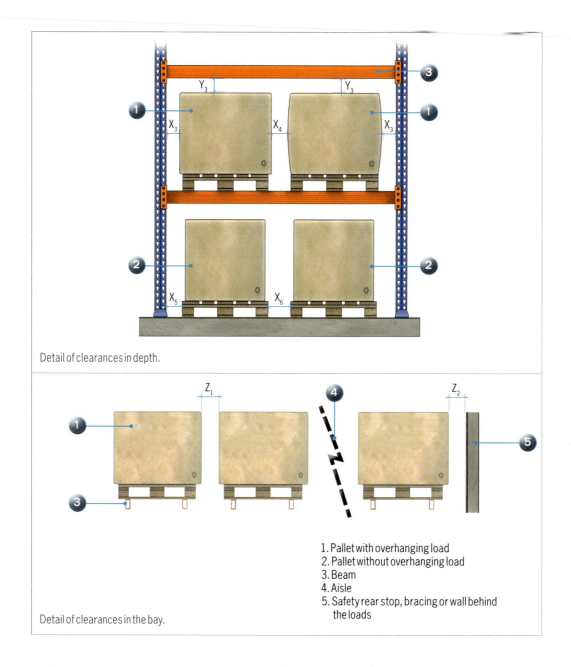

Detail of clearances in depth.

Detail of clearances in the bay.

1. Pallet with overhanging load
2. Pallet without overhanging load
3. Beam
4. Aisle
5. Safety rear stop, bracing or wall behind the loads

The diagrams here show clearances, in both the bay and the depth, when there are two pallets per bay. The measures represented by letters (X_1, X_2, etc.) are defined in the tables below.

The minimum clearances that must be maintained are defined in EN 15620 and applied depending on the class of racking unit being planned (class 100, 200, stacker cranes, or class 300, turret truck, or class 400, reach and counterbalance trucks).

MINIMUM CLEARANCE FOR CLASS 400

Height from the ground to the level of the beam (mm)	Clearances in the bay		Clearance in depth	
	Horizontal X_3, X_4, X_5 y X_6 (mm)	Vertical Y_3 (mm)	Z_1 (mm)	Z_2 (mm)
3000	75	75	100	50
6000	75	100		
9000	75	125		
13,000	100	150		

MINIMUM CLEARANCE FOR CLASS 300 (300A AND 300B)

Height from the ground to the level of the beam (mm)	Horizontal X_3, X_4, X_5 y X_6 (mm)		Vertical Y_3 (mm)		Clearance in depth	
	300A	300B	300A	300B	Z_1 (mm)	Z_2 (mm)
3000	75	75	75	75	100	50
6000	75	75	75	100		
9000	75	75	75	125		
12,000	75	100	75	150		
15,000	75	100	75	175		

In class 100 and 200 facilities, clearances are set on the basis of multiple parameters, such as the dimensions of the unit loads, the height of the warehouse, the single or double-deep layout, and stacker crane devices. Therefore, a specific plan must be developed to set the clearances in each specific case. The minimum specifications for a single-deep warehouse provided in the following table are for illustrative purposes only.

MINIMUM CLEARANCE FOR CLASS 100 AND 200

Clearances in the dock			Clearance in depth	
Horizontal		Vertical	Z_1 (mm)	Z_2 (mm)
X_3, X_5 (mm)	X_4, X_6 (mm)	Y_3 (mm)		
75	90	85	100	75

6.5.2 Use of free-moving devices

Self-supporting warehouses can be built in which goods are handled by free-moving devices (trilateral turrets, bilateral turrets, or reach trucks).

Nonetheless, one must bear in mind that turret-type devices cannot exceed 15m in height and reach trucks 10.5m. In addition, wider aisles than those normally used for stacker cranes are needed. A very flat floor is also essential, particularly if using turret-type trucks.

An important factor is that personnel are required inside the racking units to handle the load and perform operations.

Despite these issues, a self-supporting warehouse with free-moving machines is a good option and a worthwhile one too, since it is a specific construction, without pillars, and generally cheaper and faster to build than conventional building systems.

Self-supporting cold chamber with turret trucks. Source: Mecalux.

Supports for free-moving devices

Free-moving devices sit directly on the ground and, for safer, faster operations in the aisles, the turret-type truck requires a guidance system. This can be mechanical, wire-guided, or laser-guided (see Chapter 3).

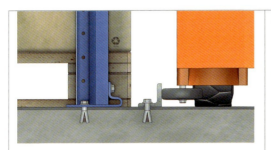

Guided with LPN 50 rail
The pallets sit directly on the floor. An L-shaped rail attached to the floor acts as the guide.

Guided with UPN 50 rail
The pallets sit on rails placed on the ground or on beams. A U-shaped rail attached to the floor acts as the guide.

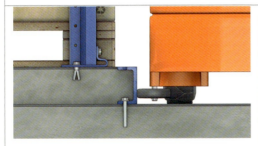

Guided with UPN 100 rail forming island
The space between the guides for the aisles is filled with concrete, forming an island on which the racking units sit.

Wire-guided
A wire buried in the ground produces a magnetic field which the machine detects and follows as a guide.

Clearances for free-moving devices

The clearances for free-moving devices are very similar to those for their fixed-route counterparts. However, one must remember that the method used to collect and deposit loads used by the first group differs from that used by the second group.

In general, free-moving devices have turning heads to collect and deposit loads on the left or right side of the racking unit. In contrast, fixed-route devices use telescopic heads.

This characteristic means that the needs in terms of aisle width are significantly different. When using europallets 1200mm deep, a turret truck will need an aisle of 1700mm to 1900mm wide, depending on the efficiency achieved with the device, while a stacker crane will need an aisle only 1500mm to 1600mm wide.

When specifying clearances in a warehouse designed to be operated with a turret-type truck, one must consider three measures when determining the width of the aisle: the distance between the fronts of the guide rails (marked as A in the accompanying illustration), the length between the fronts of the loads (B), and the separation of the fronts of the racking units (C). One must also take into account the tolerances of the flatness of the floor discussed earlier.

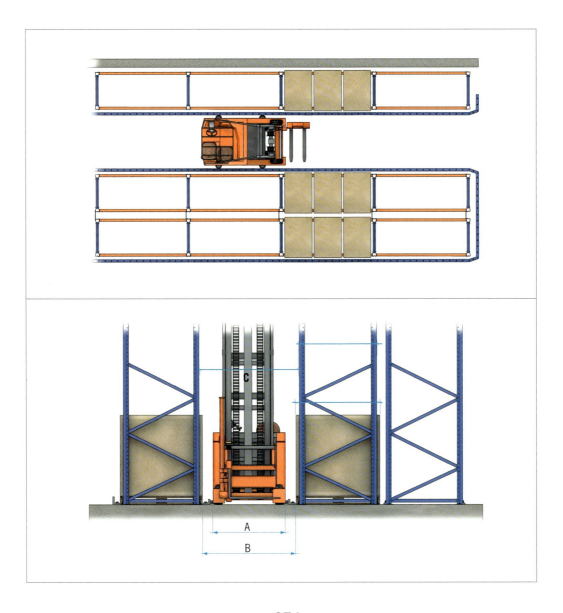

6.5.3 The external shell for self-supporting warehouses

As explained earlier, this type of structure consists of flooring on which the storage structures are built, along with the racking units between which the handling devices (which can be either fixed-route or free-moving) move. These are the main elements that comprise the interior of self-supporting warehouses and, along with the loads, are protected by two components which, together with everything inside, make up the building as such: the roof and the walls. Let's have a look at these.

A common option when creating the roof for this type of warehouse is to use steel panels that are either bolted or welded onto a frame which, in turn, is fixed to the superstructure of the racking units. This frame can be constructed as a sloping gable or shed roof, or even as a flat roof (as in the photograph below), depending on local climatic conditions.

Warehouse for a beverage company. Source: Mecalux.

In terms of elements used to cover the sides of these buildings, the wall normally consists of panels that can be fixed in three different ways: either directly to the structure of the racking units, with an intermediate frame attached to that structure, or, as a third option, with an intermediate fame attached to an independent frame.

The structure can also be enclosed using a concrete wall up to a certain height. This option is a common choice for facilities with adjacent buildings used by the auxiliary services in the warehouse.

The choice of one system or another must be made based on a range of different factors, such as the height of the building, the normal wind strength where the facility is built, the thermal and climate conditions there, and the material used for the walls. There are other important aspects relating to the structure and installation of the building in self-supporting warehouses, but these are more architectural issues than industrial design issues, and are not within the scope of this manual.

6.5.4 Combined construction systems

It is common for these self-supporting systems only to be used to build storage areas, i.e. the warehouse. Other areas, such as reception, dispatch, order preparation, etc., are normally housed in conventional low-level buildings attached to this.

This option reduces costs, since conventional construction methods are used only when strictly necessary.

Self-supporting cold chamber. First phase in service, second phase in execution. Source: Mecalux.

6.6 THE DESIGN AND CONSTRUCTION OF ACCESS POINTS

The previous sections have discussed the elements that make up a warehouse, and at times have made reference to the areas outside the warehouse. The information in this manual and its objective would not be complete without addressing this aspect, which is part of the design and planning of a facility for the storage and management of goods. Outdoor areas and access points to the facility are designed, developed, and built along with the warehouse, and play an important role in its operations, safety, and productivity.

6.6.1 Greater safety

According to workplace accident statistics, activities related to storage and distribution are among the most dangerous in terms of incidents involving people. According to insurance companies, they have the second-highest accident rate in industrial operations, with a figure twice the average rate.

Most of these accidents can be avoided through the appropriate planning of walls and access points, so it is vital to pay attention to these elements. Furthermore, proper design will not only make the facility safer, but also satisfy the present and future needs of the warehouse.

Logistics centre for a distribution company. Source: Mecalux.

6.6.2 Factors influencing access points

There are ongoing changes in the handling, storage, and distribution of materials that could dramatically affect the design of the walls. Examples include the use of the just-in-time approach for handling materials, and the use of large lorries.

The influence of just-in-time

As discussed at the start of this manual, just-in-time is an approach to product generation and distribution that seeks to adapt and adjust as far as possible to actual market demand at any time. In doing so, it aims to manufacture or store exactly the quantity of items demanded by the consumer, no more and no less. This leads to greater competitiveness, commercial capacity, and profitability.

Just-in-time (JIT) is increasingly used in large production plants. The most immediate consequence of this is that manufacturers require a constant supply of materials from warehouses or external production plants. This, in turn, leads to the need for these supply points to use JIT policies as well, and to supply components and raw materials at the rate demanded by assembly lines or supply the market with the products it demands.

To be able to offer this service, distribution centres must be very well-run warehouses capable of receiving and dispatching huge quantities of goods in very short periods of time. Therefore, it is important for these warehouses to have large access areas, equipped to provide the necessary speed and accuracy, as well as high-capacity entrances and exits in which automated loading and unloading systems can be used, such as those illustrated in the images shown here. These systems were discussed at the beginning of this chapter.

Source: Mecalux.

Large vehicles

The second most important factor in the design and development of the access points in a warehouse is the increasingly common use of large lorries. The use of these vehicles is increasing as a result of the need to reduce transport costs, since the return on each journey is greater.

The size and weight of road lorries is determined by regulations in force in each country, which generally establish a total maximum length for road trains (18m), articulated lorries (16.5m), and semi-trailers (13.6m). The maximum weight per axle cannot exceed 14 tonnes (single axle) or 18 tonnes (tandem axle), with a total maximum weight per vehicle of 40 tonnes.

However, many European Union countries have road trains longer than 18m and the disappearance of borders within the EU and increasingly common use of intermodal traffic, which combines railways with roads, mean that this trend is gradually spreading to other countries, including Spain.

It is increasingly common to see 48- and even 53-foot long containers (14.6m and 16.15m, respectively) in ports around Europe. For transport inland, these require the use of longer semi-trailers than those allowed under the directives. Furthermore, it is increasingly common for "swap bodies" to be delivered using intermodal transport. These have a minimum weight of 37 tonnes and often reach 45 tonnes. Thus, their land transport also exceeds the limitations stipulated in the directives, which set a limit of 40 tonnes per vehicle.

Long lorries create serious problems when designing manoeuvring areas for vehicles. Therefore, this issue must be addressed in advance and provision made for sufficiently large areas for this purpose.

It is not merely the length of the lorries that is limited: their height is also limited to a maximum of 4m. The manufacturers of these vehicles have designed models known as "high cube", which have larger trailers. To offer this greater capacity without exceeding the maximum height, the floor has been lowered. In terms of the design of the warehouse, this lower floor must be taken into account because it means that there will be lorries with different floor heights that must be unloaded and loaded in the docks.

6.6.3 Design of access points for warehouses

As a result of the above, great care must be taken when designing the general access points for the warehouse. Good planning will reduce the risk of accidents and minimise potential interference between lorries and people moving around these areas.

One of the most versatile access designs is in the shape of a "Y", as shown in the image below. This design offers considerable advantages: with this layout, vehicles entering the warehouse can quickly leave the road without blocking the traffic. At the same time, lorries leaving the warehouse can join the traffic on the road. Preferably, the access road to the facility must have two lanes and must be at least twice the length of the longest lorry.

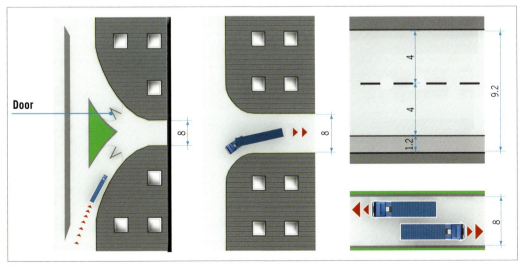

Dimensions in metres.

Service roads can be double or single. The latter are preferable, since they allow for better, safer circulation. Service roads with two lanes must be no less than 8m wide, whole single-lane roads must be no less than 4m wide. In the case of the former, these measures allow two vehicles 2.5m wide to pass each other with a space of 1m in the middle and on each side. In the case of the latter, a vehicle can move with a space of 0.75m on each side. If the road must also be used by pedestrians, a strip 1.2m wide must be added, duly separated by line markings or, even better, by a barrier 1.2m high.

6.6.4 Construction of the road surface

Given that today one must consider the possibility of working with lorries that weigh between 20 to 70 tonnes, access points must be constructed to withstand these loads. In areas where there can be severe frosts, the recommendation is to use a perfectly compacted sub-base, covered with a layer of agglomerated gravel 25cm thick, topped with another layer of reinforced concrete 25cm thick. This road surface has a minimum life of 20 years, with almost nothing more than the minimum maintenance required. In less severe weather conditions, it is enough to have a compacted base, covered with a layer of agglomerated gravel 25cm thick and finished off with a layer of asphalt 15cm thick.

6.6.5 Traffic planning

Once the access points have been designed and built, this resource must be used as efficiently as possible. To achieve this, it is essential to organise the traffic entering and leaving the facilities. The best way to do this is to establish a counter-clockwise direction of movement, as this will result in greater visibility, more safety, and maximum efficiency.

Aerial view of a warehouse. Source: Mecalux.

With this traffic planning, drivers can back into the docks with a direct view of the docks and of the semi-trailer at the same time. This is because while reversing the vehicle, the driver only has to keep his gaze fixed on the wing mirror located on the side closest to him, to the left of the cabin.

6.6.6 Access doors

The movement of vehicles and people into and out of the facilities can be controlled by doors. For the safety of the people and property, the use of separate doors for pedestrians and vehicles is recommended. Where one-way 4m wide lanes are used, the door must be 5m wide. When the access road is two-way and 8m wide, the door must be 9m wide.

6.6.7 Factors that influence the layout of the docks

Before deciding on the type of dock to be used at access points to the storage building, it is necessary to design the layout of these outside the facilities. This involves various factors.

The first is deciding whether or not a just-in-time policy will be used. If this approach will be used, the positioning of the docks can become critical and each of the areas that will be served by the docks, the types of loads, the frequency of deliveries, the accessibility of the area, the space requirements of the lorries, etc. will need to be studied carefully.

Another key aspect in determining the layout of the docks is whether they are going to be used by large capacity lorries. Current trends indicate that vehicles that are longer and wider and have greater volume than current vehicles will be increasingly common. Therefore, when planning the location of the docks, it would be useful to ensure that there is a large area for the approach, manoeuvring and build-up of large vehicles.

The third important factor in the design of docks is the existence of slopes in the land. Slopes in the dock areas must always be as small as possible: the gentler the slope, the less chance of errors and accidents. If a warehouse is going to be used by large volume vehicles, such as high cubes, it may be necessary to install special devices, such as hydraulically adjustable docks or lifts in the ground.

The aspects that influence the layout of the docks are not merely technical, but also aesthetic and organisational. When planning the warehouse, effort must be made to keep the entrance and exit areas separate from the rooms used for offices (which, in general, are adjacent to the warehouse). This is not always possible: the best position for docks is the lane to the side of the building, and the general orientation of the complex will determine whether or not this separation is possible.

There are also production factors that must be borne in mind. One option to increase the efficiency of the docks is to combine reception and dispatch into a single area. This solution drastically reduces costs and, above all, increases the use of handling equipment and personnel. However, if this is justified by the volume of the material flow, there can also be separate access points for each function (some for reception and others for dispatch).

The details taken into account when determining the positioning of the docks in the facility may have a significant influence on their efficiency. One must consider that these access points will be constantly opened and closed, so they can have a direct impact on the environmental conditions inside the building. It is therefore helpful to take into account prevailing wind directions and reduce any problems that could be caused by weather conditions.

Lastly, it is important to foresee the possible future expansion of the warehouse and ensure that any space added in the future can be incorporated into the current space in a logical manner. As a result, there must be a supplementary area where new docks can be installed without this affecting the smooth running of the activity in the warehouse.

6.6.8 How many access points are necessary?

One aspect that must be decided when designing the docks is how many docks to create.

The number of access positions to be created in the facility will depend on the flow of materials, the volume of deliveries, the time when most goods are received, the time required to unload and transfer all loads received to their destination point, and the number of handling devices available.

Nevertheless, there are three aspects that must be taken into account to ensure that the number of access points is sufficient.

First, the set of docks must be designed so that the number of docks can be rapidly increased in future developments. The initial construction can include easily removed panels in the walls, making it easier to create new doors, and covered pits, for the same purpose.

It must be remembered that the costs of remodelling a dock are substantially less when its future expansion has been planned for and this type of measure has been taken.

Second, it is recommended that a position be made available for any rejected trailers or containers. This position must be situated outside one of the doors. One of the hidden pits for the future installation of a lift can be used for this purpose.

Chapter 6 - The design and construction of the warehouse

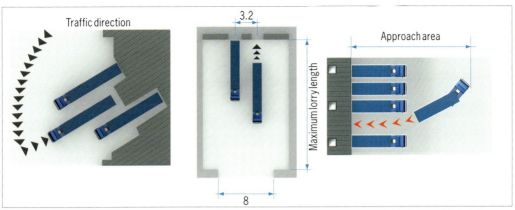

Dimensions in metres.

Finally, transport companies normally make deliveries in the morning and collections in the afternoon. This can produce bottlenecks at peak times and lead to significant additional costs. As a result, the number of positions for lorries must be equal to the maximum number that could arrive at the same time in the loading and unloading areas.

6.6.9 Asphalt and weight

When an asphalt surface is used for the access roads to the warehouse, a strip of concrete must be laid in the area adjacent to the loading docks. This measure is necessary because when the semitrailers are separated from their tractor units, they are only supported by their legs. If this separation takes place on warm asphalt, these vehicles can sink into the surface due to their great weight. The width of this strip will depend on the length of the vehicles.

6.6.10 Ramps for forklifts

Another construction issue that should not be forgotten when creating access points is the elements used so that the forklift trucks can move from the warehouse building to the area where the lorries circulate. This frequent requirement is met by the use of ramps (either concrete or with a dock lift), as explained at the start of this chapter.

6.6.11 Special features of the docks

There are other decisions that must be taken with respect to these elements, mainly what type of entry must be created in the building or in its surrounding area, its height, and so on. These issues are addressed below.

The ideal approach dock

For the approach, the ideal solution is the built-in type of dock. Its entry is almost at the same level as the height of the lorries, and slightly separated from the building to help drain rainwater.

While very easy to build, it can pose a danger to the safety of the building, particularly when using semi-trailer support legs to carry out manoeuvres. When these supports, and specifically those at the front end, are withdrawn too quickly, the tilt of the trailer can cause this to touch the walls of the building.

Sloping entrance area

When the building is located on a slope, the entry area can be sloped to give the dock the appropriate height.

The problem with this type of access is that if a lorry or semi-trailer falls too quickly, the upper part of the trailer could hit the walls of the warehouse.

There are other disadvantages to this sort of access point, such as the possible accumulation of snow in winter, which would have to be removed; probable drainage problems; and issues about safety when driving, which could require the use of accurate markings or even protective barriers.

Image provided by Hispanox.

Enclosed docks

Enclosed docks are normally ruled out due to their high construction costs, as well as the disadvantage of insufficient ventilation in the warehouse. Nevertheless, they offer a number of benefits that could justify the investment required.

First of all, it is easier to control the temperature inside the warehouse with this option, something that benefits both the goods and the personnel. It also reduces the risk of theft. Finally, it allows more use to be made of the capacity of the warehouse.

Source: Mecalux.

Saw tooth docks

Creating access points in the form of steps or a saw tooth pattern is not very common, but when there is little room for manoeuvre this configuration can be a good way to create the required number of docks. Their biggest disadvantage is that they are generally used for loading and unloading, and provide very little space for this type of work. In addition, approach traffic must be coordinated appropriately to provide good access at the correct angle.

If the use of open docks is required due to the conditions of the building, one dock may be under cover, with a minimum penetration of 6m for the loading and unloading of certain types of goods.

Image of the docks. Source: Mecalux.

Images provided by Hörmann.

Planning the approach area

Once the types of dock have been analysed, the next step is to examine how to use the space just in front of them. The approach area refers to the area that goes from the external face of the

Chapter 6 - The design and construction of the warehouse

Approach area required for the manoeuvre to enter and exit a position, with traffic moving counter clockwise		
Total lorry length	Width of berth between doors	Minimum approach area necessary
15	3.6	32
	4.3	31
17	3.6	35
	4.3	34
18	3.6	38
	4.3	37
20	3.6	41
	4.3	40

Dimensions in mm.

dock to the first obstruction found, which could be a building, fence, road, etc. The total space that needs to be assigned to this area will depend on factors such as the size of the tractor units and the semi-trailers, the width of the berths, etc.

Developments in industrial vehicles mean that their capacities and dimensions are in a constant state of flux. While the table above sets out the measures recommended for lorries of different lengths, it would be useful to confirm with the manufacturers by requesting specific data on each type of vehicle before designing this area.

Heights of the docks

Most docks for industrial vehicles are built to a height of 1.2m (in the image below, this distance is represented by X). However, there are many lorries whose cradle (the platform on which the trailer or container rests) is considerably higher or lower than this level.

If the dock is used for high-volume lorries, it must be designed for cradles ranging in height from 0.9m to 1m. Refrigerated lorries can have a floor height of 1.3m to 1.4m. Low chassis semi-trailers and removal trucks used for moving furniture normally have a cradle height of 0.9m or less. Finally, for rigid lorries one must plan for a range of heights from 0.9m to 1.2m.

Use with special lorries

On occasions, the docks can be used by special lorries with an access height above or below that of the planned dock. Measures can be taken to be able to operate with these vehicles.

One option is to use portable lifts or hydraulic jacks to lift the rear of the lorries with a low trailer. Variable height docks can also be added during construction.

If there is enough room, an extra long and variable height hydraulic dock can be used to minimise the slope produced by the height difference. There are hydraulic docks up to 3.7m long and up to 300m to 450mm high, which provides excellent flexibility and adaptability.

Lifts can also be installed in the approach area next to the dock. Using these lifts, the cradle is raised or lowered to the desired height. The fifth option is the construction of a dock under which a hydraulic lift is installed.

The following is a list of the most common types of lorries and their typical trailer height, to help with the design of the height of the docks.

TYPE OF LORRY	TRAILER HEIGHT	
	Minimum (mm)	Maximum (mm)
Container lorry	1.4	1.6
Refrigerated	1.25	1.5
Double-axle semi-trailer	1.1	1.3
City delivery	1.1	1.2
"Jumbo" semi-trailer	0.9	1.0
Removal	0.6	0.9
Van	0.5	0.75
Rigid lorries	0.9	1.2
Platforms	1.2	1.5

In conclusion, as we have seen, there are many variables that can affect the design and layout of the access points and docks of a facility. Again, in order to achieve the best result it is vital first and foremost to analyse the specific needs of the warehouse in question.

6.7 SAFETY

The last part of this chapter on the construction of warehouses addresses the installation of safety elements, an issue of utmost importance. As mentioned at the beginning of this chapter, the activities carried out in this type of plant involve a high level of risk which must be avoided at all cost.

The following sections address the aspects considered essential for providing the best possible safety conditions, such as the risk of fire, fire prevention, the reduction of the consequences of fire, and, finally, the safe layout of loads in the warehouse.

Each country, region, and local council may have its own fire prevention and health and safety regulations. The planner must keep these in mind and comply with them at all times. This will avoid problems later due to both the eventual situations which could occur, and the administrative and legal consequences arising from any breach of these regulations.

6.7.1 Fire risk

There are many building and safety standards written by experts that comprehensively address fire-related issues, how they start and spread, and how they are detected and extinguished. These are very complex issues, and not within the scope of this manual. Here, we simply aim to provide some general advice to reduce the risk and limit the consequences of any incidents.

In modern storage facilities, which have very narrow aisles and consist of structures usually between 10m and 20m high (and, in some cases, even exceed 20m), extinguishing fires manually can be extremely difficult, if not impossible. Even in warehouses with racking units only 4m or 5m high, it is advisable to install integrated sprinklers, rather than rely solely on equipment mounted in the roof of the warehouse, as is common. Part of the process of designing a warehouse must involve consulting a fire prevention protection expert.

Thus, fire safety must be a matter of primary concern when planning the facility. Leaving its design to the end can lead to consequences such as the warehouse being unsafe or the project having to be extensively modified, or even halted. The resources used to help personnel evacuate the building in the event of an incident, for example, can influence the design of spaces and even the choice of handling devices.

Under normal circumstances, the description of the facility must include detection devices (flames, colour or smoke) and automated or semi-automated fire extinguishers (water, foam or gas). It should be remembered that smoke is not only a fire risk; it also endangers the health of the personnel and the condition of materials stored.

The potential theoretical interference with handling devices may affect the layout of the racking units, their heights, their loads, and the shape of the devices. Given that the risks to be taken are the responsibility of the designer, the minimisation of these risks must be one of his or her primary concerns.

Fire prevention systems at the facility

In essence, fire prevention consists of minimising the situations that could lead to a fire, i.e. risks.

The storage of inflammable or combustible products must be avoided as far as possible. In the event that this cannot be avoided, these materials must be protected against risks arising from the proximity of smokers, faulty wiring, and any ancillary activities normally associated with maintenance teams, such as welding.

It should also be remembered that products stored in a warehouse tend to "perspire", since they are normally products of low combustibility, wrapped or packaged in cardboard, which ignites easily. Indeed, it is common to find cardboard packages which, for cost reasons, have not been treated against fire.

Fire protection system in racking units with VNA. Source: Mecalux.

Similarly, goods are normally stacked on wooden pallets, which are also likely to burn and, given their mobile nature, are also not treated to prevent fire.

These conditioning factors determine the degree of commitment required to adopt the most appropriate criteria in each business. A detailed examination of these factors can provide certain benefits in terms of risk reduction.

Cardboard, for example, may be labelled, sealed or wrapped for advertising or distribution purposes using materials that produce a large amount of smoke or toxic gases. In addition, the cardboard itself can be an inflammable material when there is a fire. In many cases, this problem can be avoided through the simple use of plastic boxes, even those of lower quality than cardboard boxes, but which offer the same functionality.

Another example of how all the details must be taken into account is the storage of loose metal parts, which, when kept in metal containers, can be a high-risk product due to the possible presence of waste oil at the bottom of the container. As a result, in the design of the operation and the warehouse, there must be a system for inspecting and cleaning these elements before they are introduced into the system.

Fire protection system in an automated warehouse. Source: Mecalux.

Shrink-wrap plastic, which is used to wrap the pallets, on the other hand, makes them more inflammable, although its main contribution to the risk of fire relates to the spread of fire, rather than starting it. As a result, a load of cans of inflammable liquid covered in shrink-wrap plastic is better protected against fire than it would be without this wrapping, because in the event of a fire the plastic acts as a barrier, reducing the increase in the temperature of the goods and delaying their point of ignition, and therefore the point at which they could burn.

In the event of a fire, cardboard packaging acts as a screen against water. Yet when the heat increases, the shrink-wrap plastic becomes dry material for the fire.

Despite taking all these questions into account and observing the regulations on this topic, it is inevitable that there will be a certain fire risk in a warehouse. Therefore, this must be understood and the required precautions and measures taken to reduce the damage from such an event, whether caused by the fire, smoke, heat, and even, very frequently, by the water used to put out the fire.

One solution that can be used in large volume warehouses, or in those in which high-risk goods must be isolated, is to divide them into compartments using fire-resistant screens.

Another good reason for dividing warehouses into compartments is the existence of a certain proportion of high value goods that could be damaged when putting out a fire with water and which, however, would not be harmed if the fire were to be put out with foam or gas (systems that can be suitable in small areas and for certain types of fire and materials).

Wall creating sectors in a general warehouse. Source: Mecalux.

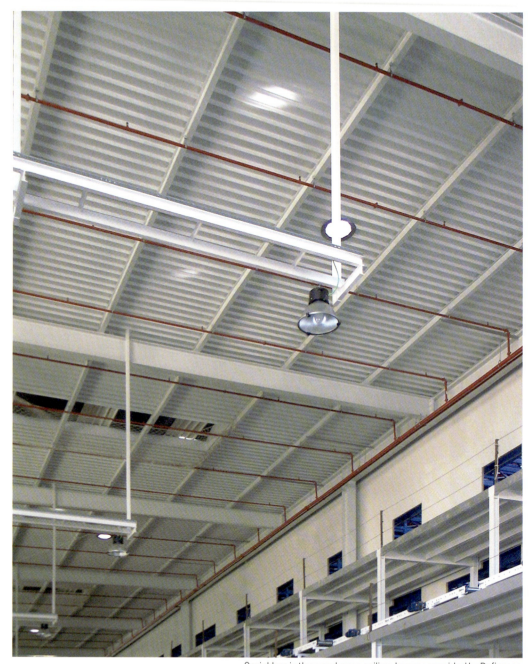
Sprinklers in the warehouse ceiling. Images provided by Pefipresa.

The use of fire-protection screens can result in the need to install fire doors for vehicles, conveyor belts, personnel, etc. Forklift trucks with retractable masts may also be required in this case, so that they can go through these doors.

The current trend is to divide up large volume warehouses, which are normally compartmentalised. At times, independent buildings are constructed and connected using automated guided vehicles. Such a system involves a high investment cost which must be studied in the context of the business strategy for the corresponding activity.

Fire prevention in the racking units using sprinklers

Even if the risk of fire has been minimised in a warehouse, racking units can be equipped with an integrated detection and extinguishing system. This applies to all racking units, both fixed and mobile. For mobile units, there are coordinated systems for supplying water that are very well developed.

Normally, water supply hydrants are located at the top of the building, with the liquid having to be taken to the sprinklers in the racking units.

The number of sprinklers that must be installed and their position on each level of the warehouse will be determined by the risks for the specific facility and what can happen on each level. Sprinklers must be strategically positioned so that they can operate without obstructions.

Often, it will be enough simply to install sprinklers on the ceiling, depending on the height of the building and the fire resistance of the products stored.

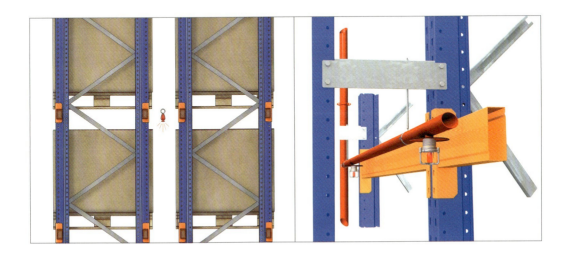

Chapter 6 - The design and construction of the warehouse

In any event, for both the installation of the sprinklers and, in general, everything related to this part of the chapter, it is advisable to seek out the support, knowledge, and experience of a company that specialises in safety issues, since the characteristics, facilities, and content of each warehouse can lead to significant changes to the recommendations set out here.

6.7.2 A safe layout within the warehouse

The design of spaces and aisles within a warehouse is addressed in earlier chapters when discussing, for example, the movement of handling devices within the facility.

Source: Mecalux.

The safe layout within the warehouse must be based on health and safety regulations in force in each country. Most of these regulations cover aspects such as the distance between evacuation doors, the intermediate areas between racking units, the specifications of working aisles and aisles for the movement of people, and the load capacity of storage devices.

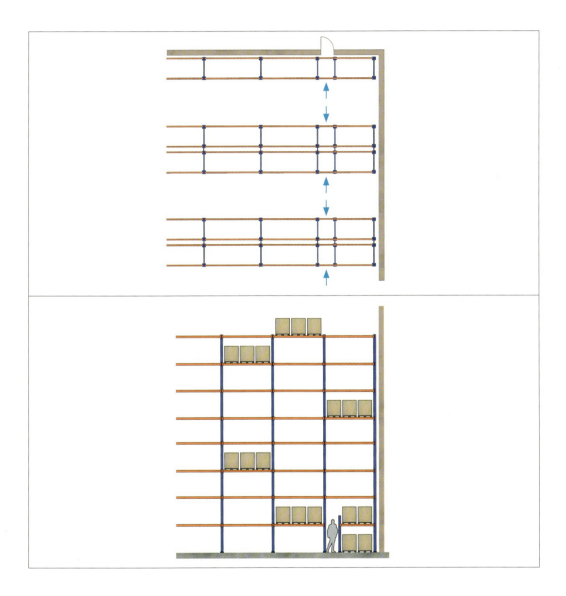

CHAPTER 7
CONCLUSIONS FROM THE TECHNICAL WAREHOUSE MANUAL

The aim of this manual has been to address almost all aspects of a warehouse, including the different approaches to its internal organisation and operation, the devices that can be used in a warehouse, safety regulations, and the types of unit loads and goods found in warehouses.

If you have read the entire document and have been paying attention, you will be familiar with the essential issues relating to warehouses and will have a solid starting point. However, it is advisable not to fall into the trap of thinking you know everything there is to know about this subject. It is not that simple: every day, new documentation and new information is being generated that will help you keep learning. Each individual circumstance and project offers new experiences which increase knowledge and, therefore, lead to greater advances.

The storage and interlogistics sector continues to evolve, so it is vital to be constantly up-to-date with the new developments taking place, as this information can be extremely valuable to these activities. In fact, the market already provides solutions that are even more advanced than those set out here (some of which are experimental) that are starting to point the way toward future techniques, particularly in the area of picking systems.

Meanwhile, for specific sectors and very particular cases (mainly for large warehouses), advanced solutions are being developed using applied engineering, which in part will be the foundation for the new solutions most widely used in the future.

These new general solutions will be addressed in future editions of this manual. Until then, we hope you have found this book useful, and that it proves helpful to you as reference material for your training, or as the starting point for launching new and interesting projects.

We at Mecalux thank you for placing your trust in us.